COMMON GROUND
ISLAM, CHRISTIANITY,
AND RELIGIOUS PLURALISM

PAUL L. HECK

GEORGETOWN UNIVERSITY PRESS
Washington, D.C.

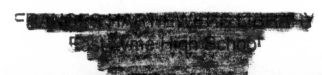

Georgetown University Press, Washington, D.C.
www.press.georgetown.edu
© 2009 by Georgetown University Press. All rights reserved.
No part of this book may be reproduced or utilized in any form
or by any means, electronic or mechanical, including
photocopying and recording, or by any information storage
and retrieval system, without permission in writing
from the publisher.

Heck, Paul L.
Common ground : Islam, Christianity, and religious pluralism /
Paul L. Heck.
p. cm.
Includes bibliographical references and index.
ISBN 978-1-58901-507-4 (alk. paper)
1. Islam—Relations—Christianity.   2. Christianity and other
religions—Islam.   I. Title.
BP172.H43 2009
261.2′7—dc22
2009007989
⊗ This book is printed on acid-free paper meeting the
requirements of the American National Standard for
Permanence in Paper for Printed Library Materials.

15 14 13 12 11 10 09   9 8 7 6 5 4 3 2
First printing

Printed in the United States of America

To My Students

Contents

Acknowledgments

THIS BOOK began as a lecture series, delivered at John Carroll University, spring 2007, under the sponsorship of the Walter and Mary Tuohy Chair of Interreligious Studies. I thank the benefactors of the fund and authorities of the university, in particular David Mason, director of the fund, for warmly supporting me during the lectureship. I also acknowledge the kindly welcome of the Department of Religious Studies, its then chair, Joseph Kelly, and the organizational support of Kathryn Merhar. Tom Schubeck was instrumental in the process, and Zeki Sariptoprak, Nursi Chair in Islamic Studies, extended his warm intellectual companionship to me on many occasions. I also thank Claude Pavur for his willingness to read advance drafts of my lectures and the many conversations that helped me to think more deeply about the relation of religion to the humanities.

Since giving the lectures, a number of people have given me opportunity to refine my thinking on religious pluralism. Tom Banchoff, director of the Berkley Center at Georgetown University, provided the support for a symposium on martyrdom in comparative perspective, November 2007. Diana Chou of the Department of Art History at John Carroll University graciously enabled me to present a lecture on the Dome of the Rock in Jerusalem as site of religiously pluralistic encounter, February 2008. Mohammad Ja'far Mahallati and David Kamitsuka of the Department of Religion at Oberlin College invited me to their beautiful campus to speak on the concept of friendship in Islam, March 2008. Gap Lo Biondo, director of the Woodstock Theological Center at Georgetown University, provided the opportunity for me to present my thinking on prophecy to the center's fellows. Todd Breyfogle of the Aspen Institute kindly invited me to participate in a workshop of ideas on the good society, June 2008.

Finally, but by no means least, the Fulbright Program gave me the chance to teach courses on religious pluralism during the 2008–2009 academic year at Muhammad V University in Rabat, Morocco. I also thank Abderrahim Benhadda, dean of the Humanities Faculty, and Muhammad Amin al-Isma'ili, chair of the Department of Islamic Studies, both at Muhammad V. In this respect, I also mention George-town University, in particular Terry Reynolds, chair of the Theology Department, and Jane McAullife, then dean of the College, for en-abling me to go on leave to pursue this kind of engagement with the Muslim world.

Last, I extend my gratitude to my students, both past and present, at Georgetown, Princeton, John Carroll, and Muhammad V. Over the last years, it is they who have provided the primary forum for me to develop my thinking on Islam, Christianity, and religious pluralism. If they have a chance to pick up this book, they will see in it echoes of past discussions and, I hope, evidence that they have had a hand in shaping the ideas at play herein. To them the book is dedicated.

INTRODUCTION

RELIGIOUS PLURALISM TODAY

I N 2007 A GROUP OF MUSLIMS presented the Christian world with a message titled "A Common Word between Us and You." This message, an expression of interreligious solidarity at a time of religious tension, spoke of a shared Christian-Muslim commitment to love of God and love of neighbor. Since then a number of meetings have been convened to discuss the document, which has received encouragement at the highest levels of religious authority and political power. There has also been caution, including a call to recognize the basic differences as well as the commonalities.

It is not surprising to find common ground between Christianity and Islam, which, along with Judaism, look to Abraham as proto-monotheist, friend of God, and father of the covenant between God and his people. At the same time religions make unique claims. Indeed, the very concept of religion may differ from one tradition to another. The common ground will always be contested. This is something for believers to take up in forging their own sense of religious purpose in today's highly pluralistic world. Unique claims will be affirmed, but there is also space to include others under the umbrella of a single truth. The 2000 declaration of the Congregation for the Propagation of the Faith, *Dominus Iesus*, promulgated under the prefecture of Joseph Cardinal Ratzinger, now Pope Benedict XVI, invites theologians of the Church "to explore if and in what ways the historical and positive elements of . . . [other] religions may fall within the divine plan of salvation." Indeed, article 841 of the Catholic Catechism states that God's plan of

1

salvation includes Muslims who "acknowledge the Creator . . . [and] profess to hold the faith of Abraham." Quite straightforwardly, a verse in the Qur'an (10:99) says that if God had wanted, all peoples would have believed together. The point, as drawn by many a Muslim thinker over the centuries, is that religious pluralism is part of the divine plan.

In principle, the study of Christianity and Islam through a single albeit refracted lens should include Judaism. Every insight in this book can be enriched by bringing in the Jewish perspective. In a way, Judaism stands at the heart of both Christianity and Islam. It has a strong sense of the messianic promise and a strong commitment to religious ethics. The common ground is ultimately tripartite. However, every study has its limits. Here, in light of the Common Word initiative, the focus is Christianity and Islam. It is hoped that others with greater expertise in Judaism will build on the initiative and offer further ideas on the various streams that flow from the figure of Abraham. The study of religious pluralism is by nature a work in progress.

There is a good deal of skepticism about religious pluralism, much of it healthy. Why cram different traditions into a single box? They may use the same language (scripture, grace, and so on) but often mean very different things. When religious communities live side by side, they often share common cultural values. Christians living amidst a Muslim majority often take on various aspects of the Islamic heritage, and the same is true of Muslims living amidst a Christian majority. But, in the end, adaptation always takes place in reference to a recognized set of truths that do not change.

There are unique truth claims, but there is also some sense of studying one religion in light of another. Scholarly inquiry is never untouched by the wider debates of the day. There is much public discussion about Islam. Is it a religion of peace? Is it a religion of violence? Insight into possible common ground between Christianity and Islam will offer direction for the wider discussion. The study of religious pluralism, then, does not aim to cram different religions into a single box but seeks to reach greater understanding of religion. Indeed, it can force us to be more precise when we use religious terminology, such as scripture and grace. What do we really mean by words like these and do they apply in the same way from one tradition to the next?

The study of religious pluralism can take up all religions, but one must have ample familiarity with the religions in question. Superficial comparison is always a danger. As a scholar of Islam, I am interested in a better understanding of Islam. I also have had considerable exposure to the study of Christianity as well as firsthand experience of both traditions. Where are the two alike and where are they different and how does that tell us something about each?

The goal here is not to review the history of Christian-Muslim relations but to seek insight into Christian-Muslim thinking. Christians and Muslims have interacted on many levels through the centuries. One can even speak of a degree of cross-fertilization: Muslims thinking about Islam in light of what Christians say and Christians thinking about Christianity in light of what Muslims say. One could, of course, focus on particular instances of Christian-Muslim interaction through the centuries, both positive and negative. The specific realities of the day do matter. For example, a community in a society where the majority does not share its beliefs may emphasize different elements of the tradition than it would if the roles were reversed. As a minority a community might speak of patience in the hope of a divinely sustained victory in an unspecified future, but as a majority it might call for some signal of God's victory in public life. There is, however, more to religious pluralism than historical circumstances. We do speak of religious traditions that endure from one historical moment to another. For Christians the way to God will always include the cross. For Muslims the Qur'an will always direct the faithful to him.

Still, because of the continuity of religious claims through the centuries, it becomes possible to think about different traditions within a single arena of religious thinking. Christians and Muslims do have the other in mind when speaking of God. What is the point of religious pluralism? What can we say about the existence of multiple religions? What are they doing together in the world? And what language best captures this? The goal here is not to offer final definitions but rather to invite reflection on religious thinking pluralistically. I do refer to specific cases but also recognize that religious traditions have their own intellectual integrity that others too can grasp.

This book began as a series of lectures delivered in the spring of 2007 at John Carroll University in Cleveland through the funding of the Walter and Mary Tuohy Chair in Interreligious Studies. A Fulbright grant to Morocco in 2008–2009, where I taught courses on religious pluralism, helped refine my thinking. However, the project's origins run much deeper. I am a Christian (Roman Catholic) who for close to two decades has been deeply engaged with Muslim society. The goal has been to study Islam, but friendships have also formed alongside scholarly pursuits. I have been struck by similarities and differences, but I have also been struck by the common drive for meaning in light of the one God. I have done a lot of listening, but I have also offered perspective. Christianity remains Christianity and Islam remains Islam: There are insurmountable differences. But there are also ways for believers of diverse faiths to enlighten one another. This has marked my own Christian relation to Islam.

Still, a book of this kind is not about personal experience. All scholars of religion develop a subjective relation to the object of their studies, but this does not make them biased observers. My readings over the years have noted common dynamics that I believe other scholars with expertise in Christianity and Islam would also notice. To be sure, my own journey may make me more sensitive to common points, but that does not mean that such commonality is not there. Indeed, a book of this kind could be written by someone without religious commitments but only competence in the two religions.

When I was delivering the Tuohy lectures, a member of the audience suggested that I might be a Gnostic. He thought I was treating two distinct religions as simply two manifestations of a single truth larger than both of them. I was, in his view, stripping Christianity and Islam of their unique truth claims. In a similar vein, one of my students in Morocco asked me whether Christians believe in God. She said this after a lecture in which I suggested that the first followers of Jesus saw the cross as God's way of guaranteeing his pledge to be with his people and, moreover, that they would not have been able to recognize this apart from the Israelite heritage to which they belonged. In her view, I had limited God's power to a set of human circumstances in which the first Christians lived. God's will, she maintained, does not depend on a set of historically limited circumstances whereby people might be able to grasp his purposes.

Religions do have their own unique claims and perspectives. Indeed, one may be true and all the others false, or they may share common ground alongside unique truths. But such a judgment can only be made in light of real knowledge. This is the role that scholars have to play in the Common Word initiative. Is the talk of common ground substantiated by serious study of religious pluralism? Does the study of religious pluralism suggest that Christians and Muslims have a common purpose in the ways they have interpreted and responded to the truths they hold across a broad range of issues: spiritual, ethical, political? There is plenty of uncommon ground, but the evidence, I argue, tilts in the direction of commonality amidst diversity. We are not, then, arguing for the creation of a common ground but instead suggesting its long-standing existence.

Amidst all of this I also challenge how we think about religion. The tendency is to think of religion in terms of identity. It is not wrong to speak about believers in terms of their distinct beliefs and practices, but it often works to keep them at a distance—those people with that identity. In fact, notwithstanding the differences it is religion as opposed to other factors that explains why Muslims today have much in common with Christians. By thinking of religion in terms of identity, we actually blind ourselves to the way it unfolds across a broad range of categories that several species of religion share. The question, then, is how to obtain a fuller knowledge of religion in light of the fact that no religion is reducible to a set identity. The study of religious pluralism is one way to get at the subjectivity of religious actors beyond so-called objective definitions of their identity. To consider Islam alongside Christianity, then, is to attempt to overcome the tendency to limit Islam to identity classification. In that way, we can understand it more fully. A pluralistic horizon asks what Islam shares with other traditions. Islam, in this sense, is not simply an object to be identified as a separate species from other objects but now a subject sharing a measure of character traits with other subjects, such as Christianity. Religions are not objects for zoological classification but dynamic actors in their own right.

The study of religious pluralism, then, can help us see that religions actually resist final definitions. The religious landscape offers us horizons, but we cannot define all its contours with precision. There is, then, an open-ended side to religion. Believers are not simply objects to label but moral agents. Thinking about religion in terms of common ground is one way to articulate this reality: Religion is not a concept that can be captured in distinct cages of identity.

In what follows, six chapters explore topics of central importance to Islam with reference to commonality in Christianity. The first two deal with the mechanics of revelation: concepts of prophecy and doubts about prophecy. The second two deal with ethics: the face of God and the existence of evil. The final two deal with politics: democracy and human rights. My conclusions support the idea of common ground but also recognize its fragility. Common ground is not immediately obvious. It requires sustained reflection on the ways beliefs are constructed and pursued even within a single tradition. Meanings and morals as advanced by religious traditions get shaped and reshaped even if general horizons are not completely malleable. The common ground may be there one moment and gone the next. But it is still there, potentially if not always actually. And, I argue, this common ground is not only for religious communities to consider and affirm or deny. It is also exciting ground for scholars to pursue in the effort to understand the nature and purpose of religion.

CHAPTER ONE

DOES THE QUR'AN BELONG
IN THE BIBLE?

O UR STORY BEGINS at the court of Rayy, a city not far from Tehran, where in the tenth century a famous debate about prophecy
took place. Abu Hatim argued for the truth of prophecy and Abu Bakr
denied it. Both were natives of Rayy and therefore shared the surname
al-Razi. Abu Hatim al-Razi, an intellectual associated with the Isma'ili
branch of Islam, recorded the debate, so it is no surprise that he came
out on top and that Abu Bakr al-Razi looked the fool.[1] Abu Bakr,
referred to throughout as the atheist, was actually quite learned.[2] He
held that the human mind is all one needs to know the truth of existence and to live well. In his view, because religion requires obedience
to revealed precepts, it belittles the mind. It is therefore foolish to follow the directives of a prophet. He thus condemned all religions as
tools the powerful use to dominate others.

To show the folly of prophecy, Abu Bakr noted the contradictions
between religions. How could any of them be true? The Gospel claims
that Jesus is the son of God and was crucified for the sins of those who
believe in him, whereas the Qur'an insists, first, that he is not the son
of God but a prophet, no different from other prophets, and, second,
that he only appeared to be crucified when in fact he was not killed but
raised up to God. In his place, the Qur'an says, another person resembling him was put to death. Thus, Abu Bakr argued, given that there is
no evidence apart from scripture to vindicate one claim over the other,

the only intelligent thing to do is to suspend judgment and give the matter no further thought. Alas, he lamented, people do not do this. Bereft of rational arguments, believers turn to violence to vindicate their claims. In the end, religion leads only to strife and bloodshed.

The existence of multiple religions does challenge the idea of a single truth, and Muslim scholars claim in response that scripture before the Qur'an is distorted. The Bible would support the truths of the Qur'an had Jewish and Christian leaders not changed its content to serve their interests. However, in this case, Abu Bakr dismissed all prophecy—Jewish, Christian, and Muslim alike. Abu Hatim was thus forced to defend the credibility of prophecy in general, putting him in the odd position of defending the truth of non-Muslim scripture. Would he be able to do this without prejudicing the truth of Islam?

Abu Hatim first acknowledged that the wordings of scripture do indeed differ from one religion to the next. Still, he insisted, they share a common meaning. The problem lies not in scriptural divergences but in the failure to interpret them properly. He argued, for example, that Jesus did claim to be the son of God in the Gospels but that Christians have erred in taking this claim literally. In fact, Jesus spoke in parable. A father loves his child and prefers him over others, and this, Abu Hatim claimed, served Jesus as a metaphor for his relation with God. In calling himself son of God, he meant only to indicate a special relation with God. Christians are led astray by taking the parable literally. The wording may say son of God, but the meaning, Abu Hatim concluded, is friend of God, a concept that indicates closeness to God and is consistent with the Muslim view of prophets as specially chosen by God.

A similar argument was made for the crucifixion. Jesus was in fact crucified—an extraordinary concession for a Muslim to make. But this, Abu Hatim claimed, does not contradict the Qur'an. The Qur'an does not say that they did not kill him but that they did not kill him for certain (4:157). This means that they did not kill that part of him that represents his true reality, namely his spirit, which God raised to himself. Abu Hatim bolstered his argument by referring to other verses in the Qur'an that speak of those killed in the way of God. Believers are exhorted to consider them not as dead but alive, enjoying a heavenly reward for the boldness of their piety. The point, then, is not that they did not kill his body but that they did not kill his spirit. He is still alive, as all those killed in the way of God, and is with God in spirit. Once again, Abu Hatim prevailed. Apparent contradictions exist only at the level of words. If Abu Bakr the atheist were to ponder the matter, he would see the harmony of all scripture at the deeper level of meaning. The problem, again, is not the scriptures but the failure to go beyond literal wordings.

What can we learn from this millennium-old debate? We like the idea of a single truth at the core of all religions. Perhaps too often we hear the statement that all religions are simply different paths to a single truth. The message of all faiths is to love God and to love your neighbor, is it not? All believers do desire to be close to God, to be in harmony with him, and to live a life pleasing to him. And yet believers are not ready to cede the literal wordings of scripture. For Christians, Jesus Christ is the son of God, not literally in the biological sense but also not metaphorically as friend of God in the sense Abu Hatim suggested. He represents God's unique word to humanity and in that sense, though human, discloses the truth of God, making him inseparable from God. Similarly, for Muslims, the Qur'an means what it says. It is the great criterion (*furqan*) that separates good from evil, the guided from the misguided, and the grateful from the ungrateful. It too originates in God as his final word for humankind—not the ink and paper on which it is written but the message communicated in Arabic. The words of the Qur'an are God's words, literally, in contrast to the words of the Bible, which do play a central role in Christian life but ultimately point to Jesus as God's message to humanity. Despite rich traditions of interpretation in both religions, we have two claims for uniqueness: the Christian one for Jesus and the Muslim one for the Qur'an. There is no person like Jesus. And there is no book like the Qur'an.

Christians and Muslims, though eager for interreligious harmony, are not about to discard plainly stated beliefs for hidden meanings. If scripture is about hidden meanings, we can make it say whatever we want apart from any clear message from God. If this is the case, why not do away with religion entirely, as Abu Bakr suggested, and rely solely on the mind as guide to life?

It is difficult to speak of common ground when it comes to the unique claims of Christian and Muslim revelation. Either we cede the message of revelation, putting the religion itself at risk, or are left to squabble about the truth of one revealed message over another. The result is either suspicion of the beliefs of others or reservation about the truth claims of all religions. This is particularly true for Christians and Muslims when it comes to the person of Jesus Christ. Yes, he is the son of God. No, he is not. Yes, he was crucified. No, he was not. The discord goes beyond descriptions. More profoundly, the two views of Jesus reflect distinct notions about the workings of prophecy.

At a basic level, Christians and Muslims see prophecy as the disclosure of three things: God, God's will, and the consequences of failing to live up to God's will. Prophets call people to piety and devotion to God as ground of all existence. However, in Christianity, and in Judaism, prophecy is never far from priesthood. Prophets call people to right living, to bind themselves to God, but also to correct worship of him, which in the Bible involves sacrificial offerings in the temple by priests on behalf of the community. The concept of sacrificial offering is not at all foreign to Islam. The sacrifice of an animal for the expiation of sins is a central feature of the pilgrimage to Mecca. But in Islam there is no priesthood. In ancient Israel, by contrast, the temple where sacrifice was offered stood at the heart of the community's covenant with God. It was the place where the people encountered the presence of God in a special way, and it was the task of the temple priests to offer sacrifices to ensure the integrity of the relation between God and his people. However, the destruction of the temple by the Babylonians in the sixth century BCE changed all that, raising questions about the nature of the covenant in the absence of the temple. To be sure, the Israelites could continue their ethical commitments as known in the Mosaic Law. These gave them a distinct identity as a people. But where would sacrifice be offered? How would God be encountered?

Some hoped for the restoration of the temple and the outpouring of a new spirit. The Israelites would devote themselves fully to the ways of God and cease from offending him. It was God's anger at the waywardness of his people and especially their leaders, some supposed, that caused the destruction of the temple and exile to Babylon. Yet, once rebuilt, the temple never regained its former status as inviolable site of the presence of God.[3] Indeed, an important scene in the book of Ezekiel shows the glory of God taking leave of the temple (10:18–22). As a result of the temple's desecration, a new vision began to take shape. Instead of the temple, the body of the prophet, the holy man of God, would ensure the integrity of the covenant. In this sense, the prophet's bodily suffering, in place of the temple sacrifice, would restore the community's standing before God. This role is noticeable already with Ezekiel, prophet and priest of the sixth century BCE, whose bodily suffering functions to restore the integrity of the community's relation with God in the absence of the temple (4:4–6). It also features prominently in the book of Isaiah, with the expectation that God will raise up his suffering servant as his chosen means of redeeming his people. For Christians, this idea reaches its unique expression in the person of Jesus Christ, whose body becomes the new temple, the site where people encounter the presence of God.[4] His sacrifice allows people to stand in the presence of God. They are still accountable for their sins, but the cross becomes a sign of hope that nothing will deprive them of the presence and love of God. It is the great sacrifice to which the church is heir.

For Christians, then, prophecy is not enough. The prophets of old proclaimed God's desire to be with his people, and this promise was fulfilled in the person of Jesus Christ. It is thus one thing to have a prophecy about God and another thing for it to be fulfilled. This is true for Muslims too. The Qur'an speaks of God, and Muslims find great solace in living according to his ways. But what holds out hope that the prophecy is actually being fulfilled by the community? Muhammad Ibn 'Abd al-Wahhab (died 1792), the eighteenth-century reformist who initiated the powerful movement in contemporary Islam known as Wahhabism, condemned the bulk of Muslims as infidels. This may have been extreme, but the question stands. How does the community know that its relation with God is sound and that it has not been deprived of the presence of God that prophecy makes known but does not itself bring into being? In one sense, God is merciful to those who turn to Him. An individual might repent of waywardness and return to the path of God, content that he is leading a life pleasing to God. As for other Muslims who may not be so pious, they can hope for the mercy of God in the life to come but risk punishment on judgment day for their religious shortcomings. Islam says that they may need to spend time in hell before admission to paradise and full enjoyment of the presence of God. But what can be said about the Muslim community as a whole, here and now? What is the evidence that the prophecy is being fulfilled and that God is present to his people? It is one thing to hope for the fulfillment of prophecy in the life to come but another thing to show its effectiveness in this world. What would be the point of having a word from God without some sign that it is being realized in the life of the community?

A ninth-century figure by the name of al-Muhasibi gave much thought to this question. He earned his name, which means the accountant, from his interest not in financial accounts but spiritual ones. How to account for the failings of a community that has possession of God's final word to humanity? To answer this question, he turned to the interior life of the soul. He wanted to know not only what the religion says humans should do but also and more profoundly the motives behind religious actions. What prompts Muslims to do the things they do, especially the things that God commands—prayer, fasting, generosity? What was troubling for al-Muhasibi was religious hypocrisy, Muslims who pursue religion not for God and a desire for the world to come but for communal approval. What motivated them in his view was not the presence of God in and of itself but favorable standing in the eyes of the world, a situation that worked against fulfillment of the prophetic message. Were Muslims ultimately about this world or the next? And if their actions, especially their religious practices, were implicitly worldly in orientation, what did that say about the presence of God in their lives?

The ninth century was a spiritually ambiguous time in Islam. The caliphate was at the height of its splendor, signaling the worldly success of a religion that had come to prevail over vast regions of the earth from Andalusia to India, known collectively as the abode of Islam. Religious fulfillment, however, remained elusive. As suggested, Muslims disagreed about the religion itself, and it was not just so-called atheists such as Abu Bakr al-Razi. Those who accepted the prophecy were also not in full agreement. There were different Sunni schools. The Shi'a too were divided into subbranches, such as the Isma'ilis. A host of sects too numerous to mention here are recorded in Islam's early literature. The prediction of the prophet Muhammad that his community would divide into seventy-two sects, only one of which would be saved, seemed to have come to pass. All others were heretics. The dilemma for piety-minded people such as al-Muhasibi was to locate the saved sect. As he noted in his *Testimonies*, he felt adrift amidst a sea of differences where many drown and only a few reach shore safely.[5]

His report of how he found the saved sect was actually a way for him to discuss more urgent issues that in his view threatened the standing of the Muslim community (*umma*) before God. He was deeply troubled by the sectarian differences within the *umma*, differences that encouraged skepticism about the existence of a single truth, catastrophically leading to indifference toward one's religious duties. Why go to all the trouble to perform them if not clearly true? It was this that most distressed al-Muhasibi because it threw the community's account with God out of balance. God has the right to be worshipped as embodied in specific religious duties—daily prayer, fasting during Ramadan, almsgiving, pilgrimage to the house of God in Mecca, and so on. Failing to meet God's rights would jeopardize the religious integrity of the *umma*.

The problem in al-Muhasibi's view was that Muslims are enamored with the world, preferring the pursuit of money over religious duties. Even the religious scholars, the so-called guides of the community, had become captivated by worldly prestige. The debt to God had increased so much that al-Muhasibi nearly despaired of finding piety to offset it and warned of God unleashing his wrath on the Muslim community for its failure to satisfy his rights. Here, then, the salvation to be obtained is salvation from God, which is achievable only by exact performance of religious duties. And yet perfect fulfillment of the conditions set by the prophetic message for harmonious relation with God was—and is—no easy matter. What could be done? How would the price be paid? As it turns out, it was not to be accomplished by crucifixion. It did, however, involve particularly pious persons who had earned God's favor. In the language of al-Muhasibi, they were God's beloved ones, his chosen ones, indeed his vicegerents on earth. They could intercede on behalf of a community with a religious account clearly in the red.

The thought that someone should undergo death to satisfy God may have occurred to al-Muhasibi. A prophetic saying (hadith) tells of a man who had committed adultery. Fearful of his standing before God, he goes to the prophet and asks him to apply the punishment, namely, death by stoning, to restore his good standing before God. The prophet sends him away, telling him to seek the forgiveness of God, but the man keeps coming back, insisting that only by submitting to the prescribed punishment will he be reconciled to God. Finally, the prophet relents and orders him to be stoned but not without remarking that his repentance is so sincere that it encompasses the Muslim community entire. In other words, his self-appointed death, intended to make himself pleasing to God so as to have access to God's presence, is evidence of pure-hearted piety. Even if represented in a single individual, it shows that the religion is at work within the community, proof that it continues to enjoy a measure of divine favor.

But al-Muhasibi did not go this way. The work of making the community pleasing to God was to be accomplished by exemplars of piety. These did not need to undergo death on behalf of the community but did have a role in ensuring the soundness of the community's relation with God. What made them pleasing to God, and through them the community, was their high level of piety as witnessed by their perfect devotion to the other world over this one. They not only performed their duties to God without flaw but had also overcome the worldly inclinations of the soul—inner urges and selfish whims that suggest a lack of full orientation to the presence of God.

It was this exclusively otherworldly orientation that preserved them from the religious hypocrisy that marked, in al-Muhasibi's view, the majority of Muslims. That he may have considered—and then dismissed—the idea of someone undergoing death to reconcile the community to God is suggested in his citation of another hadith, in which the prophet Muhammad says, "Those who cling to my precedent (i.e., model of righteous behavior) amidst the corruption of the day will have the reward of a hundred martyrs."[6] Death for God, at least in the literal sense, would not be necessary. Sincere piety, al-Muhasibi concluded, is more effective than the blood of the martyr. Still, the prophetic message alone is not enough. Also necessary were living figures whose lives visibly witnessed, and therefore mediated, a sense of sanctity. This, al-Muhasibi argued, comes about by perfect adherence to the example of the prophet who was, and is, undeniably pleasing to God. After all, God had chosen him to be his messenger, purifying him in advance for this noble mission.

As al-Muhasibi saw it, such figures rendered the community pleasing to God, staying God's wrath. In this sense, they shared in the prophet's power to intercede for the community before God. The idea that special figures might intercede in such fashion is a highly controversial but still widespread idea in Islam. It is often associated with Sufism, a long-standing part of Islam that some reformist movements, such as Wahhabism, violently reject. And today, within different circles of Sufism, reformist currents see the pious figure not as intercessor before God but spiritual guide. For al-Muhasibi, they were the saved sect the prophet had predicted. They performed their religious duties with no regard for this world. They also avoided the satanic trap of theological disputes and the religious paralysis it inevitably produced. He thought of them as religious scholars of a certain kind. What they knew was much more than the duties of religion that even the worldly minded could study and teach. The religious scholars he had in mind are figures who could claim to know not just the teachings of God but

God himself (*'ulama' bi-llah*).[7] He therefore called them friends of God (*awliya' allah*), exemplars of piety (*dala'il al-taqwa*) that protect the community from God's wrath, making them more than mere purveyors of religious knowledge. For al-Muhasibi, the community's righteousness (*salah al-umma*) depends on the righteousness of these figures (*salah al-'ulama'*). They offer visible evidence that all is not lost: The community is not cut off from God. For this reason, al-Muhasibi calls them the mercy of God for the community (*ula'ika rahmat allah 'ala l-umma*), that is, human agents of God's mercy.

In Islam, the idea that persons, not books, offer the final measure of a community's worth goes back to the prophet Muhammad, who is described in the Qur'an as a mercy for the universe (*rahma lil-'alamin*) and who is known among Muslims as the beloved of God (*habib allah*). Born, it is reported, in the year 570 into the tribe of Quraysh, at the time a powerful clan of the Arabian peninsula, Muhammad received a call from God, beginning in 610, to remind humanity of his truth. This message Muhammad disclosed gradually, as revealed to him by the angel Gabriel, over the course of nearly a quarter century until his death in 632. In the face of significant opposition in Mecca from powerful elements of his own tribe, he persevered, gathering a core band of companions. With them, he would eventually emigrate to Medina at the invitation of its leading factions to arbitrate community disputes. There he continued to preach judgment day but also set down laws for his community. In this fashion he sowed the seeds for a polity that would eventually dominate the Arabian peninsula. After his death his successors, the first Muslims, would spread Islam by conquests from North Africa and the Iberian peninsula in the west to Iran and the gates of India in the east. The point of the conquests was neither slaughter nor even conversion (indeed, the first Muslims set up garrison towns separate from the local people and did not proselytize) but rather to bring just rule to the world according to the ways of God.

For Muslims, a key moment in the life of the prophet Muhammad was his ascension to heaven on the back of the winged steed Buraq. In the company of the angel Gabriel, he traversed the seven heavens, where he met past prophets and led them in prayer, finally reaching the throne of God. From God, he received the key teachings of Islam, especially the five core practices (the testimony of God's oneness and of Muhammad as his messenger, daily prayer, fasting during Ramadan, almsgiving, and, if one is financially and physically able, pilgrimage to Mecca once in a lifetime) and the five core beliefs (belief in the one God, all his angels, all his messengers from Adam to Muhammad, all the scriptures he sent, and the judgment day to come). He also received from God divine truths (*haqa'iq*), which refer to the mysteries of Islam's spiritual life.

Muhammad's main task, then, was to convey the Qur'an, the final and decisive version of God's message to humanity. The purpose of his mission was not to establish a new religion but to restore the religion of Abraham that had been conveyed to previous communities, Jews and Christians, but that their leaders had distorted for the sake of their own interests. Although Muhammad is a prophet, having conveyed God's message, he has another role that is very dear to Muslims. He will intercede for them on judgment day.

This does not make him the bearer of sins or redeemer of the world who offsets the disordered state of the human soul. Christians too recognize that believers are accountable for their actions even in light of the good news of salvation. The Christian message of salvation does not relieve Christians of responsibility but rather of the effects of original sin, thereby ensuring that they are not cut off from the love of God even when in a sinful state: Repentance is always possible. Islam has no doctrine of original sin. Humans are susceptible to the seductions of Satan but not in any permanent or irrefutable way. The Qur'an makes clear what humans are to do. If one falls from the straight path, one is simply to repent and start again with confidence in God's mercy. That, however, is not easily accomplished without assistance. Once one has repented, how is one certain of being on the straight path, body and soul? Divine favor would be in question were it not for the favor Muhammad has earned with God. He can intercede for his community on judgment day, turning the wrath of God to mercy. His body is not necessarily the site where believers encounter the presence of God, but he nevertheless offers great comfort to Muslims as guarantor of the community's relation with God.

In this sense Muhammad is not only the bearer of a divinely revealed book. His life also exemplifies fulfillment of its message. A hadith reports that the moral character of the prophet is the Qur'an itself. In other words, the life of the prophet is a perfect realization of the prophecy, modeling for the community the message of the Qur'an. Without him it would be impossible to understand the Qur'an fully. It is for this reason that reports of his sayings and deeds have been collected as model (*sunna*) of the Muslim way of life.

In some ways the role of Muhammad in Islam echoes that of Mary in Christianity. There is great controversy over these two figures within the respective traditions. Some Muslims claim that the prophet, though human, also carries within him a divine light. In this sense, he has always existed with God even if he appeared in history at a particular moment in time.[8] For others, such a notion is a reprehensible innovation. The prophet brought the message of God, modeled it during his lifetime, and will intercede for his community on judgment day, but one should not exaggerate his nature the way Christians do with Jesus. These Muslims strongly criticize those who celebrate the birthday of the prophet Muhammad, accusing them of associating the prophet to the godhead. Similarly, some Christians show great reverence for Mary, seeing her to be the greatest of prophets for bearing God's unique word in her womb. This also makes her the greatest of intercessors for many Christians, sharing in the redemptive work of her son. But many others detest this devotion to Mary, seeing it as a kind of paganism. Whatever the case, Muhammad, like Mary, birthed the message of God to the world. Like her, he is considered immaculate, that is, without sin, and capable of interceding for believers, helping them to stand before God even when their actions do not merit it. Muhammad, like Mary for Christians, helps Muslims feel close to God.

The possibility of intercession does not relieve believers of their religious obligations. Nevertheless, the prophet, even if dead in his grave in Medina, remains alive, caring for his community, guiding them, inspiring them, visiting them in their dreams or even, for the spiritually advanced, when awake. At the same time, it has long been recognized that certain individuals share in the mission of the prophet. By embodying the character of the prophet, they, in turn, become, like him, pleasing to God. They are not—no more than the prophet—associated with the godhead but are agents of God's purpose for humanity. They too are intercessors for the community, by visibly witnessing the effective presence of God amidst the community. They are not mere conveyors of religious knowledge but instead signs that its stipulations are fulfilled.

For al-Muhasibi, a seminal thinker in early Islam, the character of the prophet can be represented by Muslims, at least the spiritual elite among them, who model their lives after his, becoming, like him, a mercy for the community. The representation of divine mercy is a perennial task. Every generation of Muslims looks for tangible signs of piety amidst the community as evidence of its religious integrity. Martyrdom, death for God, became one way to display one's piety, but it received limited approval among the religious scholars, because the intention that led martyrs to seek death could never be determined, making the status of this form of piety highly ambiguous. Moreover, it was never clear what spiritual benefit martyrdom offered the community. In contrast, the case of the friends of God was straightforward. Their holiness could be seen and measured by the impact it had on their devotees.

With al-Muhasibi we have an early example of what would later become a central idea in Islam, that the prophetic message is not enough. Living proof of its fulfillment is also needed. The prophecy speaks of God and his qualities, especially his mercy, but does not make concord with God a forgone conclusion even for the community that accepts it. This is left to persons of extraordinary charisma whose lives radiate the truth of God. Such figures sharpen communal awareness of God's presence, encouraging greater commitment to his ways. Prophecy (*nubuwwa*) is the necessary point of departure because it discloses the existence of God, but it is pointless if not fulfilled in friendship (*walaya*) with God, which, for al-Muhasibi, was achieved by perfect worship (*'ibada*) free of worldly calculations.

It has been suggested that the history of Islam is one massive undertaking to be close to God.[9] Some excelled at it and modeled the experience for others. The friends of God, offering assurance that the community is not cut off from God, have long been a spiritual consolation to the community. Their piety demonstrates that divine favor remains intact, visibly so. Yes, the saved sect can be known, not by scriptural citation or theological dispute but by eyewitness, the living exemplars of piety.

A well-known hadith states that in every generation someone will come to renew the religion of Islam. Among the different ways of conceiving this process of renewal, sainthood has been particularly prominent. Until recently it was widely thought that not having a saintly figure as focal point of one's religious devotion was to risk eternal perdition. The idea that holiness is mediated through particular persons continues to be influential across the Muslim world, but it has been hotly contested by reformist currents that make the individual—and individual reading of scripture—the vehicle of salvation rather than the saint. It is now felt in many circles that holiness is a matter of personal effort. What is the point of a spiritual intermediary? Particularly controversial is the idea that one might make a request (material or spiritual) of the dead saint in his tomb, awarding powers to the dead that belong only to God.

What might seem like a healthy development to many, the rejection of the saint's spiritual authority, has actually been a mixed blessing for Islam. It may grant the individual believer final authority over his religious destiny, but it can also have a destabilizing effect on Muslim society. If the saint is rejected as guarantor of the religious integrity of the community, the individual, every individual, becomes responsible for the piety of Islam. Yet all are not up to the task. The printing press, universal education, and now the Internet have made religious knowledge widely available, but do all have the spiritual maturity to know how to deploy it according to God's purposes? To be sure, the rejection of the saint is not unwarranted. Muslims have known many a false saint who made a business of swindling the masses by pretending to perform miracles. Through the ages, though, even the great religious scholars, experts in determining correct behavior, would visit the saints. What did they find in the charisma of sainthood that they could not find in knowledge of the prophetic heritage alone?

There have been a wide variety of saints throughout the ages, and here it will be enough to mention one, Zindapir of Pakistan, who even after his death in 1998 remains the centerpiece of a transnational network of sanctity with thousands of devotees from all stations of life.[10] For his followers, it was enough when he was alive to touch his garment or catch sight of him and now, in his death, to receive his blessing at his graveside or bask in the sanctity embodied in the shrine complex at Ghamkol Sharif, to which thousands flock every year, especially at the time of the feast day commemorating Zindapir's death, referred to as his marriage (*'urs*) or full communion with God. It is Zindapir who intercedes for his devotees on judgment day. It is Zindapir who saves them because it is his holy character that attracts them to God and thus allows them, like him, to be in the presence of God.

In this age of reformist religiosity many Muslims have come to view this kind of devotion as deviation from Islam's affirmation of one God who has no partners, no helpers, who is Creator, Lord, and Judge of all. Claims to holiness can be hollow and can be used to deceive and abuse others. At the same time, it is historically myopic to reject a special kind of friendship with God as violation of Islam's monotheism. As seen with al-Muhasibi, the idea of the friends of God—support for which exists in the Qur'an—arose not to contest the godhead but to offer a visible sign that the community's relation with the one God remained intact. This characterizes the dynamic between Zindapir and his followers. Zindapir's very person is a public manifestation and vivid expression of a life that elevates the word of God above all, making awareness of such a life available to others.

The voice of God, that is, recitation of the Qur'an, resounds throughout the shrine complex, but again, the presence of scripture, though necessary, is not enough for the fulfillment of prophecy. It is the presence of the friend of God that draws out the spiritual essences hidden in the depths of people's souls. People can recite scripture all they like, but they are only making noise, voices without authority, until the spiritual essences dormant within them are awakened, a process that the saint makes possible. His spirituality is fully operative as displayed in his character, and this animates the spirituality of others and inspires them to live according to the spirit and not the body alone. In other words, those whose inner life is still worldly in some way risk performing religious acts hypocritically. The saint, however, whose spiritual essences are fully alive, the result of his total orientation to the other world, brings about the spiritual transformation of those who enter his presence. They see in him what they are to live and embody. His existence brings to life their spiritual essences, allowing them not only to hear the divine voice of the Qur'an but also to receive it into the depths of their souls and so more effectively live out its message in their lives.

Participation in the sanctity made possible by Zindapir is most noticeable in the communal meal, a vast production that feeds thousands of visitors to the shrine, including many poor; a year-round labor of love organized by voluntary donations of grain and livestock as well as time and effort. In short, it is a sacrificial meal, operating by altruistic contribution. It offers a concrete way to participate in sanctity, a life for God, a way to live what the saint lives. The meal, which the saint mediates, represents a collective offering to God, service to God, a way to experience a life in which worldly calculations are put aside. The saint's presence ensures that such work is more than the action of do-gooders but a lived experience of sanctification through sacrifice. The acts of self-sacrifice involved in the preparation of the meal take on greater meaning in the presence of the saint, endowing them with a quality of sanctity that they would not normally have.

In all this Zindapir is able to accomplish what religious scholars cannot. They may have the expertise to inform Muslims of correct standards of behavior but do not necessarily inspire them to journey to God. Absorbed in God, pleasing to God, Zindapir's person is so imbued with the characteristics of godliness that his presence calls attention not to himself but to the shadows of the names of God that reside in persons, assigned in pre-existence and forgotten as a result of birth into this imperfect world. A mystery (*sirr*) therefore exists at the depths of the human soul, from the time of Adam whom God taught all names, including God's own. The task for Muslims is to realize their own sanctity, a process that begins with the Qur'an's revelation of the God who created humans to bear his names (i.e., attributes) and ends in a life of closeness to God.

Love for the saint therefore means identification with his body, not simply as body but as visible manifestation of sanctity. This, it should be mentioned, differs from Christian contemplation of the body of Christ. In Islam, the saintly body may bear the marks of self-denial and asceticism but not those of suffering. The reason, of course, is that the prophetic heritage of Islam is not associated with priestly sacrifice, as noted earlier. Thus the human body of the saint whose life is a fulfillment of the prophetic heritage of Islam is not the site of sacrificial offering. This is not Christian sainthood. The point is to reflect the body of Muhammad and not that of Christ. All the same, the devotee's love for the saint's spiritually marked body triggers recollection of the true character at the core of his being. From love of the saint, who embodies the character of the prophet, the devotee in turn is led to identify with the prophet, engendering love for him and his body, for it is in the body of the prophet that the purpose of the Qur'an is most visibly manifest. From this vantage point, finally, one is in a position to behold God, to be in his presence, with the saints and prophets. The prophetic message proclaimed by the Qur'an initiates a process of reminding people of the truth of God that comes to fulfillment in sainthood, that is, the bodily representation of sanctity. It is for this reason that a close associate of Zindapir can say, "Zindapir is religion. Zindapir is Islam."[11]

This is not to exaggerate sainthood in Islam. Muslims have a sense of being in the presence of God when performing basic religious duties. One can attain awareness of God without a saintly model. Still, the saint continues to play a vital function in the community as perfect model of holiness. As such, he or she is the best measure of sanctity that one might not be able to realize by one's own religious efforts. Exemplifying a life wholly for God, the saint offers insight into the reality of God, thereby encouraging heightened consciousness of God. In this sense, the saint complements the basic religious duties of Islam and models for others what they too are meant to realize.

Saints have long acted as standards of communal piety, but this is not to say that Muslims are paralyzed by their religious shortcomings. There are many ways to connect with God even if saints offer the best model. Various rituals function to expiate sin (*kaffara 'an al-dhunub*) such as purity ablutions, prayer, and animal sacrifice at the close of the pilgrimage to Mecca. Performance of these basic religious duties is the way Muslims become pleasing to God and draw close to him. Many Muslims do not read the Qur'an, at least not regularly, but do hear it recited in public places. More diffusely, then, recitation of the Qur'an in Muslim society engenders awareness of God, at funerals and marriages, on the radio, amidst the buzz of business in the bazaar. The Qur'an—divine speech—is working subtly yet pervasively to bring about a sense of sanctification of entire communities and not only of individuals.

The Qur'an, Islam's scripture, exists not to be critically analyzed, though that is important, but to be recited. It is, then, the liturgical aspect of the Qur'an that introduces prophecy into Muslim life and allows Muslims to orient themselves to it and to the God it reveals and his attributes as disclosed by the Qur'an: Merciful, Forgiving, Wise, Mighty, All-Knowing, All-Powerful, Generous, Judge, Destroyer (of evil), and so on—ninety-nine names that describe God and that one can identify with by recalling them in daily life. Ultimately, the goal is identification with the God besides whom there is no other, Allah, the name of God announced by the Qur'an as central mark of human existence.

This can happen in quite ordinary fashion. For example, the daily language of rural Moroccans includes frequent reference to the name of

God, endowing all they do with an aura of sanctity.[12] Every action—eating, drinking, rising, sitting, sleeping, walking, plowing, harvesting, buying, and selling—is initiated by invoking the name of God (*bismillah*), signaling reliance on God, entrusting oneself and all that one does to God, consecrating one's life in this world to God as goal of the next. Invoking the name of God also signals hope for God's blessing on all one does: material prosperity, health, contentment, and goodness. The community aspires to a life graced by the presence of God as heralded by his name, which can be invoked in unfamiliar and eerie places or in the face of temptation. The power of the divine name can, then, protect against evil—both the evil of others and of oneself. Recollection of his name is a way to remind oneself of the purpose of existence and in turn to be exhorted to live by it.

Other expressions imprint Muslim life with the divine name: for example, a formula praising God, *al-hamdu lillah*, uttered in all conditions, good and bad, joy and sorrow, as a sign of surrender to God's will, his divine decree, at every moment and circumstance. This is not to suggest fatalism. Muslims do their best to achieve goals. However, whatever the results may be, praise is due to God, whose will cannot be opposed but must be unconditionally accepted as wise and just even if at times obscure to human comprehension. There is a theological conundrum here, a kind of theodicy whereby all that happens, including apparently bad things, potentially receive the status of divine wisdom and justice. The concern of these rural Moroccans, however, is not theological consistency but simply acknowledgment of their created status in a world ultimately in the hands of God.

Still other expressions impregnate Muslim life with the name of God: petitions of forgiveness (*istaghfir allah*) and of protection from the seductions of Satan (*'awzu billah min al-shaytan al-rajim*), as well as supplications to God (*du'a lillah*) and imprecations against others (*la'nat allah*). Supplications accompany life's various rites of passage—birth, circumcision, marriage, and death—as a way to seek a blessing, the good, from God. Imprecations act to call down a curse on others as justly deserved punishment for transgressions suffered at their hands.

Such formulae, though not devoid of self-serving interests, point to a deep sense that all that is desired, and feared, in the end passes through divine channels.

Interestingly, the majority of these Muslims do not perform the five daily prayers prescribed by Islam. They apparently do not even frequent the local mosque on a regular basis. There may be reasons for this. In general, many Moroccans tie their piety to family rituals and annual festivals more than to regular visits to the mosque. Moreover, in rural life, it is not easy to make the demands of farming conform to the schedule of prescribed prayers. Additionally, the rural populace of Morocco is generally illiterate and has not had the opportunity to memorize verses from the Qur'an that constitute an integral part of the ritual prayers. Finally, the egalitarian outlook of the Qur'an does not overcome the deeply rooted human tendency to rank people according to social status, even in the mosque and even during the congregational prayer on Friday and feast days. People, however pious, will forgo religious duties that call attention to their lowly status in society. These people, however, are successful in living piously, inscribing the scripturally enshrined name of God into their lives through various formulae. They are thus able to color their lives with the sanctity of God perhaps no less effectively than they would if they perfectly performed all prescribed prayers. By calling on the name of God in informal but tangible ways, these people attain salvation, that is, a life sanctified by the name of God and a sense of being in the presence of God.

There has always been a Muslim drive for deeper awareness of God. Over the centuries Muslims have turned directly to the Qur'an and the names of God it discloses as a way to identify body and soul with God. The great, perhaps greatest, scholar of Islam, an eleventh-century figure by the name of Ghazali (died 1111), wrote about this subject. *The Forty Bases of Religion*, a summary of his magnum opus, *The Revival of the Religious Sciences*, treats two topics back-to-back: recitation of the Qur'an and ceaseless recollection of God's names.[13] In discussing the recollection of God (*dhikr allah*), Ghazali spoke of different levels of attainment. The first is recollection of God on the tongue. The second is recollection of God in the heart, which makes recollection of God true but may not come naturally at first, requiring a bit of effort and concentration. The highest level is achieved when one has become so habituated to recalling God in one's heart that it comes naturally and effortlessly, so much so that the act of recollection is itself no more and all that remains in the recesses of the soul, occupying one's heart entirely, is the name of the One being recalled—namely, God. One is cognizant only of one's Lord, preoccupied with nothing save him. This produces detachment from worldly concerns—a state where nothing but God is the object of one's longing, love, and attention. This is possible, Ghazali avowed, because the heart is the gateway to the heavenly realm, constituting the site where divine lights descend on humans. Through the heart, by its absorption in the name of God, one goes to God and then exists in God. It is the heart, then, that becomes imprinted by the heavenly realm (*wa-ntaba'a lahu naqsh al-malakut*), and it is in the heart that the sanctity of divinity is manifest (*wa-tajalla lahu quds al-lahut*). In this graced state, one emulates only what the world of sanctity (*'alam al-quds*) makes manifest as represented by prophets, angels, and holy spirits (*al-arwah al-muqaddasa*)—all this disclosed to the heart as the fruit of ceaseless recollection of God's name.

When it comes to religion in general, Ghazali said that recitation of the Qur'an is the best way to imbue one's character with the virtues of religion. But for those who want to go to God, that is, to the world of sanctity, ceaseless recollection of his name is best. This could be called an intensely concentrated form of reciting the Qur'an, because, after all, the core of the Qur'an, its quintessence as Ghazali calls it, is knowledge of the One whose speech it is, namely God. For Ghazali, the best litany for recalling God is "There is no god but Allah, the Living and Self-Subsistent" (*la ilaha illa llah al-hayyu l-qayyum*).

However, for most, the transformation that such practices offer is blocked by impurities of the heart and body as well as intellectual doubts and excessive scruples with the external practices of the religion—its ritual and moral norms. Alas, the sanctifying illumination offered by the Qur'an remains veiled to humanity in general. Those preoccupied with worldly concerns are unable to identify emotionally—physically and spiritually—with the verses of the Qur'an. Thus, to identify with the names of God, Ghazali suggested certain techniques. When reciting verses pertaining to divine mercy and forgiveness, one should feel one's heart fly with joy, and when the verses pertain to divine wrath, one should feel faint as if dying of fright, and when mention is made of God's greatness, one should incline the head humbly, as if beholding his majesty.

In other words, the process of encountering God is not esoteric. The word of God is not a metaphor but real. Thus the Qur'an can have no impact on the soul as a set of ideas about God but requires emotional formation—schooling in spiritual affect as guided by the verbal expressions (i.e., literal wordings) of prophecy. One is not sanctified by assenting to the idea of the existence of God: Ghazali's approach is not a rational process, though neither is it irrational. Rather, sanctification comes by joining bodily movement and emotional affect with divine speech. The only way to have one's character informed by divine and not simply human wisdom is to integrate the Qur'an into one's limbs, one's feelings and sentiments, one's gut. Only through this communion of body and soul with divine speech can one be shaped by it and so be able to represent it in word and deed for others to see. This is Ghazali at his best—limbs in unison with the heart, action conforming to knowledge of God, which for Muslims is above all the soul-illuminating knowledge of the Qur'an. The path set by Ghazali, with its emphasis on frequent recitation of the Qur'an and recollection of the names of God, is one that many Muslims follow today in their desire to live in God's presence body and soul.

All of this resonates with Christians, who seek to be with God not simply as an idea, but viscerally, bodily, in communion with God through the Eucharist, the body of Christ that Christians receive in spiritual substance (not physical form). There are, of course, various ways to experience communion with God. For Pentecostal Christians, a direct reception of the Holy Spirit, which is the result of a personal engagement with scripture and can result in the gift of speaking in tongues, is a powerful way to realize fulfillment of the Christian message.[14] This baptism in the Holy Spirit seeks to reenact in our days what Christ's disciples experienced at Pentecost after their last physical encounter with Jesus. It is not, however, separate from the work of Christ but is the fruit of Christ's work on earth, his suffering, death, and resurrection.

Thus, for all Christians, Jesus is the fulfillment of prophecy, making the true presence of God known in a way that the prophets of old could point to but not actually bring about. Knowledge of the name of God as disclosed in the person of Jesus, called the Christ, enables Christian awareness of the spiritual mystery they carry within their bodies that makes them worthy to be called children of God. It is this that for Christians reveals the true identity of God as loving father. Of course, the basic characteristics of God's way of dealing with humankind had long been known before the coming of Christ. The Israelites knew him as creator, savior, and guiding companion, but Christians believe that the triune nature of the God of Israel was fully expressed in the work of Jesus, a human person who also fully revealed the truth about God. However important the Bible might be as record of the history of God's relation with his people, it is ultimately not the Bible but the body of Christ that decisively mediates the Christian experience of God, though some Christians do tend to make the Bible the primary means of living in the presence of God. For Christians, then, it is the work of God in Christ that fulfills the eternal covenant God made with Abraham and through him with all peoples.

What does it mean when Christians speak of Jesus as the full expression of the triune nature of the God of Israel? At the end of the Gospel of Matthew, Jesus commissions his disciples to go forth to all nations to baptize in the name of the Father, Son, and Holy Spirit. The word *trinity* does not occur in the Bible, but the historical experience of God's people, Christians believe, long made known God's way of relating with humanity, especially as creator, savior, and guiding companion, aspects of God's nature that were already known at the time of the Exodus from Egypt. Speaking of God as triune, then, is not to speak of a plurality of gods but of a plurality in God's eternal and essential nature. This is a point that Muslims have trouble accepting. It is not always easy for Christians to grasp. Is Jesus God? He was born of human flesh and lived as other humans but was also born of God, realizing a divinely initiated call towards his thirty-third year on earth. His unprecedented authority, as recorded in the New Testament, attracted people to him. At the core of his message was his announcement of the kingdom of God, a reality he gradually disclosed in his own person, culminating in his own death and resurrection as the first sign of eternal life with God. He arose from the dead not to die again but to be with God as his beloved son. Christians see in Christ the divine message that they too are born for God and thus the hope that they too will rise to be with God. Jesus, then, is human but he fully revealed the essential will of God, and so Christians cannot understand him apart from God or God apart from him.

Is the achievement of Christ similar to the role that saints have traditionally played in Islam? There are some fine theological distinctions to be made. The saints of Islam, like Jesus, are agents of God's purposes, working to mediate the presence of God for the world. They help bring about its salvation. However, saints come and go in every generation, working to renew the religion. Saints in Christianity have played a similar role. But the work of Jesus is unique fulfillment of the ancient covenant, sealing it once and for all by revealing God as love. Even if Christians are entrusted with the task of continuing the work of Christ, there is nothing more to be done to ensure the fruits of the covenant. The cross is the guarantee of God's eternal presence amidst his people. The achievement of Christ eliminated once and for all the fear of humiliating this relation, staining it with the disordered state of the human soul, and bringing on the community the wrath of God, though there are some Christians who continue to make much of the wrath of God in explaining human misery. In this sense, Jesus Christ is God's unique word and therefore worthy of being called son of God.

But there is some resonance. The prophets of ancient Israel alluded to the inability of the old covenant (i.e., the Mosaic Law) to sanctify the people. They also realized that all nations, not only the tribes of Israel, were subject to God. A new dispensation was anticipated where the laws that were meant to sanctify but invariably fell short of doing so were to be inscribed on the hearts not only of Israelites but also of all peoples. By introducing God's word into the core of humanity, the sanctity to which the Mosaic Law pointed could be achieved. Christians see the fulfillment of this promise in Jesus Christ.

Similarly, sainthood in Islam, the idea of being close to God, so close that he is closer than one's own jugular vein, originates in the Qur'an. The friend of God fulfills the promise (*wa'd*) of God and wards off his threat (*wa'id*). In imitation of the prophet, bearer of God's final word to humanity, the friend of God displays the piety that the Qur'an advocates. In this sense, too, Islam is the fulfillment of the friendship that God made with Abraham and through him all peoples who submit to God. Those who walk in the way of Abraham, a person with whom Muslims closely identify while on pilgrimage to Mecca, have no fear, as the Qur'an says, and do not sorrow (*la khawfa 'alayhim wa-la yahzanun*).

As sainthood in Islam flows from the Qur'an, so in Christianity it proceeds from Jesus Christ as the ongoing representation of his spirit at work in the world. Sainthood has long been integral to Christianity, and saints are cosaviors with Christ, working to continue what he initiated. The idea that those who serve the word of God are corulers with Christ in his heavenly kingdom is as old as the book of Revelation, which speaks of the early martyrs as ruling with Christ in his heavenly realm.[15] Some branches of Christianity, though describing the living members of the believing community as saints, see reverence of past saints as a pagan practice. But to devotees, the saint, though certainly not God, continues to disclose something about God even in death. Christians do not remember the dead saint as word of God but do see him or her as servant of God's word in a very dynamic way, sharing in its agency. The body of Christ may have restored the eternal covenant with God that original sin had marred, but need for visible witness to the body of Christ remains. Saints in Christianity are not simply models of human virtue but embody the presence of Christ, just as saints in Islam reproduce the ethical character of the prophet Muhammad. Through the centuries, the saints have made the spirit of Christ visible in their own bodies for those who did not see Christ in the flesh of Jesus. Francis of Assisi is a striking example of this, actually representing in his body the wounds of Christ as sign of salvation. Padre Pio of Italy is a more recent example. Indeed, Jesus is reported to have said to his disciples that those who wish to rule with him in his heavenly kingdom will have to drink from the same cup as he. Also, as noted earlier, some groups, such as the Pentecostals, see bodily representation of the Holy Spirit as the work of every believer. The body of all Christians becomes receptacle of sanctity.

In Islam, Jesus does fulfill God's purposes but not in a unique sense. Like other prophets, Jesus is not son but true servant of God. He does open the door of sanctity, not as savior but as prophet who calls people to worship of the one God alone and not of himself. Christians, of course, do not revere Jesus as God in the sense of an independent deity, distinct and separate from God. There are not two or three gods in Christianity but one, that is, the one God. Rather, the divinity of Jesus comes from his being word of God, originating in God and making the presence of God eternally available to humankind by his sacrifice. For Muslims, God's word is revealed by a book, and the idea of God's presence being made available by the sacrifice of his son sounds odd to Muslims for whom God's word is revealed through books, that is, the books brought by the prophets, above all the book brought by the prophet Muhammad. However, for Christians, a historical witness, recorded in the Bible, precedes the mission of Christ. It is only in light of this historical witness, which Muslims do not accept, that Christians see the cross as God's means of communicating his desire of eternal life for humankind. In this sense, the work of Christ on the cross is the fullest expression of God's will. The ancient Byzantine liturgy, followed today by many Christian Arabs, especially in Syria, speaks of God "trampling death by means of death" (*bi-l-mawt wati'ta l-mawt*). The cross, then, is the means by which God embraces death and raises it to himself, eliminating its hold on humanity.

Despite varied understanding of the way in which God's word is revealed, Christians and Muslims alike recognize the word of God as highest priority, preferring it over their own will. This is not to say that Christians and Muslims never fail to live up to this ideal, but it is a shared aspiration. They recognize that truth comes ultimately from God. Is that enough to say they stand on common religious ground? Do Christians and Muslims share a single will for the elevation of God's word above all? If so, they could not be heretics to one another. This is possible, but honesty requires recognition of different teachings: Jesus as unique claim for Christians and the Qur'an as unique claim for Muslims. Christians and Muslims may share a will for truth originating in God, but is it the same truth? Are their respective teachings so different as to raise questions about the commonality of the truth to which they respectively aspire? Is it possible to have a common will for truth when the teachings about that truth are significantly different? Christians and Muslims both speak of prophecy and its fulfillment, but in Christianity, prophecy is valid insofar as it speaks of God's desire to save his people. Is this also the mark of prophecy in Islam?

To be sure, neither Christians nor Muslims see themselves as rebels against God—or at least not against the knowledge of God confirmed by the respective traditions. This knowledge is surely not the same, but does it share enough substance that we can speak of a common truth? Neither Jesus nor Muhammad claimed to found a new religion. Are the respective revelations of God so different as to nullify common ground? They both claim to share a common end, life in God. How is this life understood?

Such questions will be explored in the chapters that follow. The question here is whether these two religions complement or challenge one another. Muslims revere Jesus Christ but do not award him unique status. That would make it difficult to introduce Muhammad into the prophetic heritage on equal footing with all prophets. The Qur'an is clear that no distinction is to be made between the prophets of God. Muhammad is like Abraham . . . is like Moses . . . is like Jesus. They collectively make up the brotherhood of prophecy with Muhammad as seal and the Qur'an as God's incomparable communiqué to humanity. The Qur'an speaks more of Jesus and Mary than of Muhammad, though less than of Abraham and Moses. Jesus in the Qur'an is a sign for humans and a mercy—high-ranked (*wajih*) in this world and the next. He is called God's word cast into Mary, and he is God's spirit blown into her to effect Jesus's fatherless conception. Jesus, the Qur'an says, is divinely sustained by the Holy Spirit (*ruh al-qudus*) and is a wonder-worker, healing the sick and raising the dead. It also says, at 3:55, that God will put Jesus to death and then raise him to heaven. In Islam, not Jesus but instead someone resembling him died on the cross as Jesus was raised up to God. Jesus is destined to return to inaugurate the end of history. Thus, it is only after battling the Antichrist that Jesus will die and then be raised to God a second time in accordance with the qur'anic verse.

This, however, does not make Jesus unique. The Qur'an calls him the Christ (*al-masih*)—not as son of God but as son of Mary. His virgin birth was not so different from the birth of Adam, whom God also brought into being by blowing his spirit into his human image as fashioned from clay. This equation of Adam with Christ may be why the Qur'an makes Adam the figure to whom angels prostrate instead of Jesus, as indicated in the opening chapter of the letter to the Hebrews. The Qur'an is clear that God is not the Christ, Jesus son of Mary. This would make God one of three, along with Jesus and Mary, not singular. The point is that Jesus and Mary are pure (a hadith says that they alone were born without sin) but are not gods—not partners with God in the work of bringing history to its final climax, which the Qur'an, like the New Testament, suggests is imminent. In short, the depiction of Jesus in the Qur'an is not redeemer but prophet who calls people to the worship of the one God as means to divine favor.

That the Qur'an speaks at all of Jesus makes it a gospel in a certain sense even if not squaring with Christian belief.[16] There were gospels other than the four that made it into the New Testament, and Christians over the centuries have variously represented Jesus, sometimes in ways that go well beyond the New Testament. Even the four canonical gospels do not convey a single depiction of Jesus Christ. Only in the Gospel of John is he called God—and, again, not as God the Creator but as the one who makes God fully known and undeniably present. There are many references in the New Testament to Jesus Christ as son of God, a title the Qur'an strongly denies. But David, anointed king of the Israelites, was in his day called both messiah and son of God. The title, son of God, need not suggest metaphysical stature but rather connotes agent of God's plan for humanity, namely salvation. In the case of David, this was understood in a political sense, as savior of his people from their enemies, whereas in the case of Jesus, it took on a spiritual sense, as savior from sin in the sense of all that separates the human from life with God. The Gospel of Mark uses the title in this sense. This is how the relation of Islam's saints to God is understood, not as God's associates, which would be a potential threat to the singularity of the godhead, nor as saviors, because there is no original sin in Islam, but as agents of God's will, making them God's representatives, God's beloved.

The point is that Christianity and Islam, along with Judaism, are about a revealed message but no less so about the possibility of fulfilling it. There are key differences in beliefs but also commonality of purpose. Are Christians to reject Islam simply because it appeared after Christianity, even though it shares Christianity's ultimate purposes?[17] The book of Revelation is one example of prophecy after the coming of Christ that made it into Christian scripture. Like John, author of Revelation, Muhammad was visited by an angel and instructed to convey a message of repentance and exhort believers to hold firm in anticipation of the impending judgment day when belief would be vindicated and unbelief cast down. This is not to overlook content—the Christ of the Qur'an is not the Christ of the book of Revelation—but rather to note that Christian communities have always been open to new reception of the word of God even after its fulfillment in Christ. A key question, of course, is whether Muslims can acknowledge the Christian understanding of Christ without prejudice to the depiction of Christianity in the Qur'an. This is a complicated question. It has been suggested that the

Christians described in the Qur'an represent the beliefs of a deviant sect at the time of the prophet Muhammad that interpreted the trinity as three separate Gods. This sect, then, cannot be said to represent the beliefs of all Christians at all times. As a result, it would not be right for Muslims to take the qur'anic depiction of Christianity as warrant to classify Christians today as polytheists.[18]

This is the point. Christianity and Islam have never limited themselves to the texts of scripture. These texts, rather, are points of departure for something much more dynamic. God's message is about literal wordings but also about human responses to the possibilities these wordings hold out. Christianity and Islam are not locked in a theological duel, as if one is to be compared with another and judged to be better or worse by a set of criteria that invariably favors one over the other. To compare and contrast is not the final purpose of prophecy and may even mask its final purpose—namely, reception of the word of God in the human heart. There is, then, some sense in looking at these two religions through a single but refracted lens of religious plurality.

It is possible to speak of Christianity and Islam, along with rabbinical Judaism, as distinct commentaries on the biblical heritage. Both Christianity and Islam, in this sense, can be rooted in the book of Isaiah. There, God is proclaimed to be unique, not simply one of many, but singular, the one who alone creates and thus the one who alone is able to save, in contrast to idols, which are not creators but themselves created and thus unable to save on judgment day when all nations, not just Israel, will be held to account. It is this strand of the prophetic heritage that Islam intends to fulfill—the call to worshipful and grateful submission to the God who is alone God, none other. By emphasizing this strand of the biblical heritage, Islam does not rule out the importance of ritual sacrifice, but it is decidedly secondary in Muslim liturgical life, featuring chiefly at the annual feast commemorating Abraham's near sacrifice of his son. Rather, what stands out in Islam is prayer. Bowing down in prayerful submission to worship the one God is the ritual action par excellence of Islam, as modeled from Abraham to Muhammad.

The idea of a suffering servant, crucified on a cross as expression of God's will, does not make sense as the fulfillment of prophecy, at least in terms of the strand of the biblical heritage that Islam emphasizes. Holy people, prophets and saints, do not come into the world to be sacrificed for the sake of expiating human sin but rather to point to divinity as object of prayerful submission.[19] They are humans, specially chosen, who call people to God. Thus Hallaj, a controversial figure of the ninth century who claimed to embody divine truth and was subsequently crucified, in his view to expiate the sins of Muslims, was not accepted as a liturgical model—that is, a focal point of communal prayer—in Islam. His life and death did not reflect the part of the prophetic heritage that Islam emphasizes, prayerful worship of the unique Creator and Lord. In Islam, there are prophets but not priests. There are saints, whose bodies model sanctity, but not priests who officiate over a divine sacrifice as focal point of Christian worship. Because ritual sacrifice is not integral to worship in Islam, Muslims, who, like Christians, do conceive of themselves as a worshipful people, a people striving always to be grateful and faithful to God, nevertheless, unlike Christians, do not describe themselves as a priestly people.

The book of Isaiah contains another strand—the suffering servant who represents God's chosen means of redeeming his people. He will suffer. As agent of God's plan to redeem his people, however, he is divinely exalted (52:13). For the first Christians, their experience of Jesus was prefigured in the suffering servant mentioned in Isaiah. The various accoutrements of the old covenant—land, temple, law—all seemed to be despoiled by foreign rule of one kind or another. It was up to God to preserve the covenant for the sake of his holy name, and Christianity became fulfillment of God's promise of redeeming his people by means of his suffering servant. It is in this sense that the crucifixion has meaning for Christians as fulfillment of prophecy. Jesus is not fulfillment of prophecy in the general sense of calling people to worship God but in the particular sense of completing the ritual sacrifice that had failed its purposes. This, as noted by prophets of ancient Israel such as Malachi, only brought God's curse on the community, risking its standing before

God. As fulfillment of prophecy in this unique sense, Jesus Christ for Christians is also sacrifice, fulfillment of temple sacrifice. His crucifixion, as agent of sanctity, hence fulfillment of prophecy, is therefore consistent with the biblical heritage as read by Christians.

The variant depictions of Jesus Christ in the New Testament and the Qur'an should therefore not be taken as theological deficiency or doctrinal deviance, accusations that Christians and Muslims have cast at each other over the centuries. Christians and Muslims both have a sound biblical understanding of God as Creator and Lord of all and the one who is mercifully present to his peoples. He is not tribal deity or ancestral spirit within a pantheon of deities, but the one apart from whom there is no other. However, in emphasizing different strands of the prophetic heritage, Christianity and Islam end with different depictions of Jesus. In both, he is agent of sanctity in his work of fulfilling prophecy. But Christians do not view him simply as fulfillment of prophecy in the sense of sainthood in Islam, that is, perfect worship of God and corresponding manifestation of his attributes as disclosed by the prophecy of Islam. Christians see Jesus more specifically as fulfillment of biblical prophecy that calls for correct sacrifice as means of attaining sanctity, reconciling the community to God. This makes his crucified body, as the new temple, the focal point of worship. In Islam, prophecy is understood not as a call to perfection of temple sacrifice but to worship of the one God, who in the Qur'an as in the book of Isaiah is fully proclaimed not as deity of a particular people but as the one and only God, Creator and Lord of all, before whom submission is right and just, exclusively, apart from any other being, and who alone can sustain. In this sense, Jesus Christ in the Qur'an becomes a prophet like other prophets. He calls people to worship of the one God but does not offer his life on behalf of their sins, making it superfluous and unreasonable to envision him as priestly victim who fulfills the laws of ritual sacrifice.

Do the different teachings about Jesus, reflecting different conceptions of prophethood, make Christians and Muslims heretics to one another? Christian and Muslim teachings, as just noted, both have a biblical basis, resonating with different strands of the book of Isaiah. Thus, despite different teachings, Christians and Muslims are oriented to the same God. This is a point noted by the Second Vatican Council in the document titled *Nostra aetate*. They share a common openness to truth that comes from the same God. They have different ways of proceeding, different teachings, and different understandings of the way in which truth is fulfilled, but there is common openness to truth as revealed by the one God of Abraham.

Moreover, differences in the depiction of Jesus notwithstanding, Christianity and Islam do operate according to similar mechanics. Both see the biblical heritage as ongoing cycle of prophecy and sanctity: the first a message revealing God to the people, and the second fulfillment of the message in the community. Religion is an initiative that for both traditions begins and ends in the one God. The point in thinking of the pluralistic nature of the biblical heritage is not to compare Bible and Qur'an in the hopes of finding—or teasing out—consistencies or inconsistencies. Christians and Muslims do not understand comparative exegesis as the central point of scripture. Rather, scripture, written record of the prophetic heritage, invites believers into relation with God. Revelation as such exists not for debate about the nature of God but rather to open a way to be in his presence. Christians and Muslims alike strive for this goal. Does religion as divine initiative, set in motion by prophecy and fulfilled in sanctity, leave any room for human nature, for human thinking, for human questions and queries, even doubts, about the message of prophecy and teachings of the tradition? That is the topic for the next chapter. For now, it is enough to say that prophecy, recorded in scripture, is the point of departure for a life with God. In that, the hearts of Christians and Muslims are similarly moved.

There will always be Christian-Muslim dissonance when it comes to the literal wordings of religion, but Christians and Muslims both seek to listen to—and be moved by—the word of God, a word that is divine and has therefore always existed with God even before it is disclosed by prophecy. Christians and Muslims understand the word of God to be larger than what scripture records—it is unlimited and knows no bounds.[20] The Qur'an, for example, declares that the sea, even if it were ink, would not exhaust God's words (18:109). Christians and Muslims can therefore seek to listen to the word of God together on common ground, even in search of a common word, but both traditions have a preliminary condition for doing so. One must understand oneself to be in the presence of God to hope to hear his word clearly. The word of God may have always existed with God, but humans need prophecy to know it, and not only prophecy but also the fulfillment of prophecy as sign of God's presence amidst his people. In other words, prophecy is not the end point but rather the necessary starting point, setting in motion a process by which humans can comprehend the ultimate reality of God. And this process includes both communication of a message and its fulfillment in humans (i.e., in the believing community). Possession of the message is not enough. People are needed whose piety shows that the message engenders sanctity, demonstrating its credibility as heavenly sent. It is this piety, humanly embodied, that mediates holiness to the community, orienting it to the presence of God and thus enabling its ongoing reception of the unbounded word of God.

Christians and Muslims have unique ways of going about this. They have different prophetic heritages and different traditions of teachings, but there is a common will to be in the divine presence to listen more attentively to the inexhaustible word of God—that was, and is, and always will be. Even if recognizing unique manifestations of God's message in history, Christians and Muslims do not limit the word of God to a single time or place. It is in that idea—and not in the historical manifestations of God's message to the two communities—that Christians and Muslims share ground. But the common ground is not solid. There are different understandings of the way God's word has moved through history. Christians and Muslims will not reach a common word when it comes to scripture, that is, the sacred narrative each community affirms, but can do so when it comes to the ultimate point of scripture, that is, its fulfillment in human lives. Both communities are open to the truth of God even if in unique ways. The question, of course, is whether Christians and Muslims, in light of their unique claims, are bound to undertake this process only within the limits of their respective communities or whether in fact they share enough common ground to witness life in God for one another as well.

NOTES

1. Abu Hatim al-Razi, *A'lam al-Nubuwwa*, ed. Salah al-Savi (Tehran: The Iranian Royal Society of Philosophy, 1977), 160–70.

2. On Abu Bakr al-Razi, see Sarah Stroumsa, *Freethinkers of Medieval Islam* (Leiden: Brill, 1999), 87–120.

3. See Martha Himmelfarb, *Ascension to Heaven in Jewish and Christian Apocalypses* (Oxford: Oxford University Press, 1999).

4. See Richard Bauckham, *God Crucified. Monotheism and Christology in the New Testament* (Grand Rapids, MI: William B. Eerdmans, 1998).

5. al-Muhasibi, *al-Wasaya* (Beirut: Dar al-Kutub al-'Ilmiyya, 2003).

6. Ibid., 44.

7. This distinction is still made in Islam today, especially in the circles of Sufism. For example, see "al-'Ulama' bi-llah wa-l-'Ulama' bi-Ahkam Allah 'inda Ibn Rushd al-Jadd," *al-Ishara* 26 (2003): 26–27. This journal, now defunct, was published by the Butshishiyya, a Moroccan-based Sufi group.

8. This idea is generally associated with the mystical philosopher of the classical period, Ibn 'Arabi (died 1240). However, it is not limited to the intellectual elite of Sufism but also exists on a popular level. It is, for example, central to the Barelwi movement of the Indian subcontinent. For an overview of the idea, see Muhammad al-'Amrani, "al-Haqiqa al-Muhammadiyya aw 'Ayn al-Rahma min khilal al-Tajriba al-Sufiyya," *'Awarif* 1 (2006): 63–78. This journal is published by al-Rabita al-Muhammadiyya lil-'Ulama' in Morocco (www.arrabita.ma).

9. See Jamil M. Abun-Nasr, *Muslim Communities of Grace* (New York: Columbia University Press, 2007).

10. See Pnina Werbner, *Pilgrims of Love* (London: Hurst, 2003).

11. Werbner, 275.

12. 'Abd al-Ghani Moundib, *al-Din wa-l-Mujtama'* (Casablanca: Ifriqiyya al-Sharq, 2006), 123–31.

13. al-Ghazali, *Kitab al-Arba'in fi Usul al-Din* (Cairo: Maktabat al-Jundi, 1964).

14. For example, see Grant Wacker, *Heaven Below. Early Pentecostals and American Culture* (Cambridge, MA: Harvard University Press, 2001).

15. Martyrdom in both Islam and Christianity has a complex history. Martyrs were important for the representation of sanctity in early Christianity but would eventually be displaced by saints as normative form of Christian holiness. The possibility of martyrdom, of course, was never dismissed entirely and sometimes was actively sought out, especially in contexts of competition for the mantle of Christian truth. Martyrdom in such contexts acted as a proof of the truth of one branch of Christianity over another, as was true with the Donatists in earlier centuries and with various Christian groups of later centuries. If one were willing to die for a doctrine, surely it must be true. And yet, it was discovered, death for a cause was not enough to guarantee its truth. Other criteria were needed. See Daniel Boyarin, *Dying for God: Martyrdom and the Making of Christianity and Judaism* (Stanford, CA: Stanford University Press, 1999); and Brad S. Gregory, *Salvation at Stake: Christian Martyrdom in Early Modern Europe* (Cambridge, MA: Harvard University Press, 1999).

16. On the idea of the Qur'an as a gospel, see Tarif Khalidi, *The Muslim Jesus: Sayings and Stories in Islamic Literature* (Cambridge, MA: Harvard University Press, 2001).

17. To be sure, many Christian theologians are giving thought to this question. How is the specifically religious value of other religions to be determined? Does God's desire to be with humans work through the particularities of other religions or despite those particularities? This inquiry, too extensive to be detailed here, remains hotly contested.

18. On this question, see Jane D. McAuliffe, *Qur'anic Christians* (Cambridge: Cambridge University Press, 1991).

19. This is true even in the case of Hussein, Muhammad's grandson, whose murder in 680 CE at Karbala in today's Iraq does have liturgical significance for Shi'a. Collective remembrance of this event and bodily identification with it is a means of communal reconciliation with God. However, the wounds of Hussein are not understood to reveal the identity of God. For Shi'ism, history got derailed from the course God had intended for it, above all by the Umayyads who persecuted the true Imams and tarnished Islam by their worldly ways. The martyrdom of Hussein thus serves a vital role in the ritual life of the Shi'ism as part of the religious ceremonies signaling the community's renewed commitment to God.

20. In that sense, the possession of revealed truth should never be considered grounds for claiming a monopoly on it but rather a means of discerning its presence in the world, even beyond the bounds of a particular confession. On this point, see Daniel A. Madigan, "Saving *Dominus Iesus*," in *Learned Ignorance: An Investigation into Humility in Interreligious Dialogue among Christians, Muslims and Jews*, edited by James Heft, Reuven Firestone, and Omid Safi, in press.

CHAPTER TWO

HOW MUCH GOOD NEWS CAN WE TAKE?

A 2007 SURVEY by the Pew Forum on Religion & Public Life in the United States noted the increasing importance of those with no religious membership, roughly 16 percent of the population. Interestingly, most of them, 12 percent of Americans, believe in God but do not identify with a particular religious community. It is common to hear people claim to be spiritual but not religious. Americans have long been independent when it comes to their personal beliefs. No outside authority—governmental, ecclesiastical, or intellectual—should determine one's faith outlook. But, historically, Americans have identified with particular traditions. Why at this juncture in history is there noticeable doubt about religion? John Paul II took up this issue in his 1993 encyclical, *The Splendor of Truth*, especially in relation to moral life: How are we to know the truth and live by it in an age that exalts individual freedom? Similarly, in the Muslim world, there is discussion about some prophetic teachings that do not reflect the spirit of the age, especially regarding the role of women in society. Does this mean that the prophetic message as a whole is unreliable?[1] In a pluralistic age, marked by fierce battles between secularists and fundamentalists over the nature of human existence, the question of religious doubt is part of the rough religious terrain shared by Christians and Muslims. It is worth mentioning, too, the serious doubts today about the secular project, the idea that the world fares better without God. Here, however, our inquiry will focus on religious doubt.

Although we usually do not associate doubt with religion, it has always been vital to the welfare of religion. Ultimately, doubt ensures that religion not become reduced to a set of definitions but remain essentially a relation—known but still mysterious. Doubt about religious teachings has existed at all times and places and in all cultures but becomes more pronounced under certain conditions. The existence of multiple religions, for example, challenges the idea of a single truth. Additionally, the association of religion with violence or, alternatively, the religious rejection of scientific discoveries can contribute to religious skepticism. Indeed, the possibility of verifying the truth claims of religion is itself elusive. Is the message true? If we cannot respond with certainty, why should we commit ourselves to it? People do often act without clear knowledge. They take risks in business and policymaking. They are ready to trust others even if they do not know them fully. But it is also true that doubt can paralyze us, leaving us unable to act decisively in the name of truth. This is true in all spheres of life but especially when it comes to action for God. We cannot see God. We can neither prove nor disprove his existence. Do we have conclusive evidence that the revelation is truly a message from him, disclosing who he is and what he wants? We might have hopes but we also have reservations. If it is not clearly true, why submit to its obligations or act on its behalf?

To some extent, the Qur'an can be read as a response to this kind of doubt. Muhammad's audience in seventh-century Arabia was diverse. It included devotees of tribal gods whom the Qur'an called to the worship of the one God. Jews and Christians were also a targeted audience, charged with beliefs that fell short of true monotheism.[2] Evidence in the Qur'an suggests that they hesitated to heed Muhammad's message. They lived happily, worshipping as their forefathers had before them. They had their own prophetic message, namely the book, that is, the Bible. What was the point of another? There were apparently debates among these monotheistic Arabs about the resurrection of the body, the existence of the hereafter, and the judgment day to come; such themes feature prominently in the Qur'an, as if to quell doubts. These

Jews and Christians, the Qur'an suggests, both claimed to be the saved community, exclusively, a kind of intramonotheistic rivalry. Still, what more was there to say about God and his ways? Muhammad would have to produce a great sign if he hoped to be accepted.

This is exactly what Muhammad chose not to do. Because of the Jewish and Christian skepticism about the appearance of a new message from God, Muhammad made it clear that his was not a new message but the true message in pristine version that had once been given to Jews and Christians. The message of God to Moses, Jesus, and Muhammad was one, the very same message given to Abraham, who, the Qur'an notes, was neither Jew nor Christian. In response to the skeptics, the Qur'an claimed that the Bible had been distorted (*tahrif*). Jewish and Christian leaders had doctored the texts to support their interests and authority. A clear revelation was needed to end all divisions, but Muhammad was no soothsayer. He did not dabble in the occult and was not about to make a book miraculously descend from heaven in one piece. The truth of his message, he avowed, was plain for all to see. Just look, the Qur'an exhorts, at the alternation of day and night, the rain that comes down to renew the land, the nations of the earth that come to power, decline, and fade into oblivion. Could all this be anything but the work of a single all-powerful creator? And if so, what would save you from him if you failed to follow his directives? Why cry out to any other being for support and sustenance? Your idols have no power either to harm or benefit. They will not rescue you. Your prophets of the past were not saviors, sons of God as you claim, but only called you to worship of the one God. Yet you distorted this message by associating partners with God, claiming they would intercede for you, when in fact you alone will face the consequences of your actions on judgment day. Believe in God with gratitude!

That monotheism was not new posed a challenge for the Qur'an. The Qur'an not infrequently mentions past messengers who had brought word of the one God, associating Muhammad with this prophetic lineage. The problem, the Qur'an notes, is that people, even if accepting monotheism, have failed to live up to its implication—perfect submission to the will of the one God. Instead, they place their hopes in figures, associated with the one God, whom they presume will protect them from his wrath. But the Qur'an is clear that God's mercy extends to those who repent and believe. Others risk perdition, and, the Qur'an says, the Bible itself says so. The people in the time of Noah were wiped out for not listening to him. Pharaoh met his fate for not heeding the message of Moses. What further evidence was needed? The Qur'an only confirms this. It was therefore necessary to set forth the message once more, indeed once and for all, decisively, so that people would live up to it, unlike the other monotheists of the day. What is the point of the Bible if no one lives out its demands? Muhammad is but a warner, as the Qur'an notes, to those who ignore the message and a herald of good news to those who give ear. It was not for him to judge. All accounts would be settled on judgment day. He had been sent only to convey good counsel.

This responsibility of living in acknowledgment of the one God as Lord is a tremendous responsibility. Indeed, the Qur'an claims, when God offered his covenant to creation, even the mountains refused to bear it. Only the human being, foolishly, agreed to assume it. Muslims are therefore those who shoulder the responsibility of living up to the will of God. This idea might have applied to the first Muslims who chose to be Muslims, but what of Muslims today born into their religion? Do they also have this responsibility? And if they do not live up to it, are they no longer Muslim?

In 2006 the influential Muslim leader Yusuf Qaradawi caused a stir in Morocco, a nation where the head of state is a descendant of the prophet Muhammad and Islam is the official religion as specified in the constitution. Qaradawi ruled that Moroccans could follow non-Muslim (i.e., foreign) financial practices because they do not live in a country where Islam is properly observed. In essence, he condemned an entire nation for failing Islam and the directives of the one all-powerful God whom none escapes on judgment day. But what happens when the message is no longer compelling? The pious would attribute this to people's failure to listen to the message in full faith, preferring the allurements of this world. But times change and sentiments do, too.

God's directives may seem reasonable at one time but not so at another. Is one to adhere to the way of God simply because it is his command? One need only look at the book of Deuteronomy in the Bible. Some of its laws seem primitive and even bizarre. Are we to accept them simply because they were revealed by God to Moses? But if we do not, do we risk the wrath of God? Moreover, the gate of prophecy has been closed. The prophet Muhammad is the seal. There will be no other prophets to update the message, a belief that has caused significant problems in Muslim relations with the Baha'i and Ahmadi communities, both of which emerged from Islam in the nineteenth century with the claim of new prophecy in synch with the age.

The religious tradition itself, when it grows too large, may make it difficult to believe. Over the years, issues arise that were not treated in the original revelation, but this does not mean they stand outside the scope of God's judgment. Specialists within the community study the matter and determine a ruling believed to reflect the divine will. In Islam, for example, photography is permitted, but some have deemed it to be forbidden. This is also the case with dancing. Seafood can be eaten, but some have said it is reprehensible to do so. What about organ transplant? Gradually, God's directives are enlarged to cover life's minute details. In the end, however, it becomes impossible to fulfill them all, especially when the issues that engendered the rulings in the first place no longer exist. Is the community at risk of losing divine favor even when it desires to please God but cannot do so in the face of the endless rulings associated with his will?

One option, as discussed in chapter 1, is the saintly intercessor whose perfect piety renders the community pleasing to God. Today, however, when democratic sentiment has left its mark on religion, there is a strong sense that individuals are responsible for their own standing before God. This is one reason behind Qaradawi's condemnation of Morocco, which has a long tradition of sainthood. The belief in a hierarchy of saints, protecting the nation, remains strong in many places, but the reformist mindset objects. There are those in Morocco who, like Qaradawi, feel that for the nation to be credibly Muslim, the laws that shape its practices must be manifestly religious, not foreign. All citizens must truly live by Islam for the nation to be Muslim. It is not enough to rest on the laurels of saintly protectors. What happens, then, when those who embrace the message of the Qur'an do not live up to its teachings? The Qur'an defends itself in light of the failure of past monotheists to live up to the demands of the Bible. And now, it would seem, Muslims are no better. Were the suspicions of Muhammad's audience well founded? Even after the disclosure of the Qur'an, it would appear that people are still unable to lead lives pleasing to God.

This, of course, has not been the Muslim conclusion. A well-known hadith states that the religion will be renewed in every generation. Key leaders, renewers, will work this out in light of new developments. The religious heritage might be pared down, not the clear rulings of scripture, such as the prohibition of alcohol and pork or the command to pray, but the various rulings that past specialists had derived in response to the demands of their day but that now no longer make sense. Abridging the heritage is one way to make it easier for Muslims to follow the will of God and remain on his straight path. Muslims will, once again, be able to hope for the mercy of God, reassured that they are not humiliating the religion by failing to meet its demands.

Such a process is unfolding today, even if moving in different directions. It can cause confusion about what is incumbent on Muslims. But the point is that new needs have cast doubt on past rulings. Can a Muslim woman travel without male accompaniment? Can she initiate divorce proceedings? Should a daughter receive only half her brother's share of the family inheritance? Can Muslims live in non-Muslim society? Can a Muslim take out an interest-based mortgage to purchase a home if no other means of finance are available? Is democracy appropriate for Muslim society even when elected officials hand down legislation at odds with Islam? Can believers shake hands with members of the opposite sex? Can a Muslim woman marry a non-Muslim man who is favorably disposed to Islam but has no intention of converting? These and many other issues are under scrutiny today when the role of women is not as it once was, when males and females mix and mingle in public places unregulated, when the state claims authority to define the moral life of the nation, when Muslims and non-Muslims interact with greater frequency and sometimes fall in love. A new era might not require a new religion, but if religion is to be relevant, it will need to be renewed in some fashion.

Such issues are moral quandaries—not theological ones such as the existence of God, the immortality of the soul, or a judgment day to come. We might assume that doubts over core doctrines pose a greater threat to a religion, but the real challenge lies in doubts about its moral teachings that embody the way it is concretely lived. It is actual practices, perhaps more so than creedal statements, that are the real agents of piety, orienting the soul to God and making palpable what the doctrines set forth only as ideas. Doubts about practices, then, raise questions about the credibility of the religion as a whole. Pope Paul VI issued a papal letter in 1968, *Humanae vitae*, that affirmed the church's rejection of artificial methods of birth control. It was not at the time presented as infallible truth, though John Paul II would seem to have raised it to such a status, but it did usher in a crisis of faith for the church. And a crisis of faith cannot be addressed by a simple appeal to traditions. The traditions must make sense before they are accepted as true. Pope Benedict XVI would surely argue that *Humanae vitae* makes sense to the mind but he also notes that "if traditions are all we have, then truth has been lost. And sooner or later we will ask what in fact traditions are for. And in that case a revolt against tradition is well founded."[3]

One can speak of a revolt against tradition in Islam today. Why live as Muslims of the past if it no longer makes sense to do so? Although some think that the only way to be true to Islam is by imitating the first Muslims, including outward forms of clothing and behavior, most Muslims live according to the realities of contemporary life, reasonably but with little clear relation to Islam. Are Muslims who deposit their money in interest-bearing bank accounts sinners? Do the ethics of Islam still make sense?

Yusuf Qaradawi is an influential voice in Sunni Islam today. An Egyptian based in Qatar, he tries to make religion easy for Muslims

(*taysir*). A parallel in Shi'i Islam might be Muhammad Hussein Fadlul-
lah of Lebanon. Qaradawi is also controversial. Some years back, he
issued a statement recognizing the legitimacy of suicide attacks against
Israeli civilians. In October 2008 he precipitated a Sunni-Shi'i war over
the Internet by denouncing Shi'i missionary efforts in Sunni societies.
Also in October 2008, he vigorously condemned the attacks against the
Christians of Iraq, calling on Muslims to protect their Christian brethren, who, he added, are full members of the abode of Islam with the
same rights and duties as Muslims. In short, he has two major goals:
the stability and independence of Arab lands under Muslim rule, and
adaptation of Islam to the realities in which Muslims live today. Morocco, to return to the country whose religious integrity Qaradawi ques-
tioned, is certainly in search of a vision that combines the values of the
past with the realities of the present.

In a recent book, *Study of the Purposes of Shari'a: Between Universal
Principles and Particular Texts*, Qaradawi argues for balance: The particular teachings of Islam should not be blindly followed without understanding their rationales and purposes.[4] He rejects a literal reading of
religion but also seeks to preserve a distinctly Muslim way of life. He is
conservative but recognizes the challenge of making religion relevant
today. Qaradawi claims that every ruling has a rationale. When the
rationale that inspired the ruling in the first place no longer holds, it is
right to reconsider the teaching. He criticizes literalists but also Muslims who too easily take on non-Muslim ways of life.

For example, he defends the ruling that awards a daughter half of
what her brother receives of the family inheritance. This is reasonable,
he claims, though some might disagree, because the daughter receives
a dower when she marries whereas her brother will have to pay one,
offsetting the difference. In contrast, the ruling prohibiting women
from traveling without male accompaniment is no longer reasonable
because the rationale behind it no longer holds. When the ruling was
given, travel by camel was risky in strange lands where bandits were
ready to pounce. It would have been foolish to allow women to travel
alone. Today, modern means of travel reduce such safety concerns. A

woman who travels alone to visit friends or relatives abroad has not offended God.

One could ask whether Qaradawi has understood the rationale that originally inspired the ruling in this last case, namely, concern for a woman's sexual propriety. But that is beside the point. He wants to make it easy to be Muslim in today's world without all the complicated rulings of the past. This is especially true for Muslims living in non-Muslim society. Qaradawi has argued for special allowance for Muslim minorities to live according to non-Muslim ways, at least until things change and it is possible to live according to Muslim ways once again. So, for example, he teaches that Muslims in Europe can take out interest-based mortgages to purchase their homes.

Some hold that Muslims should not even live in non-Muslim society, basing themselves on a prophetic saying in which Muhammad absolves himself of responsibility for Muslims living among non-Muslims. This, Qaradawi contends, does not imply that Muslims are not to live in a land where Islam does not prevail. It is important to consider the historical context of the report—a state of war when Muslims who chose to reside in enemy territory needlessly put their lives at risk. In that day, Qaradawi argues, Muslim leaders were obliged to compensate for the unnecessary loss of Muslim lives under their command. The rationale is not to prohibit Muslims from living in non-Muslim society but to limit unnecessary loss of Muslim life. There is no moral dilemma for Muslims to immigrate to non-Muslim lands at peace with Islam—for study, to earn a living, and even to take up permanent residence.

All this suggests the importance of thinking more deeply about the historical factors driving doubt about religion. Of course, today, even aside from religion, there is doubt that the human mind can know truth of any kind. When it comes to religion, it is often thought that one either accepts the religion and its teachings or one does not. Indeed, many assume that religion requires one to toe a fundamentalist life—unquestioned adherence to the truth claims of scripture apart from what the mind might conclude to be reasonable or unreasonable. As a result, those unwilling to be fundamentalist conclude that religion is not for them, given that it requires them to deny the workings of the mind. Hence, they opt for spirituality or a set of philosophical principles around which to structure their life. This can be very enriching, of course, but it can also be historically myopic. It is not a question of doubting or not doubting, believing or not believing. Doubts, as we will see, actually form an integral part of religion. They do not, however, appear out of nowhere, simple products of the rational mind, but are closely intertwined with historical developments.

For example, doubts about the literal wording of the Bible were raised in the period leading up to the U.S. Civil War.[5] It was not the case, however, that people suddenly decided that it is unreasonable to believe in a book claiming to represent the word of God. Rather, historical factors were at work: The increasing distaste for slavery—at least for abolitionists—made it difficult to accept the Bible's apparently pro-slavery material, raising questions about its authority overall. Doubt, then, cannot be separated from historical realities. It is not only a question of whether the teachings of religion are believable but whether they are believable within a particular society and its attitudes to a host of ethical questions. Why people doubt is therefore a question for social scientists no less than for theologians and philosophers.

There are, of course, serious struggles for the truth of religion, and these struggles have political consequences. Many insights of modern science, particularly the theory of evolution, have posed a serious challenge not so much to Christianity but to those branches of it that tie religious truth wholly to a literal reading of the Bible.[6] Such a reading would suggest that the world is several thousand years old, not several billion as science shows, or that the human being is the direct product of divine creation without intervening (and less dignified) stages prior to our current status as homo sapiens.

The Darwinian challenge to the truth claims of religion is real, but battles over the teaching of evolution in U.S. public schools, ever since the famous Scopes trial of 1925, have been as much about preserving local control over education and its attendant values as defending religious truth per se.[7] In this sense, in very American fashion, the Bible shields a community from outside claims to superior authority, whether political or intellectual. Indeed, the First Amendment to the U.S. Constitution that deprives the state of religious authority is not so much a secular innovation as the will of religious communities, particularly Baptists. Prior to independence, the persecution they experienced at the hands of state-aligned powers, both political and ecclesiastical, led them to embrace religious freedom as a core Christian belief to protect their way of life from outside interference.[8]

Although biblically based religion can protect communities from tyranny, the commitment to the inerrancy of the Bible, which took a harder line in some Christian communities in response to the challenges of modern science, has fed into odd attempts at defending religious truth. A certain brand of Anglo-American Christianity displays a deep yearning for the end of the world, the rapture, partly out of a need to demonstrate the truth of the Bible. If all texts of the Bible are literally true, including prophecies about the end of the world, it becomes vital to realize them in history, exactly as narrated, as proof of the credibility of the religion.

Such logic follows from a reading of ancient passages that speak of a final battle between a righteous remnant of believers and the forces of Satan as prelude to the return of Christ. It is a selective reading, patching together passages from books as distant in time as Ezekiel and Revelation. In fact, a reading that pays attention to the historical and cultural context in which these passages were formulated would conclude that the intent of the author is to encourage believers to trust in the promise of God to be with them amidst the hardships they face. Instead, a literal reading produces a militant Christianity that seeks to encourage the modern state of Israel to battle its enemies, not out of a concern for the Jewish people but rather as a theater on which to enact the hoped-for Armageddon.[9] By limiting religious truth to the Bible, some Christians thus lock themselves into a choice between doubt over the literal reading of what they view as the singular source of religious truth and the need to find a political stage on which to enact some of its more obscure passages—all this to demonstrate the Bible's veracity in the face of modern science. The question of religious doubt, potentially healthful, thus becomes perverted into a political project with potentially harmful consequences. A similar process can be noted in some circles of Islam, as discussed in chapter 4.

However, religious doubt need not beget a militant piety that would battle all forces that question a literal reading of ancient and obscure passages of the Bible. It also does not generally lead people to abandon religion but rather to revise their understanding of it. Dogmatism is challenged. The purported facts of religion are thrown into doubt. This may encourage fideism—the acceptance of religious teachings apart from questions the mind might raise. In general, however, skepticism pushes believers to reconsider faith. It is not, then, simply a matter of updating the moral teachings of religion, as noted. Indeed, this can create new doubts about religion. The logic is as follows: If religious teachings are acceptable only insofar as they make sense to the minds of believers within the historical conditions in which they live, does this not make reason the final arbiter of religious teachings, at least when it comes to morals if not also beliefs about the world to come? Are we not back to the position of Abu Bakr al-Razi, discussed in chapter 1, who saw no tangible benefit in religion? If the mind determines how we are to lead our lives, then, however much people might pray, participate in rituals, and believe in God, they still end by following the dictates of their conscience in determining life's issues. Is religion up for grabs? If some things can change, cannot all? And if the religion itself recognizes the role of individual conscience, does the religion have any enduring value of its own? Religion can sometimes find itself in a Catch-22. If it adapts to new realities, doubts are raised about the eternal truth of its teachings, but if it does not adapt, doubts are raised about its relevance.

The key question, then, is whether beliefs matter for lived reality. Or are they only ideas that the mind either assents to or denies? And if they only exist in the abstract, what worth do they have? Again, skepticism is not just skepticism but a device for challenging the nature of religion. This is noticeable in one of the great controversies of modern

Christianity that pit Jesuits against Jansenists, both vigorous movements within Catholicism. Skepticism had moved to the forefront of European intellectual life beginning especially in the fifteenth and sixteenth centuries. A significant factor was the formalization of Christian plurality with the appearance of Protestantism. This confessional plurality may have been intellectually enriching but also raised doubts about Christian truth and the criterion for determining it—the authority of the church or the authority of scripture? Where was Christian truth to be found and, much more significantly, what set of rituals embodied it? The import of the Eucharist, pillar of Christian life, was at stake. Protestant-Catholic polemics, to say nothing of armed conflict, were the order of the day. There was also a spike in martyrdom, death for God, deployed as proof of one's creed. One's beliefs must be true if one was willing to die for them, no? And yet people were willing to die for different sets of beliefs. Death alone, it was concluded, was not enough to determine religious truth.[10] How, then, did religion work? This question split seventeenth-century Catholicism along Jesuit-Jansenist lines.

Jansenists, including the brilliant Blaise Pascal, responded to the skeptical sentiments of the day by arguing for an understanding of religion wholly dependent on grace as divinely revealed. Human nature had no merit in itself and thus no role in the mechanics of salvation. The problem was not the religious tradition but the fickleness of the human mind. One should have doubts not about religion but about the ability of the human mind to discover truth, let alone determine it. One either accepted the teachings or one did not, the implication being that one was either predestined for salvation or one was not. Because religious truth was seen not as something that emerged from within the human soul but wholly external to it (i.e., grace apart from nature), one simply had to conform to what scripture revealed and church authorities taught. Because human nature added nothing to religion, it was concluded that those who believed were predestined to do so by God just as those who did not were predestined for unbelief. There was no way to work at it.

The Jesuits, by contrast, were more optimistic about the ability of human nature to participate in the work of redeeming grace. There was something in the human soul, even the soul of pagans, that oriented them to God—a longing to be in a relation with God. This longing, once realized, would effectively counter the widespread doubts of the day.[11] In other words, there was something godly about human nature that led one to God and was completed by one's baptism in Christian life. This was the position of the Council of Trent (1545–1563), which countered the Reformation, affirming that human nature, though weak, is by no means entirely corrupt. As a result, the state of grace is not fixed for those whom God has chosen, but increases or decreases in accordance with the works one performs. Is it the grace of God or the human conscience that leads one to the good and true? The Council of Trent implied that both have religious worth.

Jesuits and Jansenists alike sought to face the skepticism engendered by the confessional diversity within Christianity along with the rise of scientific thinking and the discovery and promulgation of the key skeptical texts of ancient Greece.[12] However, in facing this skepticism, they arrived at two very different understandings of religion. For Jansenists, doubts were dispelled only by an uncompromising stance toward the world and a pessimistic attitude toward human nature. Truth could be found only in the faith and had nothing to do with the human condition. Jesuits also sought to establish certainty—not, however, by recourse to externals alone but also to internals. They hoped to help people discover the element within the depths of their soul—a divine light—that would lead them to turn willingly, even longingly, to God and religious life.

Jesuits, as a result, were much readier to compromise with the world, more lax, some would say casuistical, when it came to moral teachings. They saw obsession with moral probity as problematic. It could result in irresolvable anxieties over whether one's life was pleasing to God. It also caused people to focus on externals alone. Anxiety over whether the externals of one's life conformed to religious teaching might make one seem pious but could also blind one to the purpose of religion, namely, one's own internal godliness, the divine spark within human nature that resolves the dilemma of determining whether one is pleasing to God. How could human nature not be pleasing to God if it contained something of God? Human nature may be completed by the grace of God but cannot be defined in opposition to it. Attention to this inner jewel, embedded in the human soul, would animate a fully moral life, so it was argued, where moral decision making would take on a character at once both rational and spiritual—the human's response to its own godly inclinations. Are you saved and do you have anything to do with it? Jesuits would say, as a matter of fact, yes.[13]

A similar story unfolded in Islam. Ghazali, the eleventh-century scholar mentioned in chapter 1, had the lead role, but others paved the way. The ninth and tenth centuries were a dynamic time in the history of Islam. The Greco-Hellenistic philosophical heritage had been translated into Arabic, making the civilization of Islam heir to Aristotle no less than to Muhammad but also challenging religion with an alternative source of knowledge. There were also divergent understandings of Islam. Public disputation was in vogue but often ended as rhetorical contest—sophistry, not serious discussion of religious truth. Some countered with the claim that human reason has no place in religion because, they avowed, it invariably leads to doubt. Only by submitting to the literal wordings of scripture and tradition could one be a Muslim. After all, Islam is nothing if not a lived reality—tangible piety, not perplexing debate. Others argued that religion is not about this world at all. They claimed that those preoccupied with moral probity as defined by Islam were horribly deceived about the nature of religion. Reason is sufficient guide when it comes to morals in this world. Revelation, for its part, informs us of the immortality of the soul and its final destiny in the next world but does not impose on us moral burdens that do not square with reason—as if a perverse way for God to test our obedience. The controversy raged intensely for two centuries and still echoes in the *umma* today, as does the Jesuit-Jansenist controversy in contemporary Christianity.

The expansion of Islam during its first centuries also contributed to the dilemma. Muslims now lived alongside a range of peoples, diverse in morals and beliefs.[14] These people seemed to lead reasonably virtuous lives even without Islam. Where, then, was truth to be located? Different solutions to the question were offered. For a tenth-century philosopher by the name of Farabi, all religions were acceptable if they met rational criteria. People cannot live by philosophical abstracts but need particular ways of life, and religion offered that. But all religions in his view were credible insofar as they squared with the dictates of reason. If they met this criterion, religions other than Islam could also be legitimate. This was troubling to many who saw Islam as the sole religion of God. Moreover, his ideas ended by making philosophical reflection, not divine revelation, the final arbiter of truth.

This line was avidly picked up by a small but influential group, the Brethren of Purity, whose ideas caused considerable alarm in the tenth and eleventh centuries. They felt that religious practices themselves were antithetical to religion. Those obsessed with religiously defined morality made the body the focus of religion—what one could or could not do with one's body, how one was to move it during prayer, and specific guidelines for cleaning oneself after defecating and purifying oneself after sexual relations or menstruation, to say nothing of norms for commerce and finance. For the Brethren of Purity, this made a mockery of religion, which in their view was not about the necessities of the body or even the needs of society but instead about the elevation of the soul to God. Religion pointed to a realm beyond this material one, and no words, not even divine speech, could adequately represent true reality, which is something spiritual and thus incapable of being represented by a set of moral teachings to guide the human body. Divine speech existed not for its literal wordings but to be interpreted allegorically, to find in it a hidden meaning that would enable the soul to return to its true spiritual origin.

The strong challenge notwithstanding, philosophy and philosophically minded spirituality could not dethrone religion entirely. But philosophy did set the expectation that religion be intelligible. Attempts were made to reconcile philosophical inquiry and religious teachings. A little-known thinker of the tenth century, 'Amiri, did recognize ascent to God as the final goal of religion, but this goal, he claimed, could be accomplished only by adhering to the teachings of shari'a, not by abandoning them as a distraction.[15] 'Amiri felt that the esoteric ideas of the Brethren of Purity posed a danger to Muslim society, because it was the moral teachings of shari'a and not the abstract ideas of philosophy that held society together. This did not mean that religion was to be followed blindly but rather that it was more valuable to the welfare of society than philosophy. Furthermore, he argued, Islam did a better job at guiding society to happiness than other religions. 'Amiri did much to set the stage for Ghazali by arguing that shari'a not only defined the Muslim way of life but also contributed to the rational purposes of human society, namely public order. Ghazali, we will see, went further.

The subplot to all this was a concern that Islam was not working effectively. Muslims were not living up to the divine mandate. Even religious leaders were corruptible, interested more in prestige at court and influence among the populace and less in ensuring the piety of Muslim society. The caliphate was itself ineffective, a puppet in the hands of various warlords, unable to fulfill its role as leader of the abode of Islam. Ghazali's teacher, a determined theologian by the name of Juwayni, went so far as to call for the end of the caliphate. In its place, the sultanate, the real holder of power, should be invested with religious authority to coerce Muslims—by persuasion or the sword—to live up to their covenant with God. Only by political force could Muslims be stopped from bringing humiliation on Islam by failing to live up to the heavy responsibility that acceptance of the Qur'an had placed on them.

Ghazali was too wise to hope for a political solution to the religious crisis of his day. But if it was not politics that would hold Muslims together in a visible whole, what would? The city of this world had to be abandoned for the city of heaven. Religion was not to be guaranteed by worldly means, that is, politics. Yet Muslims still lived in this world. Even if politics was not the answer, Ghazali was no esotericist. Islam—if it was to be worth anything—had to be visibly manifest in the ethical character of the community. Or were Muslims now under the same indictment that the Qur'an had made against Jews and Christians—possessing a revealed book but not heeding it?

Ghazali was a prolific writer. His thought is rich and complex. His chief aim was to root the Muslim community in the heavenly city over and above the worldly one, and so he put great emphasis on the interior life. At the same time, he was a strong backer of the moral teachings of Islam. His attention to the spiritual realm was in no way an abandonment of lived religion, but he did realize that obsession with externals alone could blind one to the purpose of religion. Religion, for him, was not a metaphor to be allegorically interpreted without actually being lived or even believed in its literal aspect, but he was equally adamant that it could not be reduced to externals.

In his magnum opus, *The Revival of the Religious Sciences*, in a section titled "Blame of Deception" (*dhamm al-ghurur*), he lists various groups of Muslims who in his view think they are performing religion to the fullest but have actually missed the point. He singles out two groups in particular. First are the jurists, who spend their time issuing rulings on one aspect or another of worldly life. People come to them for a fatwa to resolve a trade dispute or to determine what is permitted and prohibited when it comes to marriage, divorce, inheritance, and so on. The jurists think they are working for religion by ensuring the welfare of this world but fail to see that issuing fatwas on worldly affairs is not the point of religion—the ultimate goal is knowledge of God. Ironically, their preoccupation with the teachings of Islam apart from its final purpose raises a veil between them and God.

Ghazali next berates theologians who spend their time debating the finer points of Islam's creeds. They exert every effort to find contradictions in the positions of their sectarian opponents. They too think they are working for religion. What could be more praiseworthy than exposing the innovations of heretics and defending true doctrine? They too miss the point. Religion is not simply eloquence of the tongue, no matter how effective in countering heresy. In the end, if not lived in the heart, it is nothing. Whereas the jurists are obsessed with rulings on permissible and impermissible practices, the theologians are consumed with the wordings of faith, that is, accurate definitions of the creeds of Islam. Both groups, then, are preoccupied with externals and fail to see that focus on practices and creeds without cultivation of the interior life poses a grave danger to one's religious welfare. It is not simply a question of hypocrisy, going through the motions with one's body and uttering the articles of faith on one's tongue without conviction in the heart. Ghazali's key concern was that the reduction of religion to factual definitions (what he termed *al-zahir*, the apparent) opens the door to doubt, given that, in the end, religious truth can never be satisfactorily encompassed in definitions, whether legal or theological. Here is where the skepticism of the day became part and parcel of religion, pushing thinkers like Ghazali to see that religion is not reducible to a factual definition. Again, he did not throw moral teachings and doctrines to the wind but sought to reassert the importance of relation with the divine over definition of it as the only effective antidote to skepticism.

Ghazali's goal was ultimately pastoral. He wanted to make religion easy, even attractive, rather than burdensome. The final goal was to get Muslims to live the religious life, ensuring that the message of Islam had not been sent in vain. He knew, however, that he had to get Islam into people's hearts for it to be embraced with enthusiasm rather than grudgingly. To do so, to define the heart as the place where religion is played out, he had to admit that human nature has a divine element to it. Ghazali defended Islam as divine initiative but one in which the human soul had a vital role and was not set aside for the simple workings of God's divine enterprise. Divine sovereignty did not contradict human nature—or the workings of the human mind.

Reservations about religion were to be countered by the recognition that the human spirit was divine. To be sure, it was not equal to God. But it was divine in that it had been created by God and implanted by him in humans as a mechanism to ensure their orientation to him. Making the human spirit the focus of religion could effectively counter doubt. How could humans doubt something integral to their nature? Ghazali called this godly element of the human spirit the rational soul; it shared in the rationality of the universe that God had created and therefore distinguished humans from beasts, making them worthy to be in the presence of God as capable hearers of divine speech.

This, however, does not happen without effort. Humans have to prepare themselves. The divine essence of the soul, Ghazali claimed, gets cluttered with worldly concerns and attachments. All this needs to be cleared away to ensure that the word of God not remain at the apparent level (i.e., sayings and deeds) but penetrate to the heart. A twofold process is necessary: first, intellectual demonstration that God is indeed the human being's greatest good; and, second, ascetical and spiritual discipline to purge the soul of its worldly ambitions and false desires until all that remains is a desire for the face of God.

Such things were hardly new in Islam. Muslim circles of piety had long aspired to this kind of saintliness, as discussed in chapter 1. Ghazali, however, wanted to make this inner-oriented religiosity more widely available by grafting it to the basic duties of Muslim life. In a section of *The Revival of the Religious Sciences* titled "Wonders of the Heart" (*'aja'ib al-qalb*), Ghazali sums up his thinking by citing a hadith: "If it were not for the demons hovering over human hearts, people would behold the kingdom of God."[16] In other words, Ghazali wanted to make sure that Muslims orient themselves to the kingdom of God in all they do. It was for this reason that he reorganized all the branches of religion under what he called the science of the other world (*'ilm al-akhira*), to which the heart alone has access, not the physical senses. He thus instructed Muslims, when undertaking religious duties, to imagine the mysteries these duties represent, so as to combine religious practice with heavenly truths. In this way, he wanted religion to take root in the heart.

For example, the duty to pray can be fulfilled by motions of the body and movements of the tongue, but this is potentially hypocritical, devoid of conviction, and thus nonsense. Ghazali taught that such externals should be accompanied by corresponding movements of the heart. The duty to undergo ritual purification in preparation for prayer should similarly not be confined to the parts of the body that are wiped and washed (head, hands, feet)—one should simultaneously purify the heart. Pilgrimage, also, is more than simply travel to Mecca so that one might boast of performing the ultimate religious duty—that is, visiting the house of God. Travel must be accompanied by a heart occupied by nothing other than the thought of being in God's presence. Ghazali thus emphasized the two sides of the faith: external and internal, bodily actions and movements of the heart. Life with God was initiated by God, by the workings of grace in external practices revealed by God (that is, religious practices). But they would be meaningless, not only hypocritical but also susceptible to doubts about the truth they represent, if unaccompanied by godly stirrings within.

Ghazali ceaselessly called attention to the causal relation between the morals and beliefs of Islam and the transformative impact they have on the soul. He referred to this as the descent of divine lights onto the human heart, illumination of the soul, a concept beyond the ken of both those who limit truth to God's grace apart from human nature and those who limit it to human nature apart from graced insight. The one thinks only of the dictates of grace and not the human response to it, and the other, limiting existence to material reality, loses the ability to wonder. Ghazali's recognition that the essence of the heart contains a godly element means that human nature has place in religion no less than a divinely instituted set of norms and creeds. Religion is not just duties but also the performance of duties whereby the heart experiences the hidden realm of the other world, beholding heavenly truths as the prophets and saints did. This would dispel, once and for all, doubts about truth or scruples over one's standing before God. The evidence needed exists in the depths of one's soul, the door opening to the mystery of relation with God.

Because the human soul contains something of God, human rationality merits a legitimate role in the religious arena. In this way, Ghazali brought Islam into partnership with philosophical reflection. This did not reduce Islam to human rationality but did mean that Islam could not be unintelligible to the human mind. For Ghazali, God's directives—to fast, to pray, to follow certain norms of marriage and commerce—did not exist as test of blind obedience. They have a purpose and embody a recognizable good that the human mind can discover if not wholly determine. Reason was not to be feared as something that would inevitably lead to doubt. Recourse to human standards of judgment would not distort God's will or cause people to abandon the prophetic venture because it was demonstrable that the rational soul—indeed the logic of the universe—is oriented to God no less than the prophetic message of the Qur'an. In short, rationality is no less relevant to Islam than prophecy.

This insight has tremendous import today. When it comes to religion, it is often assumed that one is either a fundamentalist or a skeptic, that there is no third option. For Ghazali, reason no less than revelation was religious food for the soul. He certainly did not expect Muslims to be philosophers. In his opinion, only an elite group should pursue philosophy. Rather, he wanted to show that the teachings of Islam are not obscure but instead stand in harmony with universal truths and verifiable certainties. This does recall the ideas of Farabi and the Brethren of Purity, as well as other Muslim philosophers, such as Avicenna, but it differs in one crucial respect. Ghazali did recognize the integrity of reason, but in contrast to the philosophers he claimed that it could not function fully apart from revelation. Such a view bears some resemblance to the ideas of John Paul II as spelled out in his 1998 encyclical on the religious life of the mind, *Fides et ratio*. Reason is at its fullest when it wonders, and it is religion that opens the mind to wonder. In this sense, the conscience does not exist merely for individual self-expression but also to be attracted to a truth greater than itself. The heritage of Islam would happily concur.[17]

In various places in his magnum opus, Ghazali showed a pastoral concern for the everyday Muslim who would have been exposed to aspects of the intellectual conundrums of the day but would not have possessed the scholarly expertise to respond to doubts about the credibility of the prophetic message or the reliability of its transmission from Muhammad. Perhaps it had all been made up! How could Muslims know for certain that what was taught as Islam had actually issued from the mouth of the prophet? Ghazali realized that study alone is not capable of dispelling doubts, that indeed it could add to them. Knowledge of the religious heritage is not enough, because, as noted, it could be oriented to worldly concerns. He would classify the study of shari'a, usually considered the heart of the religion, as a worldly rather than otherworldly science, given that it in fact applies to the actions of believers in this world and not to the spiritual realities of the next. Also, in his view, by identifying religion too closely with the study of religion, people were distracted from its heavenly purpose, and this put Islam in jeopardy. The problem was not the Muslim failure to live up to its teachings, casting suspicion on why it had been sent in the first place. The issue was not the revealed message, but rather that Muslims did not perform religious duties with the otherworldly orientation that the Qur'an had made the criterion of true religion.

Humans, to be sure, were not to save themselves. But there had to be something in humans that enabled them to orient themselves willingly—with the help of revealed teachings—to the other world. Ghazali claimed that this divine mystery at the core of humans made them worthy to receive the divine lights of sanctity (*anwar ilahiyya*) as the purpose for which they had been created. Such a purpose could not be realized if there was not something about human nature that actually shared in heavenly being.

Ghazali, first of all, put great confidence in the rational faculty with which humans had been endowed. The mind—if open to reasonable discourse—begins the process of orienting the soul to a world beyond this one. To demonstrate this, Ghazali occasionally modeled arguments with skeptics, those who sow doubt by claiming that death is a mere nothing (*'adam mahd*).[18] This, for him, was the crux of the matter. If there is no hereafter, what is the point of religion? As noted, the science of the next world is queen in Ghazali's reframing of the various branches of religious knowledge; thus shari'a is not the purpose of religious study but simply the departure point. Awareness of the next world is the final goal. In this schema, the mind has a key role to play, for it brings skeptics to admit at least the possibility of the life to come. This gives the mind a claim on Muslim obedience, because it is by the power of the mind that people admit that what is truly of lasting value is manifestly not something of this world; deniers of the next world could be shown the contradictions of their own doubts.

Ghazali asked his skeptical interlocutors a number of questions: Had they understood something that all the prophets, saints, and sages of the past had overlooked? Did they have proof for their denial of the next world? Or were they only following the fashionable thinking of the day? Did they indeed have knowledge they had independently verified or were they simply parroting things they had heard on the authority of others, pseudo-philosophers, not people with real authority? Was their denial of the eternity of the soul certain knowledge, akin to the statement that two is greater than one? If not, if they could not irrefutably demonstrate that the next world did not exist, it was wiser, indeed logically incumbent on them, if they were intellectually honest, to give thought to their ultimate fate. After all, even happiness in this world requires knowledge and action, and one would not abandon efforts to attain success in this world even if it were not certain but only possible. Had the prophets and saints lied about what they claimed to witness? If they were not liars, then they were truthful, making religious life a rational option once again. Our minds direct us to avoid dangers in this life, even when such dangers are only possible and not quite certain. Why should the same not be true in our estimation of the things of the next world? Indeed, if one obeys the rational faculty rather than the baser passions of human nature, one is led to the conclusion that preparation for the next world is a truth manifestly evident to the intellect.

Because the intellect has such significance for Ghazali's project, demonstrating the rationality of the truth of the next world, he awarded it religious authority. He thus permitted a measure of metaphorical interpretation of revealed texts that would otherwise violate human rationality: for example, the verse of the Qur'an that says that God has a hand, that is, a bodily limit, or the hadith that says that the prophet Muhammad saw paradise on a wall. The reference to God's hand is merely symbolic of his might and when Muhammad said he saw paradise on a wall, he didn't mean paradise literally but instead an image of paradise he had formed in his mind. However, things in scripture that do not violate human logic cannot be read metaphorically. Thus, because people read scripture in different ways, depending on intellectual acumen, it is necessary, Ghazali argued in one of his last works, to recognize the validity of several approaches.[19] For some, a literal reading is convincing, but for others, a more intellectual reading might be in order. A Muslim who did not attest to the literal truth of the tradition in all its details should not, then, be threatened by *takfir* (condemnation as an infidel), putting his life and property in jeopardy. To ensure against intracommunal strife, Ghazali formulated a simple criterion for determining fidelity to Islam. One only had to affirm that the prophet Muhammad was not a liar, that he was truthful at some level of interpretation. Those who declare that he was not a liar are safely Muslims.

Ghazali thus laid out a framework for the reconciliation of the different sects and schools within Islam, to put a stop to the destructive practice of *takfir* that threatened to tear the community apart. He too had been object of attack. More important, in creating a framework in which diverse readings of the Qur'an all had legitimacy, he hoped to undercut the perception of religious division in Islam—a plurality of contesting truths that were so serious as to cast doubts on the integrity of the religion, leaving believers so dazed as to throw in the towel altogether.

The divine core of the soul therefore embraces the rational faculty, which Ghazali referred to as a light. However, this light is fully illuminated (properly functioning) only when it receives the divine lights of grace, which Ghazali called light upon light.[20] In the end, all that remains is the soul in communion with its divine friend, the thing to which it is truly attracted, and for that reason Ghazali classified the love of God as highest virtue, a love that will make performance of religion—practices and all—effortless endeavor, even attractive, because these practices now constitute the forum for intimacy with the divine beloved. Love for Ghazali was not a philosophical virtue, but a mystical one, only realizable with and in God, through the heart's mystical appropriation of divine speech, as noted in the previous chapter, especially the names of God as disclosed by prophecy.[21]

In short, Ghazali was saying to Muslims, "If you want to know the truth, model your life after the prophet." The prophet not only established Islam's way of life but also perfectly oriented his soul to the next world, that is, eternity. His soul surely was detached from worldly ambitions and thus fully capable of receiving revelation without doubts or scruples. And the Qur'an did descend onto his heart, illuminating his life for others to see and witness and so be convinced of the rightness of the worship of the one God, Creator and Lord of all. The process of dispelling doubts thus includes the human soul, the interior working of the heart. The heart is content in its Lord when it recreates the experience of the prophet who for Muslims is known as the beloved of God, whose soul is in intimate communion with God, and who not only knew but also perfectly lived the way of God—shari'a. By doing what the prophet did, by living as he did, by embracing prophecy in all its details, Muslims realize what he realized and see what he saw—the divine mysteries descending into one's heart.[22]

One might not be convinced of divine truth by the academic study of religion or the various theological arguments deployed in its defense, but how can one argue with the stirrings of the heart? The heart is the mirror of divine mysteries. It is there that the rational soul is to entertain knowledge of God—in synch with what most closely corresponds to its true essence. Thus, in modeling oneself after the book of God, one is fully rational, fully following the dictates of the rational faculty, which, Ghazali noted, is the only thing that distinguishes humans from beasts: "Those who shed from their skins their base passion and arm themselves with the shield of shari'a will have their hearts gladdened by the light of divinity and their faith kindled by the light of God's unity."[23]

Ghazali's final purpose was to show a necessary connection between what Muslims did outwardly in their particular practices and what they experienced inwardly in their deepest convictions, giving shari'a a meaning much more profound than mere injunction, not simply wordings of the law but realities of the soul, mysteries at work in the heart and not only rulings to regulate conduct of the body. Conjoining spiritual insight to the everyday ethics of Islam, Ghazali advanced a conception of shari'a that made it attraction of the heart and not simply obligation of the body. In this way he sought to increase the faith of

Muslims in troubling times. By recasting shari'a so that it operated at both external and internal levels, he broadened the ethics of Islam. Shari'a included the actions entailed by religious practices: prayer, purification, pilgrimage, as well as rulings for commerce, crime, and a host of other things. But it also touched the heart and mind, the very soul of the human, and thus could only be true. In sum, Ghazali integrated the two realms of Islam, the outer and the inner, more systematically than had previously been done.

Ghazali shows us how doubt can be a fruitful part of religion. What appears as a threat to its teachings can actually offer a way to embrace them at a more profound—and reasonable—level. Indeed, his intellectual project aimed to preserve shari'a as the visible side of Islam and to convince people of its truth as a worthy guide for human action. More significantly, his appreciation for human rationality as the lynchpin of belief made it integral to the religious project. The details of shari'a are not something one might come up with on one's own, but, with Ghazali, there could be nothing that violated the dictates of reason. He thus made it possible, even necessary, to introduce philosophy into the religious sphere, even while respecting the bounds of each. He equated the moral character of the prophet Muhammad with the four cardinal virtues known from Greek philosophy: wisdom, courage, temperance, and justice. How could those who claimed to be wise doubt the message of Islam if the prophet's character reflected the best insights of philosophy?

This was not a clever way to reduce the ethics of Islam to philosophical ideas. For Ghazali, religion instilled an ethics beyond anything philosophy might offer. For example, love is a religious, even mystical, virtue. It thus requires the prompting of divine revelation to be fully realized. However, that religion has more to offer than philosophy does not mean that the teachings of Islam can violate virtues universally acknowledged by all peoples. The rational soul may not be able to generate all truth but must be able to grasp it when it sees it: Truth is divine but is still to be weighed in the balance of the mind. This, Ghazali claimed, is no less true of shari'a. Building on his intellectual predecessors, Ghazali claimed that shari'a is not simply a matter of tradition and precedent, to be followed whether it makes sense to the mind. He was certainly not against the idea of precedents if backed by a rationale. It is not enough to apply shari'a. It must be applied with justice, that is, reasonably and not arbitrarily. In a discussion too complex to spell out here, Ghazali argued that there were reasons why God had given shari'a to Muslims. These reasons he summed up in a set of universal principles that all humans recognize as true. In other words, shari'a in all its details has to be sensible. It cannot be reduced to a divine test of human obedience and cannot violate principles that the human mind recognizes as true. Islam, in this view, aims to fulfill a rational purpose for this world.

In this, Ghazali did not turn Islam into a set of abstract ideas; tangible practices served as signposts on the way to God. Rather, he aimed to show the harmony of shari'a with universally recognized truths. He formulated a list of universal principles that continues to inform shari'a reasoning and called them the five necessities: preservation of religion, life, progeny, intellect, and property. They are called necessities because without them society would plunge into chaos. Thus a precedent that opposes one of these principles poses a threat to the welfare of society, thereby contradicting the purposes of shari'a, making it right to overturn it. For example, a ruling that prohibits selling goods before actually having them in one's possession can be tabled if it causes hardship for the trade of goods that are normally bought and sold before actual production, such as fruit and vegetables. As guarantor of the common good of Muslim society, shari'a cannot undermine development, including effective trade. It has been given for a purpose, the welfare of Muslim society, and cannot be applied in a way that undermines that purpose.

The history of doubt in both Christianity and Islam is vast and greatly understudied. Every generation of believers has to face its doubts. The question is how. The rise of modernity has led some Christians and Muslims to cling to literals—clear definitions of belief and behavior—without rational inquiry into their meaning. The fear that

doubt about the visible components of religion will lead to the abandonment of religion entirely tags doubt as enemy of religion. The conclusion is that reason has no place when it comes to the pursuit of
religion. Its application to the religious heritage will only undermine it.
The covenant with God will be something that humans define rather
than God—the warning of the Qur'an to the monotheists of its day.
Yet Ghazali—and the Jesuits after him—showed that doubt can in fact
enrich the faith without jeopardizing its core practice and beliefs, calling Muslims and Christians to the wonders of the interior life through
traditional rituals. The idea of faith as a ritual activity is something the
modern mind has trouble grasping, because it is accustomed to think of
faith as assent in the mind and rituals as hollow by nature.

What do believers do with doubt? This is a central part of the common ground that Christians and Muslims share in the skeptical age in
which we live. Some place emphasis on what the religion has always
taught as fundamental to the covenant of God—for Muslims this is the
set of core practices, beliefs, and spiritual teachings that Muhammad
received during his night journey to God. Others speak of broader principles that the Qur'an contains and that reason affirms: monotheism,
development of human civilization, and peace. Most, however, find
they need both. Whatever definition of religion individuals reach, and
today more than ever religion is the choice of individuals as much as a
tradition of ancient truths, doubt will be central to the process. The
respective Christian and Muslim response to doubt, either in fear and
trembling or in wonder and joy, will greatly influence the ongoing relevancy of religion in the world. It has never been clear whether religion
is necessary for determining human welfare and the moral order necessary to promote it, but it does provide people with great hope for a life
to come, and that, ironically, holds tremendous value for this world, as
we see in chapter 3.

In the end, then, the mind has a place in religion, and doubt in the
mind is not the enemy of God. The mind does not determine what the
religion is—only God can do that. In Islam, the realities that the mind

is called to contemplate are not the abstract truths of philosophy but the divine names the Qur'an discloses and believers can behold beyond the material appearances of this world. For Christians, the object of contemplation is the kingdom of God as revealed by Jesus Christ. It is a point of human orientation and not an empirical fact to be demonstrated in a laboratory. In this sense, religious experience is a matter of both heart and head. That is, the religious practices that orient the heart to God need not be seen to detract from the power of the human mind. But to reach such a conclusion, one may have to start with doubts, serious doubts, about religion itself, doubts that may lead one either away from religion or to a deeper appreciation of its nature at the core of one's being. In the end, what can be said is that for Muslims and for Christians, piety is not irrational. It is possible to be both devout and thoughtful, both believer and intellectual. To be fully intellectual, one should be entranced by what God has revealed to humankind. To be a full believer, the workings of the mind should be completely operative. This, significantly, does not mean reducing religion to esoteric ideas. In this, Ghazali's musings have import for questions of religion and reason in our own day. Doubt is integral to religion. It can challenge it to refine its message in response to shifts in society. More significantly, it shows that religion is not properly a set of definitions, legal or theological, because such definitions are never completely satisfying, but is more exactly understood as a deposit of relations that are revealed but never fully describable in words or deeds, even if those too are part of it.

NOTES

1. For example, see Abu Ahmad 'Abd al-Ghafur, "al-Tashkik fi Sunnat Khayr al-Anam: Silah al-Mustaghribin li-Hadm al-Islam," *al-Sabil*, no. 44 (December 16, 2008): 9. This is a Moroccan journal associated with Salafi currents.

2. See, for example, G. R. Hawting, *The Idea of Idolatry and the Emergence of Islam: From Polemic to History* (Cambridge: Cambridge University Press, 1999).

3. Joseph Cardinal Ratzinger, *God and the World: A Conversation with Peter Seewald* (San Francisco: Ignatius Press, 2002), 35.

4. Yusuf Qaradawi, *Dirasa fi Fiqh Maqasid al-Shari'a: Bayna Maqasid al-Kulliyya wa-l-Nusus al-Juz'iyya* (Cairo: Dar al-Shuruq, 2006).

5. Mark A. Noll, *America's God: From Jonathan Edwards to Abraham Lincoln* (Oxford: Oxford University Press, 2002).

6. See, in general, George M. Marsden, *Fundamentalism and American Culture*, 2nd ed. (Oxford: Oxford University Press, 2006).

7. See Jeffrey P. Moran, *The Scopes Trial: A Brief History with Documents* (Boston, MA: Bedford/St. Martin's, 2002).

8. See, for example, Rhys Isaac, "Evangelical Revolt: The Nature of the Baptists' Challenge to the Traditional Order in Virginia, 1765 to 1775," *William and Mary Quarterly* 31, no. 3 (July 1974): 346–68.

9. Key figures in this kind of Christianity include Hal Lindsey, author of *The Late Great Planet Earth* (New York: Zondervan, 1970), and John Hagee, author of *Jerusalem Countdown: A Warning to the World* (Lake Mary, FL: FrontLine, 2006). See David D. Kirkpatrick, "For Evangelicals, Supporting Israel is 'God's Foreign Policy,'" *New York Times*, November 14, 2006. For a Christian response to this outlook, known as premillennial dispensationalism, see Laurie Goodstein, "Coalition of Evangelicals Voices Support for Palestinian State," *New York Times*, July 29, 2007.

10. Brad S. Gregory, *Salvation at Stake: Christian Martyrdom in Early Modern Europe* (Cambridge, MA: Harvard University Press, 1999).

11. This idea has had important impact on subsequent Catholic teachings about religious pluralism. See Daniel A. Madigan, "Saving *Dominus Iesus*," in *Learned Ignorance: An Investigation into Humility in Interreligious Dialogue among Christians, Muslims, and Jews*, edited by James Heft, Reuven Firestone, and Omid Safi, in press.

12. Richard H. Popkin, *The History of Skepticism from Savonarola to Bayle* (Oxford: Oxford University Press, 2003).

13. This is one reason why in the Catholic tradition of Christianity as opposed to the Calvinistic one, it is held that "justification happens within the believer and not completely in Christ." David P. Scaer, "Evangelical and Catholic—A Slogan in Search of a Definition," *Concordia Theological Quarterly* 65, no. 4 (2001): 325.

14. See Paul L. Heck, "Doubts about the Religious Community (*Milla*) in al-Farabi and the Brethren of Purity," in *In the Age of al-Farabi: Arabic Philosophy in the 4th/10th Century*, ed. Peter Adamson (London: Warburg Institute, 2008), 195–213.

15. See Paul L. Heck, "The Crisis of Knowledge in Islam (I): The Case of al-'Amiri," *Philosophy East and West* 56, no. 1 (2006): 106–35.

16. al-Ghazali, *Ihya' 'ulum al-Din*, 4 vols. in 2 (Cairo: Dar al-Salam, 2003), vol. 3, chapter on *'aja' ib al-qalb*.

17. For a discussion of the conscience in the ethical heritage of Islam, see Nuha al-Qatarji, "al-Akhlaq fi Mafhum al-Islam," *Majallat al-Mashriq* 2004, no. 2: 363–88 and 2005, no. 1: 177–214.

18. Ghazali, *Mizan al-'Amal*, ed. Sulayman Dunya (Cairo: Dar al-Ma'arif, 1963), 185–86.

19. Sherman A. Jackson, ed. and trans., *On the Boundaries of Theological Tolerance in Islam: Abu Hamid al-Ghazali's Faysal al-Tafriqa bayn al-Islam wa-l-Zandaqa* (Oxford: Oxford University Press, 2002).

20. Ghazali, *The Niche of Lights/Mishkat al-Anwar*, ed. and trans. David Buchman (Provo, UT; Brigham Young University Press, 1998).

21. See Mohamed Ahmed Sherif, *Ghazali's Theory of Virtue* (Albany: State University of New York, 1975).

22. This is the key point of Ghazali's autobiographical work, *Deliverance from Error*.

23. al-Ghazali, *al-Ma'arif al-'Aqliyya*, ed. 'Ali Idris (Safaqis, Tunis: al-Ta 'adudiyya al-'Ummaliyya lil-Tiba'a wa-al-Nashr, 1988), pp. 73–83.

THE FACE OF GOD

A Social Good?

HEAVEN AND HELL have long featured in the Christian-Muslim imagination. Satan is no less real than God. However, although religious teachings are meant to guide one to a happy outcome in the hereafter, there are reservations about making final statements on the status of souls in the life to come. The church does on occasion declare someone a saint. In addition, some Christians maintain that they alone are saved, a matter that God has determined in advance. Some Muslims avow that Islam has a monopoly on salvation, leaving non-Muslims outside God's mercy. In general, however, Christians and Muslims admit that such matters lie beyond human control. It is God who judges. But it is also God who loves his creation and regards it with mercy. In the end, Christians and Muslims recognize that the fate of souls, including sinners, is not ours to decide.

Still, there are clear teachings about wrong and right. There is, of course, diversity and disagreement, but there are also long-standing positions on marriage, care for the poor, and norms of worship, to name only a handful of issues. Is God's revelation solely about laws, to follow or disobey? And what determines the truth of God's ways? For Christians, there is the Bible, but there is also natural law. For Muslims, there is the Qur'an, but scripture alone does not determine the appropriate ruling for every situation. For that, a host of other jurisprudential tools exist, including the precedent of the prophet, the consensus of the community, local custom, and even what religious scholars deem best in a given context. Indeed, for every clear ruling there is also a dispensation if the situation warrants it. A pregnant woman is dispensed from the obligation to fast during Ramadan, and Muslims are permitted to eat carrion (i.e., the flesh of dead animals) in time of famine. In other words, reality is also a factor in determining the will of God.

In the end, a greater ethic lies beyond all the teachings. Christians aim to live in the love of God, Muslims in the mercy of God. This does not mean that believers are relieved of moral responsibilities toward fellow creatures and toward society in general. Rather, the love and mercy of God point to the purpose of religious teachings, namely, encounter with the face of God.

Does this encounter have a contribution to make to the welfare of society or does it apply only to the world to come when believers behold God in his full glory? When it comes to prosperity in this world, we look to politics and economics to explain how things work and how they might be improved. The face of God, for some, represents an artistic possibility, an icon disclosing divine transcendence in familiar form. Others see it as a focal point for religious contemplation, a way to draw closer to God. But we do not take it into account when considering matters of this world.

Does the face of God have ethical import that might make it relevant for the sustainability of human societies? We often assume that the way we interact with others in society (right and wrong, including punishments for transgressing the rights of others) is the state's to define. The state exists to keep the peace; it has a role in regulating the economy if not actually intervening in it; it has a monopoly on the legitimate use of force, because the results are invariably disastrous when individuals take the law into their own hands. Some claim that the state also has a religious purpose, a matter considered in chapter 5. Here the question is one of ethics, that is, the values by which a society exists. What is the source of our ethics? If we say it is the state, we are assuming that a nation's prosperity, including its ethics, is the work of political institutions alone. Moreover, making the state the source of our ethics also affects the way we view ourselves. It suggests that all authority, and therefore all meaning, is secular in origin.

That all ethics is not secular (i.e., cannot be handed over to the state) does not mean that religion is to fill the gap, especially in pluralistic societies. Awarding the state the authority to define the ethics of society can be dangerous, however. It risks reducing the core of our being to a political definition, namely citizenship; the human spirit is too complex to be reduced to a set of definitions to be translated into state policies governing society. There is always something about the human being, both good and bad, that cannot be so reduced, cannot be made the object of state law. In other words, the human being is part mystery. This might be called the inner life, which, depending on its quality, can lead people to do things their conscience tells them are wrong but that the state has not explicitly prohibited, just as it can lead them to do things for the sake of others, acts of kindness, that the state does not require of them. By relying too much on the state to monitor the ethics of society, we lose sight of this fundamental part of our human constitution.

Moreover, by leaving ethics to the state to define, because, after all, it represents us, we assume that care for society is not our responsibility. Why aren't they doing more about poverty? Why have they so misman-aged our relations with other nations? To be sure, watchdog groups, including the press, keep political authorities honest. But another mat-ter is in play. We are easily seduced into thinking that we are not bound by ethical limits in areas not regulated by the state. This type of think-ing is disastrous for societies and economies. Indeed, it lies behind the current financial crisis with roots in a host of banking practices, such as subprime (or predatory) lending, that are ultimately parasitical. Such practices, however, are not the work of hardened criminals but of repu-table bankers and many others who break no laws—and therefore, in their minds, operate ethically—but are still led by a greed that has re-cently devastated the national and international economy.

The point is that legal definitions and laws are not enough because they are easily twisted for self-serving purposes at odds with the intent of the law, which is to protect the common good. Reducing the human condition to a set of state-regulated definitions causes us to forget that we are not primarily about definitions but about relations—with others—and that these relations have claims over us irrespective of society's laws. The state is not enough to ensure the welfare of society—character is also needed. Our conscience tells us what is right and wrong. We are not moral imbeciles by nature, and yet we fail to do right and choose to do wrong, sometimes with little remorse. The corporate scandals of recent years bear this out, Enron being only the most celebrated of many cases. Well-educated men and women with tremendous resources of their own thought nothing of destroying the lives of others.

Thus, though the democratic state effectively ensures a people's aspirations and vital needs, other elements go into the ethics and welfare of society. Christianity and Islam both affirm this, especially in the attention they pay to the character of the human soul alongside legal norms. Character is understood as the fruit not merely of keeping to the law but of one's inner life. Spirituality therefore has import for the ethics of society, helping bring about harmonious relations with others, whether human or divine—or even animal or mineral.

There are different kinds of spirituality, some nontheist. To speak of spirituality as an encounter with the face of God is to speak of only one kind of spirituality, based on God's revelation of himself and therefore common to Christians and Muslims. All spirituality, if true, speaks of harmonious relations with others and with the universe entire. Moreover, secular spirituality is not entirely unlike its theistic counterpart but also requires a critical and questioning detachment from the world and its ways.[1] Spirituality, though, is never in the end a wholly secular concept. A spiritual way of life can be achieved without revelation of a kingdom to come, but revelation does set the bar in refusing to take this world as final end in preference for transcendental meaning. There is much reflection to be done if we hope to consider spirituality in a world that contains not only the spirituality of theists of varied stripes but also of equally diverse nontheists. William James, pioneer in the psychology of religion, saw ethics as the fruit of the religious experience, and that will guide our discussion of the face of God here.

Does awareness of God in the human psyche have an impact on our ethical horizons? All cultures, history suggests, have equal amounts of good and bad. The ethical fruit that comes from encounter with the face of God may be as much possibility as reality. But the troubling absence of ethical sensibility in public life, from leaders on down, compels us to look beyond this world in the hope of finding ethical meaning. Some call it the kingdom of God. Indeed, that is the heart of Jesus's teachings, especially in the Gospel of Matthew. It is a kingdom that is not of this world and yet, ironically, exists in our midst. There have been many interpretations of the heavenly kingdom and many thoughts about how to make it visible in this world—through prayer and missionary work, by serving the weakest members of society, by looking at catastrophes, whether natural or manmade, as signs of the end times and God's millennial rule. Of the many parables Jesus uses to describe the kingdom of God, one of the most compelling is that of the mustard seed, which is the smallest of seeds but has the potential to grow into a large bush. In other words, the cultivation of ethical dispositions in the depths of the soul, even if not apparent to others, can bear much fruit in our interactions with others. The good of society, then, is staked not merely on the existence of standards of right and wrong but also on the possession of enough character to adhere to them.

To be sure, all states of the soul are not the same. The encounter with God can lead some to disdain or even terrorize others. Theological definitions are therefore necessary to ensure that the spirit at work in one's religious life is truly godly. But whether a believer's comportment is consistent with religious teachings, the ethical agent is not knowledge of the law but awareness of God in the psyche. For Christians and Muslims, this spiritual awareness, if properly cultivated, generates an expansive ethics that embraces not only those dear to us (family, friends, fellow believers) but all we meet, including those we do business with and even those we despise.

Spirituality, in this sense, can contribute to the sustainability of society in allowing us to be with others in ethically harmonious ways. Is this merely a nice idea? A series of conversations I had in 2008 with members of the Butshishiyya, a spiritual brotherhood based in Morocco, suggests that spirituality does have practical import for society. As a leading member of the brotherhood put it, spirituality teaches you humility.[2] It reduces egoism, which facilitates your ability to enjoy good relations with your neighbor and with all people. Because you live for the face of God, he explained, you do not feel resentment toward others, and this reduces conflict in society. Indeed, it makes you more aware and tolerant of others, regardless of creed. That all have their origin in God makes it possible to embrace them even while committed to the specific teachings of Islam. Another member noted that he had never been able to live up to Islam's teachings until he joined the brotherhood and took on its spiritual way.[3] Employed in Morocco's judicial system, he mentioned that this spirituality gave him peace of soul, allowing him to detach from the world's temptations. Although fully in the world, including circles of government, he is not tempted to take advantage of a situation for his own interest. He does not live for himself. And this, he concluded, has had great benefit in his family life and in his relations with others. Spirituality, in this sense, fosters a detachment from the ways of the world but, ironically, allows for richer engagement with it.

Spirituality, then, does not necessarily add to standards of right and wrong but can encourage inner dispositions that make it less difficult to adhere to them. It is not enough to know a system of ethics. One must find a way to live it. A society in which self-regard is the norm risks extinction. Can spirituality play a positive role in commerce and business? Material interests stand at the heart of business, and hard decisions are sometimes made, but business breaks down without the trust that others hold to a system of ethics and do not simply maximize short-term gains at all costs. This is not only a matter of adhering to the norms of a contract but also of doing right by others even in areas not mentioned in the contract. Without a sense of decency, a city, no matter its resources, has no future. Spirituality is not a call to live in isolation but rather to live in the world with a measure of freedom from it. It can therefore encourage us to limit or even forgo our own interests for the sake of honest and ultimately prosperous relations with others.

We do not need revelation to know right from wrong, but it may expand our ethical horizons beyond what the state requires or even beyond what our mind determines on its own. The prophet Micah of ancient Israel spoke of acting justly, loving mercy, and walking humbly with God (6:8). This requires knowledge and awareness of God. The perception of the transcendent can engender a healthy freedom from the standards of this world. Such detachment from possessions, prestige, and power does not mean suspension of worldly activities, but instead sacrifice of one's attachment to them for the sake of a positive relation with God.

Do Christians and Muslims pray to the same God? The Second Vatican Council, in a document known as *Nostra aetate*, suggests that they do. But do they conceive of God in the same way with the same characteristics? In one sense, the question is beyond verification. Despite theological definitions within the respective traditions, it is impossible to define with precision the way Christians and Muslims each encounter the face of God. Such is the nature of spirituality. Notwithstanding potential differences in the Christian-Muslim image of God, it is still to be asked: Does the encounter with the face of God bear similar ethical fruit, namely, enhanced capacity to act justly, love mercy, and walk humbly with God?

In contrast to the state, religion questions not only the actions and intent of the wrongdoer but also the state of his soul. In this sense, wrongdoing is viewed not only as infraction of the law but more profoundly as a failure to trust in God entirely as ultimate source of well-being. From this viewpoint, religion would say that because the presence of God is unlimited, we should be oriented to God at all times, and this unrestricted consciousness of God bears ethical fruit: humility, self-control if not self-denial, and the freedom to give from our want as well as from our bounty. This awareness of the presence of God at all times begets a shift in attitude from self-regard to altruistic attentiveness to others.

Such an outcome is not guaranteed and depends on a host of other factors. People, Christians and Muslims, have taken the presence of God in their midst as warrant to attack others judged to be God's enemies. This makes it all the more urgent to understand the theological dimension of religious experience. What is the theological outlook that makes encounter with the transcendent a source of violence? We consider that question in chapter 4. Here, spiritual awareness suggests a human purpose in living for God and not for one's own standing, reputation, possessions, and pride; one willingly sacrifices such things for the face of God. From a psychological viewpoint, the ego may need to be nurtured as part of the process of human development, but from the spiritual viewpoint, it is ultimately to be overcome and transcended as by-product of belief in God. This, in turn, transforms the way we view and deal with others. We are willing to make sacrifices for the sake of a heavenly reward, which can be experienced in this life no less than the next. It is, ironically, the poor who are custodians of blessings that the rich receive in caring for them. By sacrificing for others, we express a love for God. This is captured in Jesus's teaching that what we do for others, especially the least among us, we actually do for him. It is also captured in the words of a fourteenth-century Muslim scholar, Ibn Qayyim al-Jawziyya, who understood sacrifice as patient adherence to the will of God. His point is that believers sacrifice for the sake of a relation with God. This idea in Islam has its origins in the prophet Muhammad who, though maligned and attacked by the tribal leaders of Mecca, displayed a willingness to forgo a just retribution for the sake of peace in society. Was this simply an astute strategy to win over his adversaries or the mark of a man whose character was formed by a deep awareness of the presence of God?

Spirituality has import for the welfare of society because it reduces greed—greed for prestige and property, which generates conflict and endangers society, to say nothing of increasing the desire for revenge. The deleterious impact of greed on society has been noticed as far back as ancient Greece.[4] We are familiar with the concept of secondhand smoke. Billions of dollars have been handed over by tobacco companies to nonsmokers. We are not yet familiar with the concept of secondhand greed. Banks recklessly extended lines of credit, allowing people to live beyond their means. The accumulated debt hurts the fiscal health of the nation, adversely affecting those who live within their means. Is it not reasonable to oblige banks to hand over billions of dollars for harming the welfare of those who live moderately but have suffered from secondhand greed?

The link between spirituality and ethics is made in the Sermon on the Mount, in which Jesus, herald of God's presence, exhorts his listeners to something beyond simple adherence to the law. It was not his intention to abolish the law but to point to an ethics of the spirit that could enhance understanding of it. The human soul, aware of being in the divine presence, will refrain not merely from murder and divorce but even from anger and lust. This idea is found in a well-known hadith in which the prophet Muhammad says, when asked about the essence of Islam, "Don't become angry [and, the exegetes add, paradise is yours]." How else might one endure attacks against one's standing in this world with equanimity if not by cleaving one's whole life to God in the hope of encountering him in a life to come? Restraining anger here is not a matter of stoic indifference, that is, the mind's conquest of the soul's baser passions, but readiness to sacrifice worldly inclinations, counted as little next to the face of God as object of one's true desire. As the Qur'an notes, "You will not attain righteousness until you sacrifice what you love" (3:92). Ethics here is not simply about everyone getting their due but unique by-product of living in the presence of God.

How does one live in the presence of God? What is the image of God that makes it possible to live in his presence? The Bible at times talks of God's wrath and his displeasure with his chosen people but also of his loving kindness and unshakeable commitment to his covenant with them. They may go astray, risking his anger, but he always seeks them out, enticing them back to him. For Christians, this notion was fulfilled in the person of Jesus Christ who, as Paul says in his letter to the Colossians, reconciled all creation to God by the blood of the cross.

This gives Christians the confidence that they will never be deprived of the presence of God, but it does not do away with the need to repent for wrongdoing—confession, penance, making amends, and so on. Christianity may say that hell has no hold on humanity but has not done away with the idea altogether. The fate of sinners on judgment day looms large in Christian art of the past even if less so now.

God is described in the Qur'an as having ascended his throne. He is positioned to command right and forbid wrong, that is, to promulgate his way of life, shari'a, for those who submit to him. The Qur'an also mentions the face of God: majestic, ennobling, and omnipresent. Wherever one turns, there is the face of God. Indeed, it is the sole reality—all perishes save the face of God. It is also closely associated with acts of giving and sacrifice—feeding the poor for the face of God, enduring patiently out of a desire for the face of God. Here, giving is not merely a charitable stratagem but an act of mercy performed for God. Does the face of God as depicted in the Qur'an correspond to the divine countenance that Christians behold in Jesus Christ—merciful and kind, self-sacrificing, edifying, consoling, transformative, loving?

Muslims do not speak of God as father.[5] Some might conclude from this that they do not have a sense of being in God's presence that the image of a loving father would trigger. It is certainly human to feel guilty at times. Do Muslims experience God as source of guilt? All kinds of believers do at times, and nonbelievers are by no means free of feelings of guilt. Do Muslims feel beloved by God, totally and decisively? Does their image of God evoke a sense of being beloved by him? Or do they feel they always come up short in the effort to please him? They may not speak of God as father, and some Muslim leaders may be more inclined to speak of humans loving God rather than God loving humans, but Muslims do have the religious resources not only to stand in the presence of God but also to feel touched by his love. Is this unconditional love? Or does it depend on perfect obedience to his will? Do certain persons act as objects of God's loving gaze on behalf of the rest of the community—akin to what Christians see in Jesus Christ? Indeed, there is one person, the prophet Muhammad. He is not God's son, but Muslims do call him God's beloved (*habib allah*). Does he, then, model for Muslims what it means to be so beloved?

Some Muslims, though experiencing God's presence, would like a clearer definition of that presence in terms of love. In a meeting between Muslims and Catholics in Rome in November 2008, Muslim participants noted that God's love, originating principle of the universe, precedes the love humans have for him. They also cited a hadith that God's merciful love for humanity is greater than a mother's love for her child.

God for Muslims is no abstract concept but is known by ninety-nine names, descriptors of his divinity as revealed by the Qur'an: Kind, Just, Wise, Affectionate, Creator, Compeller, Destroyer, Strong, Knowing, Living, Self-Subsistent, the One who gives life, who puts to death, and who will raise humans to life again on judgment day, and so on. Despite the fact that loving (*muhibb*) is not one of the ninety-nine names, Muslims, as noted, would associate it with his primary quality as merciful. The most common name given to God is in fact merciful (*rahman*), functioning almost as his proper name. God, the Qur'an attests, has ordained mercy for himself (6:12, 6:54), and one of the most common double-descriptions of God in the Qur'an is forgiving compassionate (*ghafur rahim*). Muslims do not know God as distant or merely transcendent but, through his names, tangibly close—a face at once majestic and beautiful. This diversely described face of God, poking into history through the Qur'an, is meant to attract the attention of Muslims at all times and places. God's names evoke an unmistakable, palpable sense of being in his presence, and this is reinforced by a well-known hadith: "Worship God as if you see him, and if you do not see him, know that he sees you."

Ghazali, the eleventh-century Muslim scholar mentioned in earlier chapters, includes a section on the love of God in his magnum opus, *The Revival of the Religious Sciences*. In speaking of the love of God (*mahabbat allah*), he means both the love of humans for God and God's love for them. He does not point to a decisive act of love on God's part as Christians see in the cross but rather focuses on the idea of loving

God as the greatest of human pleasures and the beauty of God as the basis of all beauty.

This recalls the thought of Bernard of Clairvaux, the twelfth-century monk and doctor of the church. In his famous commentary on the Song of Songs, Bernard characterized all human love, above all the love of married couples, as a metaphor for real love—namely, the love between the soul and its divine lover. Human love, then, which seems real, is actually the metaphor and divine love the reality. For Ghazali too, God was the only reality and therefore the only object worthy of our love. And so knowledge of God, if it is true, inevitably leads to love of him. He is beautiful and all beauty is only a reflection of his beauty. A parallel to this theological view of beauty in contemporary Islam is evident in the writings of Farid al-Ansari of Morocco. It is this that attracts the human soul to him—godly beauty—as embodied in the character of prophets, saints, and the righteous, who enkindle in others a desire to be similarly godly.

Ghazali's point is that we love others for their inner character and the relation it bears to God's character. We see them as kind (*muhsin*), and we are drawn to their kindness, even if not recipient of it, because it is beautiful in itself. This idea of kindness (*ihsan*), it should be noted, is self-consciously acknowledged by Muslims as the peak of Islam's ethical system and perfection of its morality. In Christianity, it is the third of the theological virtues, along with faith and hope. Kindness, then, in both Islam and Christianity, is that virtue achieved only through awareness of God, unlike other virtues, such as justice, which humans know apart from the revelation of God's face. This, of course, does not mean that only believers can be kind, but rather that the disclosure of a world to come makes kindness in this one a divine mandate.

Ghazali, though speaking of the beauty of kindness as witnessed in others, affirms that this kindness originates in God as the final cause of all kindness. And so it is through the expression of kindness by creatures in this world that we can know God and be drawn to him in the other world as the origin of all kindness. What we believe to be attraction to the kindness we see in the character of others is actually attraction to God. Ghazali even went so far as to criticize those who love

God out of hope for paradise or fear of hell. God is sufficiently attractive, even perfectly so, without such incentives. Those who realize this are able to see God in this world indirectly (i.e., through creatures whose character traits reflect his attributes) and will behold God directly in the next world. These are the pure-hearted, whose faces will manifest divine truth (*haqq*) on judgment day, or, as Paul wrote in his second letter to the Corinthians, "with faces unveiled, we all reflect the image of the Lord's glory as in a mirror."

All of this assumes that one has conformed oneself to God and his ways. Does this differ from the Christian notion that God comes to humans, even before compliance with his ways, clothing himself in humanity so as to be with humanity without prior condition? The Qur'an says that God took Abraham as his friend, that is, God initiated the relation of affection. Christians and Muslims both affirm religious practices as a way to open the mind to the presence of God. There must be awareness of God's self-revelation for God to do what he intends to do, that is, be with humanity. This is where Ghazali shifts to God's love for humans. God, he says, calls people to companionship with him and hastens to love them. Indeed, God implanted his light in the hearts of those who long for him, creating the necessary condition in them by which they might turn to him and he come to them.

To be sure, Ghazali was thinking of spiritual masters. This is also true of the ninth-century figure, al-Muhasibi, who wrote a short work, *Aiming to Return to God*, in which he stated that evidence of God's love for humans can be found in those figures whose entire lives are ordered by the presence of God. To Ghazali it made sense that some are closer to God, not in physical location but in spiritual character. They are more aware of God's presence and more fully conform to it. This spiritual hierarchy notwithstanding, God has created something in all human hearts that longs for his favor, making humans worthy object of God's love and delight, such that God might gaze on them, Ghazali wrote, as a tender compassionate mother (*walida shafiqa rafiqa*)—in echo of the hadith that God's mercy is greater than a mother's compassion for her child. The world, then, is part of God's merciful self-contemplation, and the human constitutes a focal point of his gaze.

This dynamic may be fully realized only after humans attain a character that adequately reflects God's gaze, but the point is that God's gaze is there and humans are its object. God, then, is the originator of love. He entices humans by the pleasure of intimacy with him, occasionally lifting the veil between them and him, disclosing knowledge of himself to attract their attention. God's love for his servants is expressed in his drawing them close to himself, which, Ghazali claims, he does by driving away their worldly preoccupations, purifying their interior state from the muddiness of this world, and lifting the veil from their heart, so that they might see him.

The omnipresence of God's face means that the ethics of Islam is not limited to the dictates of law but expands to include kindness to all (*ihsan*). How could one be anything but kind to others if aware of being in the presence of God at all times? And this is echoed in the Qur'an's description of the prophet Muhammad as a mercy for the universe (*rahma lil-'alamin*). But what does God think about sinners? Does he not hate them? Are they not objects of his wrath? Or does he love them too, as Christians understand God to love sinners no less than the righteous? The Qur'an describes God as loving the kind, pure, just, and patient, and not loving transgressors, wrongdoers, the proud and arrogant, unbelievers, the wasteful, and those who sow corruption on earth. It would seem that God's love is partial and conditional. Still, the Christian notion of God's love for sinners is meant as a spur to their conversion and not encouragement to persist in sin. Given that, as Muslim theologians maintain, God is not affected by human sin, it might be best to take the references to his not loving the sinful not as a limitation of his mercy but as inducement to repent. And God is himself ready to initiate the process of repentance, as signaled in the description of God in the Qur'an as the one who in his compassion turns to humans (*tawwab rahim*), "Thus did God turn to them so that they might repent. Indeed God is oft-turning and merciful" (9:118).

It is common to think of Islam in terms of laws and punishment for transgressing them—shari'a justice. For many Muslims, Islam is about personal devotions, communal prayer, fasting during Ramadan, pilgrimage to Mecca, celebrations on feast days, and certain rites at marriage and death. But religion is also about the ability to endure, sacrifice, even suffer, for the sake of God, even to the point where the concept of enemy is no longer a reality and all is viewed through a single lens of kindness: "Don't become angry (and paradise is yours)." The Qur'an calls for kindly dealing with one's enemies (60:7). Similarly, the Sermon on the Mount in the Gospel of Matthew expands the goal of religion beyond mere justice to include the endurance of sufferings of every kind for the sake of Jesus, the Christian face of God. Is one willing to suffer for the sake of the good and beautiful?

A spiritually enhanced ethics does not do away with the basic teachings of the faith. Jesus came to fulfill the law, not do away with it. In Islam, the basic system of morality could be described as a tightly regulated economy of rights (*huquq*) owed to others, to God, and even to oneself. God has the right to be worshipped, as embodied in various ritual duties, but has also revealed sanctions against theft, adultery, false accusation of adultery, alcohol consumption, and brigandage. Believers who commit such crimes will have to pay the penalty either in this world or the next. There is also the possibility that God will cover over (*satr*) people's sins in his mercy (*rahma*). Members of society also have duties to one another, and God has forbidden Muslims from transgressing the life, property, and dignity of others unless there is right cause (e.g., if the person is a murderer and is judged to deserve death or an unrepentant blasphemer who wages war against society). Spouses have duties to one another and to their children. The community as a whole has a duty to care for the weak and poor, and relations between individuals are to be guided by justice, that is, everyone getting their due, especially when it comes to commercial relations. Islam therefore places great emphasis on keeping promises and fulfilling contracts. When obligations are not met, justice is to be served, but the aggrieved can act mercifully toward others in imitation of the prophet. Rulers are to be obeyed so long as they do not transgress the rights of God and his servants (human beings). This could imply just rule or rule that does not offend the morality of Islam or, at a minimum, rule that does not prevent believers from performing their ritual duties (i.e., praying, fasting, and so on).

To be sure, the legal norms cannot be ignored, but neither can the idea of character (*akhlaq*) or, more specifically, nobility of character (*makarim al-akhlaq*), which in Muslim parlance amounts to selflessness. In a well-known hadith, the prophet says that he was sent to perfect nobility of character so as to model it for others. The laws, shari'a, are there, but so is the possibility of perfecting them in the form of kindness to all creatures—*ihsan*.

Ethics here has two interrelated dimensions—communalistic and universalistic. The first works through the particulars of religious practice, rituals and laws (what could be called the identity of the religion) but is to bear fruit in universally recognized character traits—humility, generosity, magnanimity, love, kindness, and the like. The communalistic side of ethics in Islam is expressed in the teachings of shari'a. But these teachings are a means to something greater. The goal is to live in the mercy of God, a state that encourages nobility of character in one's relations with all. Islam would not be Islam without its particular religious forms and norms, but it also would not be Islam without the kindness to strangers and guests for which Muslim society is so well known.

A problem arises when the communalistic side—the particulars of a religion—is seen as a singularly valid form of human existence. The particulars are never abandoned, but when limited to its particulars, religion ceases to be a way of life and becomes exclusive identity. Its final purpose gets lost in favor of the elements that constitute its particular identity. When shorn of its universal perspective, a religion has trouble embracing all life beyond the confines of the believing community. Does possession of the religion of God (*din allah*) require goodness only to fellow believers or to all?

A widely used term today, identity—ethnic, political, religious, and so on—sets a person or group of people apart from others, creating boundaries that supposedly define their existence. Is this term fairly applied to religion? Religion defies boundaries as much as it conforms to them, unfolding across cultures, nations, and other categories of human existence. In the end, it is difficult to say where religion ends and nonreligion begins. Some Muslims, like some Christians, have latched onto the idea of religion as exclusive identity distinguishing them from all else—culture, nation, other faiths. This is partly a reaction to the perception that the world seeks to eradicate Islam. Nevertheless, it ends by limiting piety to a set of particular laws (i.e., identity) to be implemented as a political project, locally and globally. This trend is considered in chapter 5. For our purposes here, it is enough to note that this development, the reduction of Islam to worldly identity, reflects attempts over the course of the last century to strip the ethics of Islam of its spiritual outlook. Once shorn of the sense of being in the presence of God, religion becomes a worldly project like any other, easily exploitable for political and even terrorist purposes. Indeed, when religion is limited to group identity apart from consciousness of the unlimited transcendence of God, it can turn into a quest for group supremacy rather than an ethics of love over hate, kindness over vengefulness, regardless of creedal boundaries.

Muslims are not about to set aside the norms of shari'a but do recognize that they exist within a wider religious vision. In Islam, norms apply to ritual prayer, finance, marriage, and a host of other concerns. Muslims have different opinions about these norms, however. Some see Islamic banking as a way to shield the investments of Muslims from corporate greed. For others, it is a way to hide shady dealings behind the cloak of religion. Some see the laws of inheritance as a way to keep family bonds intact, given that estates are distributed by a complex set of norms that takes into account the extended as well as the nuclear family. For others, it is unjust to adhere to these norms because they can favor unfamiliar relatives over one's own children, especially daughters, in an age when the nuclear family is increasingly the norm.

When thinking about Islam, inordinate attention is given to shari'a by Muslims and non-Muslims alike, making it seem that Islam is about shari'a and nothing else. This, in turn, makes God in Islam seem angry, vengeful, and unforgiving. He lays down laws and then gets angry when people fail to obey them, forcing him to want to punish them. In discussions about Muslim society, the focus, almost obsession, is on the very infrequent cases of stoning adulterers and executing apostates. This is not to make light of such human rights violations, which I consider in chapter 6. We cannot, however, judge Muslim society entirely on such cases when in fact Muslim society is more about neighborliness and mutual support. This myopia is compounded by the assumption that Islam is oppressive to women. Concealed behind veils, their sole reason for existing, it is believed, is to bear children. Moreover, it is often asked, is it not the husband, even an abusive husband, who alone initiates divorce at will and takes additional wives as he wishes? What kind of religion would allow this?

In response to charges that Islam is at odds with modern liberalism, some Muslims respond that the welfare of human society is more effectively preserved by Islam than by modernity. They point to the breakdown of the family in the West, the high rate of divorce, the prevalence of unwed mothers and fatherless children, the unabashed delight in gross forms of substance abuse and intoxication, the ease with which people enter into sexual relations with others they hardly know and may never see again, and the absence of any credible deterrence to crime, whether by gangs or white-collar executives. Yes, they admit, the punishments of Islam are harsh, but the modern world needs them, if only to survive.[6] The argument is also made that Islam is better for women, requiring the man to support her and her children, relieving her of financial worries that would force her to work and limit her ability to care for her children, exposing her and them to exploitation by potent as well as not so potent men.

The relation between sacred teachings and human freedom, not to mention human dignity, is complex. This complexity was captured at the UN summit for interreligious dialogue in November 2008. Muslim representatives called for international commitment to respect for the sacred symbols of all religions, reflecting Muslim sensitivities about insults directed at the prophet. The political chiefs of Europe, with no religious figures among them, balked at this, defending freedom of expression even at the expense of religious sentiment. Finally,

George W. Bush stated that he had been led in his policymaking, including his war-making, by a desire to defend the freedom to change one's religion. One was left with a sense of three different viewpoints about the nature of religion with little hope of mutual understanding or reconciliation.

To put it generally, Muslims seek respect for their religion in the eyes of the world. Europeans worry that the growing presence of Islam in Europe threatens their right to be unencumbered by religion. Americans see individual freedom as the very essence of religion. We are faced with a quandary that could lead to a clash of identities. To earn respect for their traditions, some Muslims assert them over the rest of the world. Some secular liberals, to demonstrate their tradition of unhindered freedom of expression, create art offensive to believers. Do Muslims have the ethical resources to be kind to others in a world that does not understand them? Do secular liberals have the resources to be kind to others even when the law gives them the right to insult them? Is our behavior limited by our laws? We live in a highly pluralistic world and cultural values diverge in radical ways. People are not going to give up these values and the identities they embody, but if we are about nothing more than our identities, then perennial clash is the likely outcome of the human condition. The question is whether the various traditions of the world offer something in addition to identity, whereby people can meet others harmoniously even when differing from them in profound ways.

It is impossible to encompass all Muslim societies in a simple description. One can find polygamous marriages in Islam, formed at the discretion of the male whether or not the state in question permits it, but most marriages are monogamous and do not end in divorce. There have been highly celebrated cases of adultery and apostasy in places as varied as Nigeria, Pakistan, Saudi Arabia, and the Sudan, but the death sentence has not always been carried out. Even in these cases, the problem is not Islam per se. The tradition, to be sure, has effect. There are rulings that call for the death of the adulterer and the apostate, but there are also controls to ensure that they are not pursued for political ends, as is invariably the case today, when Islam has become a political football rather than, as in the past, a source of moral stability for society.

The point is that the religious tradition itself is broader than shari'a. This is true for other systems. U.S. law calls for punishment of murder, theft, the sale and use of drugs, and, in some states until recently, sodomy. Most Americans, however, do not spend their days thinking about such things. The daily ethics of American life is about waving to one's neighbor, acting kindly to those one meets, patiently enduring the day's trials, inviting friends to dinner even if one is not going to be thrown into jail for not doing so. This is also the case for Muslims, who do not spend the day thinking about crime and punishment à la shari'a. Indeed, despite perceptions, the bulk of shari'a is devoted not to crime and punishment but to ritual practices. Muslim lives are shaped by a religious heritage that calls for justice but also encourages people to get along with others. This makes it necessary to reconsider the ethics that Muslims find most meaningful.

Those who travel or live in Muslim society are often struck at the welcome they receive and the spirit of hospitality and generosity. Certainly, no society is free of anger, violence, or corruption, but in all societies values help preserve harmony. In Islam, this is known as nobility of character (*makarim al-akhlaq*), working in tandem with state law for the welfare of society. This is not to suggest that Muslims have a nobler character than non-Muslims. Every individual, Muslim and non-Muslim, is to be judged on personal merit. Rather, the point is that the ethics of Islam is much broader than questions of crime and punishment. At heart, it is about the cultivation of interior dispositions that ultimately depend on recognition of the merciful face of God as ground of existence. For the sake of God, one remembers to be kind. For the sake of God, one remembers to be clement. For the sake of God, one is willing to sacrifice for others. This is the mark of ethics in Islam, much more so than shari'a, or at least not the impoverished view of shari'a as identity marker.

In what follows, we consider some of the different formulations of this tradition of ethics in Islam. It is worth emphasizing that the ethics of religious traditions are not simply theory, but affect the way people think about day-to-day realities. An article in *Nursing Science Quarterly* suggests that in our willingness to relinquish what we treasure, we fortify our relations with others and affirm who we are before God. Interviews with patients disclosed "stories of sacrificing something important in the name of friendship and connecting with the divine. In each case, a cherished something was reluctantly offered in the hopes of strengthening a connection with another."[7] Although originating in a Christian heritage, this insight recalls the dictum in the Qur'an to have no love for anything like your love for God. Spirituality in this sense offers the possibility of transcending self and self-attachment in one's relations. More effectively than the power of reason alone, orientation to the face of God as ultimate relation, for the sake of which all else can be sacrificed, mitigates, if it does not wholly eliminate, the egoistic inclinations of our souls—inclinations that are themselves the by-product of our fears of losing our most prized possessions.

A certain historical myopia exists today among some Muslims, who feel that enthroning Islam as master of the state is key to restoring the glory of Islam. The idea that Islam has been eclipsed by the so-called West raises anxieties about divine favor. Why is God favoring the West if his chosen religion is Islam? What can Muslims do to regain God's pleasure, restoring the glory of Islam? Some, arguing that Muslims have humiliated Islam, respond to this anxiety by calling for a fuller implementation of shari'a as state law at the expense of all other considerations. However, it was never shari'a alone that made Islam great but rather nobility of character (*makarim al-akhlaq*). It was always a willingness to forgo brazen self-interest for the face of God that created environments of trust as necessary precondition for a healthy society. In other words, a precondition for success, even individual success, in business, in education, in all spheres of life, is trust—trust that what one does makes sense and that one's efforts are not meaningless. A society that encourages lying, cheating, and bribery over truthfulness, promise-keeping, and merit-based competition will face a crisis not only of legitimacy but also of prosperity.

This is not simply a nice theory. The Gülen movement, a global network of Turkish Muslims, recognizes that a simple implementation of shari'a at the state level will not guarantee the success of Islam. They do not seek control of politics, which would be only a superficial solution to the problems of corruption that have plagued Turkish society in recent decades. Rather, they aspire to reinvigorate the ethical life of the nation on the basis of what one scholar has called pre-contractual solidarity, the trust and moral decency necessary for activity to make sense.[8] As a result, the Gülen movement, which oversees a variety of projects, notably schools and interreligious initiatives as well as conferences that aim to heal secular-religious animosities in Turkish society, operates through an ever-expanding network of shared ethical expectations that offer an alternative to a life based on self-regard. To be sure, followers of this movement are known for a keen sense of competitiveness—in business, in education, in all spheres of life. But the shared commitment to a common ethics not only fortifies relations between people, both inside and outside the movement, but also establishes the preconditions for the success of the movement's activities. It is worth making sacrifices for the face of God when those whose society you share also take seriously the notion of a life devoted to the face of God as highest good. And this goodwill pays off by inspiring people to do great things. Sacrifice for the sake of divine favor and prosperity can go hand in hand. The model of the Gülen movement therefore differs significantly from Max Weber's analysis of the spirit of capitalism. Wealth is not evidence of salvation. Rather, it is an ethics-based solidarity. Through self-sacrifice for God, wealth is generated in unexpected ways.

Despite the politicization of Islam in recent decades, a strong commitment to nobility of character (*makarim al-akhlaq*) as key element in facing today's troubling world remains. A recent work, available in bookstores from Casablanca to Damascus, speaks to this Muslim desire for an ethical vision beyond politics. *The Character of the Muslim: His Relation to Society*, written by Wahba Zuhayli, a prominent member of the Sunni establishment in Syria, does not treat shari'a per se, even if assuming it, but argues that the ethics of Islam is primarily altruistic concern for others.⁹ Zuhayli writes about shariʿa elsewhere but here focuses on everyday ethics as the actual arena where commitment to God is affirmed or denied. Over the course of 464 pages, Zuhayli pursues his stated goal: "refinement of the human being, elevation of his sentiments, and encouragement to be good throughout life entire, to be constructive, and ethically upright."¹⁰ He notes a potential contradiction of Muslim life. It is easy to declare beliefs and perform rituals at appointed times, but these beliefs and rituals become hollow if they do not bear ethical fruit in one's private and public conduct, that is, visibly impact Muslim character. This, Zuhayli writes, is the touchstone of Islam's credibility. Indeed, what would be the worth of religion if believers were cheaters, liars, and backstabbers?

In chapter after chapter, the underlying theme is the need to recreate an atmosphere of trust in Muslim society. The author opens with great emphasis on truthfulness (*sidq*), seeing its antithesis, lying (*kidhb*), as the greatest enemy of Muslim society. All action that shows altruistic concern for others is considered a kind of divine worship: removing a stone or thorn from the road, giving water to a thirsty dog, presenting neighbors and friends with the occasional gift to eliminate unspoken animosities, bearing a pleasant countenance, smiling and optimistic rather than mean-spirited and frowning. The details are at times overwhelming. When saying farewell to others, one should exhort them to piety and good conduct. On holidays, one should help the needy, visit family and friends, exhibit affection and joy. In eating, one should begin by invoking God and end by praising him. When invited to dinner, one should show appreciation for the food and refrain from sitting arrogantly as if a master to be served. One should recognize the social rights of others, seeking to reduce conflict by acting gently and tolerantly and with pity and mercy toward the needy, for a hadith has it that "whoever does not act with mercy will not be treated with mercy." One should always return another's greetings, visit the sick, attend a fellow Muslim's funeral, bless someone who has sneezed, offer helpful advice to others, and support victims of injustice. In echo of a prominent idea in early Christianity, that movement away from evil is a movement toward God,[11] a hadith is cited that says that those who cannot do good should at least not do evil because there is heavenly merit (*sadaqa*) in refraining from evil (*tark al-sharr*).

Zuhayli's goal is to make human solidarity the hallmark of Muslim society, where injustice is absent, anxieties lifted, unintended mistakes overlooked, and there is no deceit and deception, no betrayal, dishonoring of others, lying, extortion, or deal-making that serves personal interests rather than the common good. There will be no defense for the unjust on judgment day, including not only those who exploit public office for personal gain but also those who harm the property and reputation of others and transgress their rights or break good faith with them, dishonoring promises or breaking contracts. An important conclusion is that the believer acts justly because he relies on God and trusts in him for his sustenance, whereas the unbeliever in his heart fears not God but poverty, leading him to covet wealth and possessions even at the risk of his ethical integrity. Again, in echo of early Christian thought, the goal of ethics here is not punishment for transgressing laws but formation of character, known in Islam as refinement of the soul (*tazkiyat al-nafs*), to reflect the likeness of God.

Drawing on prophetic teachings and the example of the first Muslims, Zuhayli has advanced a notion of Muslim life where a person is evaluated by his righteousness and goodness towards others and his readiness to meet the needs of others. For this he will be compensated with a heavenly reward. In other words, the revelation of another world, a kingdom to come, means that you can suffer in this world, endure hardship and deprivation for the sake of the values of the next one, engendering a broader ethical framework where you are both just and kind not because you expect it in return or hope for a benefit here and now but because of divine favor anticipated in paradise.

Is it all pious niceties? Do Zuhayli's exhortations have any relevance for this world? What is it that holds a society together, especially an urban society of multitudes with no blood ties to bind them, with nothing in common but proximity? Evangelical Christianity acted as cohesive force for the American republic in its infancy.[12] It was not state institutions or even laws but networks of people who willingly sacrificed for one another, whose ethics were imprinted with a desire for both liberty and virtue, and who thereby established common expectations of behavior by which people were made to feel part of a single nation. Religion in the case of the early republic was democratic in its assessment of tyranny as demonic but also expected citizens to be virtuous. Religion can play a significant role in creating a shared national culture in which people willingly invest body and soul.

This is Zuhayli's point when he writes of "a love that expects nothing in return and is not motivated by personal interest." Many countries in the Middle East, which has a historically rich civilization, are today desperate for ethical renewal of the type that the Gülen movement has initiated in Turkey. Corruption, driven by the interests of the ruling class, is pervasive, eroding the social fabric of entire nations and decimating the will to live of peoples who are by nature spirited and intelligent. The greatest victim of this ethical breakdown is the economy of the Middle East, which in many places suffers because there is little sense of investing oneself in it if one cannot trust in society, hope for decency, and see one's interests not in isolation but as part of the good of the whole. Zuhayli's aim, then, is not simply to make believers good believers, but to reinvigorate the spirituality of Muslim souls, compelling them by their own accord to be truthful, upright, and prosperous, renewing a national culture so that activity, especially economic activity, might make sense. To this end, he quotes a hadith in which the prophet says, "By him in whose hand is my soul [i.e., God], you do not enter paradise until you believe, and you do not believe until you love one another. Shall I guide you to something that will allow you to love one another? Spread peace among yourselves."

This kind of thinking is hardly new in Muslim society. A tenth-century work by Ibn Abi al-Dunya, *Nobility of Character*, includes reports about the first Muslims, suggesting that they saw Islam as building on and perfecting the ethical heritage of Arabia.[13] The early Christians thought similarly of Christian ethics as building on and completing the ethical heritage of Greece and Rome.

At the same time there was good reason for the first Muslims to define their values as religious rather than tribal, despite their tribal heritage. The beginnings of Islam, even if embedded in the tribal context of seventh-century Arabia, were primarily urban, and the call to faith was accompanied by a call to leave tribal life, tribal kith and kin, for citied life, first in Medina, for a new way of relating with others based not on blood ties and tribal alliances but on faith and piety. The values of tribal Arabia—generosity, magnanimity, clemency, endurance, and fortitude—were adopted by Islam but reoriented to the face of God rather than to personal and tribal reputation. Ethics was now to have a religious purpose, namely, heavenly reward, informing relations with all peoples regardless of affiliation. If Islam was to succeed as ethical venture, it had to broaden the scope of ethics beyond the prevailing tribal assumptions of the day. Thus Islam nurtured a system of universal kindness based on notions of neighborliness and friendship and driven by a longing for the face of God, that is, a heavenly reward above and beyond strategies and calculations for maximizing tribal standing and personal reputation. Sacrifice for God, not pride in oneself and one's clan, was to become the central mark of Islam's ethics.

A social system in which cohesion is based on shared faith rather than blood ties or tribal alliances means that one's relations with God will be reflected in one's relations with others. God, after all, is no tribal deity in the possession of a single clan but Creator and Lord of all. The awareness of the one God expanded the ethical horizon of Arabian society. The demand of God for exclusive devotion apart from any partners means that wherever one turns, there indeed is the face of God, combining in a single religious formula worship of the one God and ethical dispositions necessarily universal in scope.

Rightful relations with others are protected by shari'a, encompassing both God's rights to be worshipped and the rights of fellow humans to justice. But mutual relationships, epitomized in kindness, are the lynchpin in a sliding dynamic between the encounter of the merciful God and merciful encounter of others. Ibn Abi al-Dunya begins his work with a hadith stating that "a man's generosity is his religion, his virility his intellect, and his stature his ethical character." Another hadith describes God as "generous and loving generosity, magnanimous and loving magnanimity." In short, the Qur'an's disclosure of God—besides whom there is no other—initiated a new criterion of action where self-denial made sense in light of one's final destiny in God. As one hadith puts it, "Strive for truthfulness—even when it seems to lead to destruction, it brings salvation. Put aside lying—even when it seems to lead to salvation, it brings destruction."

Islam, then, decisively rejected the idea that one's position in this world is the final measure of success, and this gave a new grounding to the soul in its relation to the world and the things of it, as noted by the statement that Ibn Abi al-Dunya attributes to one of the first Muslims: "The believer is not content to see his neighbor injured or a relation in need but is rich-hearted without possessing anything in this world. He is not misled in his religion or deceived. For him, this world is no compensation for the next, nor miserliness for magnanimity." Gradually yet perceptibly, the ethical norms expected from tribal relations were redirected toward other believers and potentially towards all. To this end, Ibn Abi al-Dunya marshals forth the following hadith: "Whosoever believes in God and judgment day should honor his neighbor. No believer is full while his neighbor goes hungry." His point is that this ethical disposition, made possible by the exclusive monotheism of Islam, is predicated on interior freedom that looks beyond worldly notions of gain or loss, as epitomized in the hadith that "a believer will not attain purity of faith until he repairs relations with those who shun him [cut him off], gives to those who have deprived him, excuses those who have wronged him, forgives those who have insulted him, and acts kindly to those who have harmed him."

Ibn Abi al-Dunya goes on to record the top-ten list of ethics in Islam as passed down by 'A'isha, beloved wife of the prophet and leading figure in early Islam. "Honest speech, sincere fortitude in obeying God, giving to the suppliant, repaying good deeds, strengthening family ties, keeping faith, acting honorably to neighbors, acting nobly to friends, extending hospitality to guests, and chief of all is modesty

(*haya'*)." Modesty, which is better translated here as humility, is the
result of the experience of standing before God and giving him his due
as Creator and Lord of all. It assumes the presence of God—a spiritual
orientation that transforms dispositions in the heart towards others.
Another hadith equates lack of humility with unbelief (*kufr*). Humility
is described as a kind of forbearance and clemency, even chastity, that
is, modesty in one's dealings with others as opposed to immodesty and
greed—traits that undermine society, as signaled in another hadith:
"Ask God for relief [from greed] . . . and so [be free] of discord, enmity,
covetousness, and spite; be servants of God as brothers."

Something similar was at play in the fellowship practiced by early
Christians. Christianity not only offered a new perspective on the ancient Israelite faith but also attempted to create a new kind of society
based not on kinship ties but on shared devotion to the face of God as
revealed in the person of Jesus Christ. Rodney Stark makes a compelling case for this in *The Rise of Early Christianity*, arguing that early
Christianity flourished largely for the new ethical vision it wrought in
the morally troubled cities of the Mediterranean world then under
Roman imperial sway. The focus of Christian ethics is mercy, com-
manded by God in this life and rewarded in the next. As Stark notes, a
Christian ethics of love and charity that went beyond family and tribe
was a tremendously attractive and galvanizing force against the chaos
and misery marking the urban life of the day. It brought consolation,
trust, solidarity, mercy—all the result of a willingness to sacrifice for
the face of God, to view as small and inconsequential the things of this
world next to the promises of the next. The idea that God loves humanity demanded that Christians love one another if they were to cooperate
with divine favor. This required not only witnessing to the claims of
the Gospel but also creating the conditions by which society might
more effectively cohere and flourish at a time of ethical ambiguity and
social deprivation, that is, amidst a situation that encouraged selfishness
rather than selflessness, and bitterness and vengefulness rather than
kindness.

The new orientation that Islam brought to the ethics of seventh-
century Arabia was variously elaborated over the centuries. Ibn Hazm,

tenth-century scholar of Andalusia, was one of many who gave a philo-sophical character to the ethics of Islam. The only thing of lasting value, he argued, is God.[14] Therefore, the only thing worth working for is God. Everything else ends in sorrow, but the person who is oriented toward God (*al-tawajjuh lil-llah*) and works for the next life (*al-akhira*) is never the object of envy and enmity. He is even gladdened by set-backs, obstacles in his way, trials and tribulations, because these too are counted toward the goal to which he aspires, that is, heavenly merit. For Ibn Hazm, self-transcendence is the goal of life in this world, as he says, "Expend your *self* only for a cause that is above it [higher than yourself], and that can only be God." If you choose such a path, he says, you will no longer pay attention to the speech of people, who delight in accusing and shaming one another, but only to the speech of the Creator. In fact, he says, to be perceived as blameworthy is preferable to praise, which leads to pride and self-satisfaction, whereas patient endurance of blame and insults will be rewarded in heaven.

Ibn Hazm goes on to discuss the human faculty of discernment, the capacity for rational decision-making, which distinguishes humans from beasts and associates them with angels. Religion, he says, com-mands us to avoid living according to our passions and instincts, and for this we must use our reason, the tool given to us to hold in check our baser inclinations that come from the irascible and appetitive aspects of the human soul (emotions such as anger and physical cravings of the body). Human reason is thus integral to the ethical disposition that religion commands, empowering believers to refrain from living accord-ing to natural inclinations alone. He sums this up anecdotally: "Whoso-ever does ill to his family and neighbors is the most ignoble of them. Whosoever responds in kind to their ill treatment is like them. And whosoever does not respond in kind to their ill treatment is the noblest of them, the best and most virtuous."[15]

Is this the Muslim equivalent of the Christian turning the other cheek? Ibn Hazm, of course, identifies it with the ethics of the prophet Muhammad, who, he affirms, was sent for the purpose of perfecting noble character (*makarim al-akhlaq*). If you want to be virtuous, Ibn

Hazm advises, you should not accompany those who seek prestige, material comfort, and pleasure, because vicious dogs do the same. Were it not for worldly ambitions, people would not seek to bring one another down. Ambition is the cause of every anxiety, avoiding which all peoples and nations agree is the goal of life. The opposite of anxiety is emancipation of the soul (*nazahat al-nafs*), a virtue that ennobles one with courage, generosity, justice, and understanding. In Ibn Hazm's view, a believer is not led by his irascible and appetitive faculties, but is discerning—not simply discerning but discerning in light of the revelation of God: "Whosoever affirms the vision of God [i.e., in the next life] has intense longing for it, is greatly inclined to it, and is not content with anything that falls even the slightest degree short of it, because it is his ambition."[16]

Islam's understanding of the ethical fruit of the spiritual life reaches a climax in Sufism, which has had immeasurable impact on Muslim society, especially its combination of longing for the face of God (intimacy with God) with an ethics that calls for enduring the evil of the world so as to be kind to all (i.e., suffering not for its own sake but for an ethical end). Such a stance, Sufism claims, is possible only by the empowering disclosure of the face of God. Sufism, despite popular perceptions, does not consider this world as simply a test and trial in preparation for the next. For Sufism, it is not a question of putting up with this world as a passing illusion but of embracing existence entire as reflection of the face of God. That is, all that exists is able to exist only insofar as it shares in the existence of God, making creation the site of God's self-disclosure no less than the scripture of the Qur'an. How could one ever spite others, seek revenge for suffering at their hands, if they in some measure reflect the face of God, that is, the names of God, which for the architects of Sufism are actually countless in number, forming the spiritual reality behind the world's material appearances? To be so oriented to God necessitates spiritual training, refinement of the soul. And the goal is detachment not only from worldly concerns but even from one's self. After all, self-attachment is ultimately what keeps one from total orientation to God and through him to others as partial reflection of his image.

Here, then, the merciful face of God is the departure point for both spiritual and ethical existence. The cycle of existence begins with God's self-introduction in the Qur'an as merciful and ends by giving the soul a godly coloring: "The color of God, and who is better than God at coloring?" (2:138). It is this godly coloring of the soul that is to mark one's relations with all things, especially other humans, because it is humans above all creatures who are glimmers of the face of God made manifest in creation. This idea is well captured in a letter on the universalistic dimension of Islam's ethics by Ibn 'Arabi, a thirteenth-century intellectual whose thought continues to be both influential and controversial today:

> Kindness is obligatory . . . for the prophet said, "Indeed I have been sent to perfect noble character" . . . and [for that purpose] God introduced Himself into companionship with humans. . . . So, you undertake noble character only through the companionship of God exclusively. Do what pleases God and avoid what displeases Him, whether towards Him or towards others, for conduct towards others is counted among the things that please God. . . . All Muslims and non-Muslims are edified by those who are attentive to the presence of God [i.e., the friends of God, *awliya' allah*], and God has a claim on every Muslim in their conduct with all God's creatures, without exception, from every class of angel, jinn, human, animal, plant, mineral, and inanimate creature, whether believer or not.[17]

These words capture the idea, mentioned earlier, that it is *makarim al-akhlaq*, not shari'a, that gives Islam's ethics its universalistic dimension; shari'a may be the necessary departure point for beginning the journey with God, but it cannot be the end, if the purpose of God's religion is to be realized. The ethics of Islam embodies a universal kindness through recognition of the unbounded presence of God—the face of God, which, the Qur'an says, one encounters wherever one turns. A high stage of spiritual development is assumed here, as noted by the great mystical poet of the thirteenth century, Rumi, who declared in one of his quatrains that God has given the world saints as exemplars of his mercy to all created beings, noting in particular the universal scope of their mercy which reflects the scope of his mercy.[18] How could it be otherwise when one realizes that all belongs to God, as Abu Hafs al-Suhrawardi, another mystical virtuoso of the same period, put it, "Whoever claims possession of something, his altruistic outlook is not sound, since he considers his *self* more entitled to the thing by possessing it . . . altruism is the mark of those who see that all things belong to God."[19]

The spiritual heritage of Sufism worked to cultivate high levels of Muslim self-detachment and interior freedom (*hurriyya*), because the face of God that constitutes exclusive object of one's longing is universally accessible, as heralded by the Qur'an. Here, Islam, like Christianity, opens a potential horizon where the concept of enemy no longer exists, as illustrated by al-Qushayri, eleventh-century author of a popular manual on Sufism that continues to be widely read today. He wrote that spiritual realization occurs "when one finds no difference in eating with friend or infidel."[20] It is not only a question of a universal morality, extendable to all, but also the recognition that the quest for revenge is an illusion, and al-Qushayri described kindness (*ihsan*, the height of noble character) as "patiently responding to reprehensible behavior with kind behavior." He illustrated this with a story about a Muslim tailor and his Zoroastrian client who would pay his bills with counterfeit dirham:

> The tailor would [always] take it. One day, when he had business away from his shop, the Zoroastrian came and paid counterfeit dirham to his assistant, who would not accept it, and so the Zoroastrian paid authentic dirham. When the tailor returned, he asked, "Where is the shirt of the Zoroastrian?" When the assistant related what had happened, he said, "What evil you have done! He has been treating me like that for some time, and I've borne it patiently, casting his counterfeit money in a well, lest another be harmed by it."[21]

In other words, enmity, the desire for retribution, is an illusion that leads us to perpetuate the cycle of evil, but a spiritual disposition focused on the face of God is able to absorb the world's evil and counter the deception of seeking vengeance. This undercuts at least one part of the motivation to hate one's enemy, removing a portion of evil from the never-ending cycle of revenge. The ability to suffer patiently, then, is indicant of spiritual maturity, as noted in a Sufi manual of the thirteenth century by Abu Hafs al-Suhrawardi, "Getting along with all folk, children, neighbors, friends and all people entirely, constitutes the [noble] character of Sufism, for by enduring insult and injury, the essence of the soul is made manifest."[22] Islam, no less than Christianity, affirms the importance of justice, but both also possess a logic that goes beyond justice. Al-Suhrawardi told a story about his uncle, Abu l-Najib al-Suhrawardi, a spiritual luminary of the twelfth century:

> I was with our sheikh [Abu l-Najib] on his journey to Damascus when one of the villages sent food to him in the presence of Crusader captives who were in chains. The table was set and the captives were to wait until he finished, but he said to a servant, "Fetch the captives so that they might sit at the table and eat with the brethren." He brought them, seating them at the table in a single row. The sheikh got up . . . walked over to them, and sat with them as if one among them. He ate and they ate, and it was made manifest on his face the humility before God that was at work within him, the contrition and detachment from pride over them on account of his faith, knowledge, and action.[23]

Where has all this gotten us? It may be impossible to determine whether Christians and Muslims have the same understanding of God's countenance in all its contours, and, indeed, there may be a reason not to want uniformity. Perspectives on the God of Abraham are not exhaustible. After all, we speak of God as a mystery to be in relation with and not a fact to be defined. Certainly there are similarities in the spirituality of the two religions, the sense of standing in, even cleaving to, the unbounded presence of God and longing for the ubiquitous face of God. There is also similarity in the ethical potential that follows from encounter with the face of God. The revelation of God for Christians and Muslims alike affirms self-sacrifice, not in a stoic sense of emotionless indifference, but rather in the sense of acting for God, for the face of God, for a relation with the divine friend. There is a common Christian-Muslim desire to reduce the ego before the revealed presence of God, with a resulting readiness to forgo self-interest for the sake of a relation with God, that is, for the sake of divine favor as ultimate goal, above any worldly standard of success. In both Christianity and Islam, reverence for the one God, who is not limited to tribe, expands one's ethical outlook.

Does Christian affection for the face of Jesus Christ line up exactly with Muslim attentiveness to the names of God as revealed by the Qur'an? What is clear is that for Christians and Muslims alike, the revelation of the face of God announces the good news (*bushra*, a term used by both Christian and Muslim Arabs), that is, the good news of the divine presence amidst humanity, offering spirituality to humans, freeing them from the limits of self-interest and self-regard in preference for a loving and merciful kindness inspired by the face of God. Regardless of the unique contours the two traditions give to the divine face, Christians and Muslims alike are moved by the realization that spirituality, the dispositions one cultivates in the soul, are necessary precondition for the formation of a truly noble ethical character, something, it would seem, which is desperately needed in society today, not simply for the sake of ethical harmony but even more so for the good of society.

NOTES

1. See, for example, Pierre Hadot, *Exercices spirituels et philosophie antique* (Paris: Études augustiniennes, 1981).

2. Abdessamad al-Ghazi, interview, November 2008.

3. Tahir 'Attaf, interview, November 2008.

4. See Ryan K. Balot, *Greed and Injustice in Classical Athens* (Princeton, NJ: Princeton University Press, 2001).

5. At least not officially. For example, in Morocco, the Berbers sometimes refer to God as Father Lord (*baba rabb*).

6. Taqi Usmani, "The Islamization of Laws in Pakistan: The Case of *Hudud* Ordinances," *Muslim World* 96 (2006): 287–304.

7. Kristine L. Florczak, "The Lived Experience of Sacrificing Something Important," *Nursing Science Quarterly* 19 (2006): 139.

8. Elizabeth Özdalga, "Outside or Redeemer? The Gülen Community in the Civilizing Process," *Muslim World* 95, no. 3 (2005): 429–46.

9. Wahba al-Suhayli, *Akhlaq al-Muslim: 'Ilaqatuhu bi-l-Mujtama'* (Damascus: Dar al-Fikr, 2002).

10. Ibid., 21.

11. For this notion in early Christian thought, see Robert Louis Wilken, *The Spirit of Early Christian Thought: Seeking the Face of God* (New Haven, CT: Yale University Press, 2003), especially chapter 11.

12. Mark A. Noll, *America's God: From Jonathan Edwards to Abraham Lincoln* (Oxford: Oxford University Press, 2002).

13. Ibn Abi al-Dunya, *Kitab Makarim al-Akhlaq*, ed. James A. Bellamy (Cairo: Dar Ibn Taymiyya, 1990).

14. Ibn Hazm, "Risala fi Mudawat al-Nafs wa-Tahdhib al-Akhlaw wa-l-Zuhd fi l-Radha'il," in *Rasa'il Ibn Hazm al-Andalusi*, ed. Ihsan Abbas (Beirut: al-Mu'assasa al-'Arabiyya lil-Dirasat wa-l-Nashr, 1983), 1:322–415.

15. Ibid., 397.

16. Ibid., 363.

17. Ibn 'Arabi, *al-Wasaya* (Damascus: Dar al-Iman, 1997), 57–58.

18. Rumi, *The Mathnawi*, ed. and trans. R. A. Nicholson (London: Luzac, 1940), 4:721.

19. Abu Hafs al-Suhrawardi, *Kitab 'Awarif al-Ma'arif* (Cairo: Maktabat al-Qahira, 1973), 250.

20. al-Qushayri, *al-Risalat al-Qushayriyya* (Beirut: Dar al-Sadir, 2001), 46.

21. Ibid., 159.

22. Abu Hafs al-Suhrawardi, 245.

23. Ibid., 241.

CHAPTER FOUR

JIHAD

Is It Christian Too?

AT DIFFERENT POINTS in his letters, Saint Paul speaks of his struggle to announce the good news made manifest in Jesus Christ. The term to describe this struggle in the Arabic translation of the Bible is *jihad*. Although Paul admits his own weakness, he claims that his is not a human jihad (2 Cor. 10:3). His efforts to make the word of God known represent a great jihad (Phil. 1:29–30; Col. 1:29–2:1; 1 Thess. 2:2), one for which he would greatly suffer. Surely, Paul is not calling humanity to violence or even just defense of a political order. Christianity does recognize the reality of this world and the necessity of human governance to preserve justice, protect human life, and maintain the common good. But an explicit word from God is not needed to know the purpose and virtues of human governance. Paul's jihad was a struggle for something beyond this world. It is the kingdom to come, knowledge of which transforms the way believers live in this world even as they anticipate the next. For this he willingly suffered, not simply to suffer, but to make the good news known.

The prophet Muhammad also had a jihad. Was it the same as Paul's? In Islam, jihad means struggle to make God's word highest. It too is not a struggle for a human system but for the reign of God. This struggle had great urgency for Muhammad. Like Paul, he set his sights on the great day of the Lord. For both, it was not enough to live justly in this world. One needed to prepare to meet God and be saved—or lost.

Additionally, both Paul and Muhammad acknowledged Satan as opponent of this divine mission. They did not so much hold him responsible
for worldly injustice as see him as the spoiler of God's good news,
seducing people from attentive focus on the world to come, from their
faith and the great struggle they too share as recipients of God's word.
Struggle is at the heart of the human experience, but in Christianity
and Islam, it goes beyond normal affairs.

Since the days of Paul and Muhammad, Christians and Muslims
have sought to announce the word of God to the world by various
means. One is by locating evil and combating it. The concept of evil
was supposed to disappear with the death of God and the rise of psy-
choanalysis in his place. It persists, however, along with its classical
persona, Satan, serving as a useful way to label one's political enemies:
the axis of evil, as George W. Bush once described Iran, Iraq, and
North Korea; or the great Satan, as Ayatollah Khomeini labeled the
United States. Politics aside, for Christians and Muslims, evil, characterized as Satan, is the enemy of God's good news.

Today as in the past, Christians and Muslims struggle to manifest
God's good news in a world that fails to grasp it fully. Billy Graham
spent his life calling people to Christ for the salvation of their souls.
But the effort to proclaim the news of a world to come invariably gets
caught up with worldly matters. In a speech delivered in December
2007, Mitt Romney, a presidential candidate of the Republican Party,
responded to certain Christians who felt that his Mormon faith disqual-
ified him from holding the presidential office. Interestingly, though
affirming the First Amendment's separation of religious authority from
the state, he also recognized that religion, all religion, is very much part
of national life. This commitment to protect people's liberty to pursue
religion freely in the public space is, he maintained, what makes the
United States a great nation with a mission to defend religious freedom
at home and abroad.

How exactly is the nation to represent religion? Christians, to speak
only of the largest category of believers in the United States, express a
range of opinions about the relation of God's purposes to the nation's

destiny. Some understand the United States to have an explicitly Christian identity, giving Christians the right of dominion over it. In this view, the integrity of the Christian mission is tied to national identity, making national authority something only Christians can rightly claim. Other Christians, though they hold the nation to moral standards, do not link God's word to the nation's destiny so explicitly. The reasons for this divergence are complex. It is partly because of the way Christian morality is understood. Some see the Bible as singular source of morality. Therefore, if the nation is to be moral, it must be grounded in an explicitly biblical mandate; Christians of this view claim that the Founding Fathers intended to establish a Christian nation.

By contrast, other Christians speak of multiple sources of moral truth. In addition to the Bible, there is also natural law. Human life has an order to it. This order originates in God, but the human mind can recognize it apart from revelation. There is, then, an objective moral order apart from religious inclination or personal choice. The morality of the nation is therefore not tied to revelation but instead to recognizable truths. Such truths, in this view, would apply to marriage, defined as the union of a man and woman for the sake of procreation, and to human life, which is to be protected at all stages, in potential (as a fetus from the moment of conception) no less than in actuality (once outside the womb). They would also apply to care for the poor and weak, also members of a society that functions organically and not simply as a collection of disconnected individuals.[1] Christians of this type are keen not simply to preserve so-called traditional values. They also recognize a higher purpose to life, represented in a special way in the family and society as arena of God's creative action, but they do not necessarily speak of the nation as having an explicitly religious identity.

Of course, we live in an age when the theory of evolution raises many questions about the existence of a moral order determined by higher truths. The human has become the measure of all things, including moral choices. Many Christians accept this. For them, religion inspires individuals as they grow in their personal relation with God but does not translate into a moral order by which society as a whole must live.

Still other Christians take the implications of God's word in a more militant direction, looking to violence in the Middle East in the hope that it will usher in the great rapture as first step toward the inauguration of God's kingdom on earth.

How, then, is God's word to be made highest in this world—by care for the downtrodden or by fighting the infidel? It would be difficult to determine which Christian outlook best reflects Paul's self-described jihad. And that is the point. Believers pursue the mandate to uphold God's word in diverse fashion. This is also true in Islam. In the Qur'an, the essence of jihad is struggle in the sense of sacrifice: sacrifice of one's worldly possessions and even of one's self for the sake of making God's word manifest, indeed highest, in the eyes of the world. How exactly is that to be accomplished? In some places in the Qur'an, jihad has a militant tone and is linked to fighting, though it is important to understand how Muslims read such verses. After all, the Bible also contains divine calls to violence (such as Num. 31), but Christians do not read them as directives to be carried out. In other places in the Qur'an, jihad means struggle in the sense of Paul's mission for Christ, witnessing a life for God above all else, even to the point of suffering for it. This ambiguity is also at play in the Sunna. In one hadith, the prophet says he has been ordered to fight until people submit to no gods but the God, and in another that the best jihad is to speak justice to oppressive rulers. Here too, it is important to ask how Muslims read these reports.[2] What human activity appropriately represents religion in this world? Is violence a way to witness to the glory of God beyond worldly standards of justice? In a well-known New Testament passage, Jesus equates service of the deprived and downtrodden with the kingdom of God. And a well-known hadith speaks of seven things that will earn God's shade on judgment day: a just leader, a youth reared in the worship of God, a person with a heart bound to the mosque, two people whose mutual love is based on a shared commitment to God's will, a person who rejects improper sexual offers, a person who gives charity discretely, and a person who is overcome with tears when recalling God even in private (i.e., his tears are not pretended piety).

A key question, then, is representation of God's word in the world. After all, God's message knows no borders. How is the good news to be spread? How is the world to be evangelized or qur'angelized? A terrorist figure such as Osama bin Ladin claims to be struggling to elevate the word of God over the world. Some Muslims took satisfaction in his attacks on the United States, viewing them as just requital for what they perceived to be a U.S.-led war on Islam. Many condemned al-Qaeda from the start, but many others did so only when fellow Muslims became targets, making al-Qaeda a threat to the interests of Muslims and not only the so-called West. Indeed, although al-Qaeda still attracts youth to its ranks, its religious vision has come under heavy attack from those who once shared it. The leaders of Egypt's Islamic Group and the erstwhile jihadist ideologue, Imam Sayyid al-Sharif, remain committed to the global supremacy of Islam but realize that terrorism actually hurts the cause.[3] Their main criticism of al-Qaeda is its failure to distinguish the battle for the other world from political conflict in this one. Confusing God's battle with political conflict encourages indiscriminate violence against all who reject one's religious view. Rather, they argue, Muslims should proceed with prudence in addressing the wrongs committed against them by the world's powers.

Like Christians, Muslims have a variety of ideas on appropriate ways to make the word of God highest in this world. Some do so by preaching the message of the other world, focusing on the rewards and punishments that Muslims can expect in the hereafter. Tablighi Jama'at, a global group with origins in the Indian subcontinent, exhorts fellow Muslims to perfect adherence to religious rituals apart from political considerations. The point is to store up rewards in the kingdom to come to offset the tribulations of the grave. Likewise, the Gülen movement, mentioned in chapter 3, advances the word of God in this world apart from political considerations. Unlike Tablighi Jama'at, it does not preach fear of punishments to come but focuses on acts of kindness, representing the ethics of the next world through merciful behavior toward others, Muslim and non-Muslim alike.

In short, the struggle to represent God's word is a perilous undertaking. Standards of justice and other human virtues such as wisdom, moderation, and patience do not depend on disclosure of a world beyond this one. Although Christians and Muslims embrace these standards, they also speak of something more, calling people to God in word and in deed. The manner of carrying out such a mission is fraught with confusion. When does jihad become jihadism? When does the struggle to represent God's word as highest standard in one's life turn into a mandate to dominate others? The revelation of a world to come has inspired Christians and Muslims to great acts for God, but they have also stumbled along the way. It is therefore vital to think carefully about what representation of God's word entails. The Bible links the kingdom of God to service of the least among us, but it also speaks of great battles before the coming of the kingdom. Likewise, Islam links jihad to the battle between good and evil in one's soul, but it also recognizes jihad by the sword to defend and extend the sovereignty of God's ways in the shape of a particular legal order. To be sure, there are key differences in the way jihad is conceived by Paul of Tarsus and Muhammad of Medina, yet at heart jihad is the struggle not only to ensure justice but also to exhort believers to live in anticipation of judgment day. It becomes jihadism, however, when it turns into a battle for supremacy of one group over another. Are there instances when the Christian mission also ceases to be jihad and becomes jihadism?

The legitimacy of force to correct wrongs has long been recognized by believers and nonbelievers alike: wrongs committed by one group against another, one nation against another, a tyrant against his people. But in times past Christians and Muslims saw other reasons to use force. Theories of just war have varied through the centuries no less than those of jihad. The need to defend a people against external aggression was widely seen as legitimate, and religious motive was never entirely ruled out. There was a sense in both religions that infidels and apostates needed to be brought into a properly ordered relation with God, by force if necessary, and that for their own good (the betterment of their souls). In Christianity, the goal of converting others—or at least getting them to hear the word of God—offered legitimate grounds to use force. In Islam, force was legitimate not so much for the sake of conversion but to spread the rule of Islam as representative of God's order. In an age of human rights, such thinking, though persistent in some circles,[4] has no place. Defense is the only just cause for warfare. However, even when Christians and Muslims saw religious order as a legitimate pretext for force, moral guidelines still applied. Force could not be used indiscriminately.

Is this the case today? The international order forged over the last century in place of religiously based empires is a remarkable achievement, but it has been accompanied by unprecedented levels of violence, including indiscriminate violence. The past century has witnessed military projects that sought not to defend a people and their land but to spread a particular view of human perfection. Here, violence has no clear end but is used indiscriminately to eliminate those who do not fit the definition of human perfection, whether cast in racial, political, or religious categories. It is when representation of God's word becomes conflated with group supremacy that religion takes on a terrorist hue. This is also true of secular movements with ideological philosophies that separate purportedly correct from purportedly incorrect forms of humanity.[5] Secular philosophies too can take on jihadist hue. Whether religious or secular, identity supremacy becomes a guiding principle, even at the expense of moral considerations and even at the expense of human life—collateral damage of the jihadist kind.

When it comes to the jihadism of al-Qaeda, the enemy is secularism, viewed as satanic threat to the long-term fate of God's word. The deeper fear is that the eschatological horizon that opens on the world to come is in danger of disappearing in the face of secular sentiment that makes this world the end of human existence. The victims of al-Qaeda's attacks, then, are collateral damage in a larger, much more complex, and ultimately unnecessary battle for supremacy between religion and secularism. The struggle to keep the kingdom of God credible in the face of the perceived menace of secularization need not take terrorist form. Indeed, in Muslim society, tyranny has often been secular, represented by colonial overlords and postcolonial dictators who have used secularism to justify domination. It has been argued that the religiously minded are unable to grasp the ways of modernity and therefore must be forced to accept them. Yet even in the face of such tyranny, Muslims have not lost sight of the fact that the struggle to make God's word known cannot proceed willy-nilly. It must take a form that works for—not against—the greater interests of the *umma*, a standard that the indiscriminate violence of al-Qaeda does not meet.

There is a larger context. The peoples of the world, Muslims included, were once enchanted with modernity and its promises. It was supposed to explain the mysteries of the universe and eliminate all problems. Modernity has offered much, new political forms such as democracy and scientific discoveries that alleviate suffering, but it has a darker side. Many thought it would make religion obsolete. The human mind, coupled with technical expertise and economic efficiency, would bring about the good of all through the workings of a hand that was invisible but no longer divine. The goal was to liberate people from long-held systems of beliefs seen as obstacles to progress, especially the ability to inquire critically and express oneself freely.

All of this led to great advances but also to bizarre and tragic results. The mind alone, unchecked, cannot guarantee the moral life. Some modernists sought to justify racist theories—and therefore imperial dominion—by comparing the brain size of different races. For the biologically fit, it would be just a matter of time before history would end and all enlightened peoples overcome their native passions by remaking themselves in the European image. Despite its accomplishments, modernity not only held out promises that failed to materialize. It also had a decidedly supremacist aspect, and Muslims were usually placed outside that circle. In reaction to this disdain of Islam, some Muslims responded in kind, calling for the supremacy of Islam over the rest of the world. Moreover, science has proven capable of serving destructive no less than productive ends, and capitalism, having bested socialism, is demonstrably ill equipped to save the world: only a lucky handful tend to thrive. Indeed, the once-vaunted claim of secularism as neutral thinking no longer holds. For many Muslim societies, secularism has not been guarantor of tolerance but rather pretext for regimes to claim moral authority over citizens in the name of helping them progress toward modern life: Ba'thism in Syria and Iraq, Kemalism in Turkey, Nasserism in Egypt, and Suharto's New Order in Indonesia. The U.S. attempt to introduce democracy to the Middle East has been viewed similarly. Based on experience, many Muslims conclude that the incapacity for God in the human mind as by-product of modernity has been morally disastrous for the world. There is some sense to this. One need only look at the violence of twentieth-century Europe, perpetrated in the name of the modern state and accompanying secular ideologies, such as national socialism and international communism. For some Muslims, there is urgent need to make the word of God manifest once again to overcome the tyranny of secularism.

Indeed, God now seems to be breaking out everywhere. Is this to be understood in the biblical sense, where God breaks out whenever displeased with the failures of his people to live up to the demands of their covenant with him? Or is it simply worldly ideologies now in religious clothing? Is it God breaking out or the Antichrist? As suggested, the highest aspirations of religion are never very far from evil.

Supremacism is based on the myth of perfection and its attainability in this world. For Nazism, perfection was defined in terms of the German race, and those who did not fit into this racial myth, the Jews, were depicted as the Antichrist, the embodiment of evil. In the Soviet Union, communism represented the perfection of human history, requiring elimination of the bourgeois class for the sake of proletariat rule. The jihadism of al-Qaeda therefore does not originate in Islam. It is a response to modernist ideologies seen as a threat to the sustainability of the Muslim way of life.[6] Long defined primarily as a moral force, to correct manifest injustice, jihad has now been forced into the service of ideological ends. Key figures of the past century, notably Abu-l-A'la Mawdudi of Pakistan and Sayyid Qutb of Egypt, paved the way for jihadism by recasting jihad as revolutionary ideology—in other words, a very modernist take on jihad.[7]

In this way, the defense of Islam against the secularizing menace takes on a supremacist hue—an antimodernism that is Muslim only insofar as it has harnessed its wagon to jihad. Moreover, in its determination to push back against an arrogant secularism, jihadism claims that the secular never had a place in Islam alongside the call to God. This assertion, however, ignores history. A core principle of classical Islamic political thought is the need for balance between the realities of this world and the demands of religion. Sultans were expected to adhere to standards of justice but were never expected to perfect this world in the image of the next. Nor were they declared agents of idolatry (*tawaghit*) if their rule fell short of religious ideals. Certainly, excessive injustice, it was recognized, would eventually lead to the demise of a sultan's rule, but the only criterion used to declare rule as insufficiently religious was the ruler's own declaration of his infidelity. Today, however, because of jihadist overcompensation, a new standard has been asserted whereby a Muslim ruler who fails to represent religion flawlessly is subject to jihadist attack. The reverence for secularity, long a hallmark of Islamic political thought, is lost on al-Qaeda. Similar instances of this historical myopia exist in Christianity. In the sixteenth century, Anabaptists, by discarding the heritage of Christian thinking that recognizes secular authority, aspired to realize the kingdom of God on earth in communities set apart from the world. In one instance, this zeal turned into a reign of terror as the Anabaptists of Münster, Germany, sought to eliminate all life that fell short of Christian perfection.[8] Just as secularism can get out of control when it turns into a mission to correct believers, so religion too distorts its own purpose when it loses the reverence for secularity that has long been part of its heritage.

This is not to say we should let go of our myths and the ideals they embody, whether religious or secular. We should examine them critically to ensure that they are true and not false. All the same, they inspire us to live and to achieve great things. Our myths become dangerous, however, when we turn them into a political project to be achieved in this world. The moment we demand the world to conform to our myths of perfection, we run the risk of tyrannizing and even eliminating others who stand in the way, that is, the risk of collateral damage. And so again, when it comes to the highest ideals of religion, it needs to be asked whether it is the word of God or the Antichrist that is being served.

Article 676 of the Catechism of the Catholic Church states that "the Antichrist's deception already begins to take shape in the world every time the claim is made to realize within history that messianic hope which can only be realized beyond history through the eschatological judgment. The Church has rejected even modified forms of this falsification of the kingdom-to-come under the name of millenarianism, especially the 'intrinsically perverse' political form of a secular messianism." That is, the pursuit of jihad remains true only as long as it recognizes the imperfectibility of this world. It becomes jihadism when it turns the announcement of the world to come into a political project to be realized in this one, a move that immediately legitimizes violence not for moral purposes but to achieve divine perfection here and now. Jihadism mistakenly insists on the total victory of God's word in this world even when the Qur'an makes clear that such victory is to be had only at an unspecified future judgment day.

Jihadism, then, may feed on demands for greater justice in this world but ultimately stems from anxieties about the godly character of the *umma*. Is it living up to its divine mission to make God known or has it become hopelessly compromised with secularist calculations as advanced by infidel nations and apostate rulers? If, as jihadists claim, secularizing processes are gradually closing off the Muslim mind to the ultimate reality of God, something palpable and dramatic needs to be done to prove the power of God's word to the world. The anxiety over the sustainability of religion in the face of a secularizing world becomes cause to introduce the kingdom of God into this world, to make it visible for all to see—in short, to turn it into a political project. Jihad becomes jihadism. One is ready to die, even kill oneself, and to pursue death actively, if it will offer a visible witness of ultimate reality before the eyes of this world.

Religion is back in a very public way, seeking to muscle secularism aside as lead global ideology and advance its authority over the secular state. But what are the risks? We had Hitler, der Führer-Savior of Nazi

Germany, and Che Guevara, the messiah of international socialism. Both were willing to build utopian orders over the bones of those who stood in their way. More recently, we had Khomeini. Some saw him as the Hidden Imam, returned to save the Iranian nation (and Iranian political rhetoric continues to harp on the return of the awaited Mahdi), but he sent hundreds of thousands to their death on the battlefield with the promise of paradise. And now Osama bin Ladin challenges U.S. global hegemony with a particular kind of martyrdom, designed to proclaim the power of God over the world through indiscriminate display of lethal and suicidal piety.

At play amidst all this are competing definitions of religion. Is religion about a deeper consciousness of transcendent meaning as conveyed by revealed messages or is it about a sometimes very narrow expression of group identity? If group identity, religion easily coalesces with worldly agenda and political projects, mobilizing believers to kill and be killed, not for the flag but for God apart from the flag. How does the divine symbol, God, resonate with patriotism? In one sense, religion has long aligned with political membership. Subjects were to follow the religion of the ruler. But Christianity and Islam have also challenged the reduction of religion to the interests of a single people, whether tribe, nation, or even empire. The promoters of modernity have been naïve in thinking that religion would gradually disappear in the face of secular progress, but the struggle for religion has taken on odd contours that make it seem entirely worldly in its manner of proceeding. Religion has become, unwittingly to many of its purveyors, almost indistinguishable from the ways of the world. This is in part the result of the ascendant definition of religion as group identity. We remain at a critical stage when it comes to jihad. Jihadism will not succeed. No utopianism ever has. But it has the potential to create a good deal of havoc and to recur periodically. There is great need for Christians and Muslims, along with others, to consider its true purpose, and a key issue along the way is a fuller grasp of the nature of religion. Oddly, in many places across the Muslim world, there seems to be an inability to identify Islam without accompanying negative reference to the so-called West. The assumption, then, is that religion is simply an identity. Therefore, because the West is not Islam, the logic goes, it must by definition be anti-Islam. This rhetoric continues to pose great harm to Muslim youth, closing doors to positive interaction with other peoples.

As noted earlier, the sense of jihad as used in the Qur'an is righteous struggle for the way of God, but Muslims have nuanced jihad in a myriad of ways over the centuries. In general, the tradition speaks of two jihads: a lesser one of force to preserve the moral order of Muslim society, and a greater one of spiritual combat against the baser elements of one's soul that prevent it from adhering to the will of God. The evil to be combated is both external and internal—a disorder in both society and the soul that blocks harmony with the way of God. Muslims therefore have options in deciding which concept of jihad best serves their interests in today's world.

In Islam, belief in God is itself an essential part of repelling injustice. In a popular hadith collection compiled by the thirteenth-century Syrian scholar al-Nawawi, the prophet directs a person who had asked about the meaning of righteousness to inquire of his heart because, Muhammad said, "Righteousness (*birr*) is what makes the soul content while sin is that which leaves the soul troubled." In this context, righteousness connotes belief in God. Thus, faith in the soul is integral to the moral life. The idea is elaborated by another Syrian scholar, Ibn Qayyim al-Jawziyya, who lived a century after al-Nawawi. In *Steps of the Seekers*, he speaks of two kinds of polytheism. The greater one, associating partners with God, is not pardonable and will be punished in the hereafter, but other kinds of belief that fall short of true monotheism, even if not explicitly associating partners with God, may lead to a failure of justice in this world, requiring political redress of some kind. Polytheism is the greatest sin in Islam, but can be viewed as a cause of injustice in this world and not only a theological deficiency.

On the one hand, polytheism (*shirk*) is evil because it transgresses the Qur'an's revelation of God's oneness. It is thus injustice not against other humans but against God. Yet the Qur'an identifies *shirk* as a great wrong (*zulm 'azim*) that harms human society. Adam and Eve wronged themselves by putting themselves before God. The Israelites at Sinai wronged themselves by worshipping the golden calf.

Injustice according to the Qur'an results from the worship of beings other than God. If one truly believes in God, Creator and Lord of all, who rewards and punishes on judgment day, if one truly believes in God as singular reality, as opposed to the things of this world, if one truly believes in God who alone sustains and saves, one would not commit moral outrages or transgress the rights of others. And so, by qur'anic reasoning, recognition of the one God results in righteousness. It is not simply a matter of a happy outcome in the world to come. Rather, acknowledgment of the one God checks people from elevating themselves over others on the pretext of having divine allies. It is the word of God that is to be highest and not the word of particular individuals or groups.

In other words, the Qur'an is decidedly antisupremacist. Its brand of monotheism counteracts the tendency of humans to dominate others on the pretext of possessing gods alongside God. In the end, they only wrong themselves, that is, human society as a whole. The point is that *shirk* is actually a human trick, a pretext to ignore the ethical implications of monotheism by becoming master rather than servant of others. Evil here is seen through the prism of idolatry, which is not simply about bowing before graven images. More profoundly, it is a disorder that results when humans make themselves the purpose of existence. It is no coincidence that the Qur'an's call to monotheistic worship is accompanied by horror at humanity's moral failings: social hierarchies, political ideologies, disregard for the weak and needy, elite monopolization of wealth and power.

The failure of monotheism, in this sense, results in the decay of society—injustices that cause economies to fail and people to abandon cities, undermining human civilization. The Qur'an warns of past nations that did not heed the counsel of prophetic messengers. They set themselves up as arbiters of justice, arrogantly justifying a hierarchy of power through idolatrous religiosity. In the end, the Qur'an says, they wronged only themselves, for they will be held accountable before God on judgment day when the weaker elements of society, whom they duped into following them, will ask them, their worldly overlords, why they led them to prefer their way over the way of God. Corruption (*fasad*) is the outcome of false belief that parades as truth but is really a version of human supremacy pretending to divine purposes: glorification of oneself, one's class, one's race, one's nation, one's religion over others. The Qur'an castigates Jews and Christians for claiming that they alone will be saved, a confessional arrogance that some Muslims admit is now also true of Islam. It is this confessional partisanship that can make it difficult for some Muslims to accept international condemnation of political figures implicated in great atrocities, such as in Iraq under Saddam Hussein and now in Darfur under Omar Bashir, simply because they are Muslim in name. Here, ironically, as the Qur'an warns, false belief masks itself as true belief, putting the survival of society at risk by making good evil and evil good.

Indeed, monotheism has its own supremacist tendencies. This is noticeable in Wahhabism, which is politically quietist in principle but can morph into jihadism when made into a political project.[9] Wahhabism is allegedly inspired by the teachings of Ibn Taymiyya (died 1328), revered by many as the greatest scholar of Islam. However, his teachings, though strict, are not adequately represented by Wahhabism. For example, in a treatise on communal harmony,[10] he argued that the moral corruption in society is the result of the failure of Muslims to agree on a single form of monotheistic worship. It may strike us as odd to think of ritual diversity as the cause of social degradation, but for Ibn Taymiyya, it raised doubts about the singularity of truth, and this, in turn, leads to a lack of moral rigor. In his view, the failure of Muslims to follow a single form of worship raises a significant question. Which, if any, represents the correct way of worshipping God? Moreover, if Muslims are not worshipping God in singular fashion, the conclusion could be drawn that they have lost sight of the singularity of God. In turn, Ibn Taymiyya avowed, this drift away from monotheistic singularity leads to injustice in society. That is, people will make decisions according to partisan interests rather than the truths of Islam. Instead of singular devotion to God's way, people will prefer the authority of those who serve their particular interests over those who are more competent in governing society's affairs justly. Thus, for Ibn Taymiyya, what starts as theological laxity ends in a cronyism that jeopardizes the public good.

In this sense, his ultimate concern was the welfare of Muslim society. Here, religion is not a tool to affirm group identity but a moral project, preventing people from associating partisan interests with God's decrees. For Ibn Taymiyya, then, belief in God reduced the likelihood of bias in assessing the interests of society. It is for this reason that he condemned the introduction of innovations into religion, not simply because they confuse monotheistic truth but more so because they can be politically exploited, leading to communal disunity, intra-Muslim conflict, and loss of moral harmony.

Ibn Taymiyya's ideas were troubling to many in his own day. He was accused of introducing innovations into the faith and disturbing the peace, and he would die in prison. But there was a moral vision behind his drive for doctrinal unity. Wahhabism, in contrast, tends to place doctrinal purity above all other considerations, turning religion into a question of identity. In this sense, it can offer grounds for war-making in the name of religious identity apart from moral considerations that all would recognize as legitimate grounds for war-making.[11] Wahhabism shares Ibn Taymiyya's horror of religious innovation (*bid'a*) as the summit of evil but takes it in a different direction. Whereas Ibn Taymiyya was concerned with the moral implications of doctrinal confusion, Wahhabism places greater emphasis on doctrinal purity in assessing the worth of human existence.[12] Infidels, including Muslims who do not accept the principles of Wahhabism, are potential enemies of God not because they represent a threat to the moral order but because they fall short of the demands of religious identity. As a result, they have no moral worth if not clearly Muslim. In a reversal of Ibn Taymiyya, Wahhabism can actually exacerbate conflict within Islam, encouraging Muslims to condemn one another not for moral failings but for alleged deviation from true Islam.[13] Although not the cause of jihadism, Wahhabism feeds into it, making sense of fighting and even eliminating others for failing to place the call to religion above all other considerations. Force is justified not to achieve the moral purposes of monotheism but in the name of a creed. Others, Muslims included, may lead moral lives but become legitimate objects of attack if deemed inadequate representatives of the interests of the other world. Jihad becomes jihadism when a particular definition of religion offers grounds for violence against those who fall short of religious perfection.

Believers of all types have long posed questions about evil. How can it exist if God is all-powerful and loving? Is it a test of faith, a kind of backdrop to religious commitment, where those who resist its seductions are rewarded in the life to come? Or does it have a reality of its own, embodied in systemic perversities in human society that produce poverty, homelessness, and exploitation of the weak? Why does God, who has decreed mercy for himself, allow humans to suffer, to say nothing of his permitting natural catastrophes such as hurricanes and tsunamis? Theologians may claim that evil is actually the absence of good, amounting to nothing next to the infinite goodness of God, but this is little comfort to victims of abuse and terror and neglect. And if religion claims to be the enemy of evil, why has it become easy prey to violent conflict?

In April 1993, seventy-four members of a Christian group known as the Branch Davidians were killed in a fire sparked by a botched police attempt to penetrate the group's compound in Waco, Texas.[14] The police had initially sought to apprehend the group's leader, David Koresh, accused of sexual improprieties, but they soon found themselves involved in a larger conflict. Koresh viewed the standoff through a biblical lens. He saw it as a sign that the kingdom was at hand. Prophecies spoke of battles between the forces of evil and a righteous remnant. There would be conflict. Some would be slaughtered. But Christ's reign would follow. Surely the military-like siege of his compound was evidence that the process had irrevocably begun.

Federal authorities were blamed for the tragic outcome, accused of not understanding the nature of the sect they faced. Koresh is not entirely innocent, however. His brand of piety led him to welcome violence as potential fulfillment of scriptural prophecy. He saw biblical predictions of violence as the culmination of scripture without considering their deeper intent. As a result, he could not distinguish the message of scripture from the events of the world around him. The police at his gates were the forces of evil, come to initiate the final battle in which Christ would eventually triumph.

Scripture, both Christian and Muslim, does speak of cosmic battle that pits good against evil. Believers become part of this battle. They too are responsible for the struggle for God's way over Satan's. But how is this struggle to be pursued in this world? There can be a tendency to read the cosmic battle between good and evil into particular political confrontations. Ronald Reagan did just that in his speeches against the Soviet Union, which he referred to as the evil empire, although his willingness to negotiate with the Soviets showed that he did not actually consider the political confrontation to be spiritual warfare. To be sure, equating worldly battles with spiritual warfare may be justified if there is a truly moral cause. Thus, in Islam, it is necessary for the military leader first to wage war on his soul and its baser ambitions to ensure that when he goes to war, it is not for his own political interests but for a truly noble cause.

Alongside this is the particular way scripture is read. Some fear that anything short of a literal reading of scripture is tantamount to questioning its divine origin. Believing in the divine origin of scripture is not problematic in itself, but a literal reading of scripture without attention to the historical context in which it was written can have unfortunate consequences. That is, reading scripture in such a way makes it easy to transfer its narrative from one historical moment to another. In turn, such a fundamentalist reading of God's word can make it difficult to distinguish between scriptural narrative and the events unfolding at the moment. The spiritual warfare that scripture urges is thus read into political battles that are in fact all too worldly. The worth of scripture, including the battles it narrates, is tied to its fulfillment on the world stage. Violence in the world reflects God's word and takes on divine purpose. Jihadism therefore follows closely on the heels of projects that confuse a worldly entity, such as the nation, or a worldly cause, such as global supremacy, with God's purposes. Violence for the sake of a worldly mission is misconstrued as religious mission. It becomes reasonable from this perspective to think that we can fulfill the purposes of religion by worldly stratagems. The political foe is understood as God's enemy, making negotiation and reconciliation much more difficult. To take an example, the United States, though its policies sometimes lack purpose, is generally a positive presence in the world. But in the jihadist mindset, it is God's enemy, stripped of all worth. It embodies evil, it is an agent of idolatry (*taghut*), making it the antithesis of God. This, in turn, makes sense of perpetual violence against it. Also, some Muslims, associating the United States with Christianity, run the risk of viewing Christians in general as political enemy as well as religious deviant.

Christianity has not been immune from such associations. It became implicated in worldly projects, such as European colonialism and even Nazism, which some Christians saw as fulfillment of God's purposes. In some circles of U.S. evangelicalism, there is a tendency to equate Christianity with U.S. policymaking.[15] This can translate into particular support for the state of Israel, which one evangelical leader has called God's foreign policy. There may be political reasons for the United States to support Israel, but to see it in biblical terms is to turn the United States into an agent of religious promise. It is not wrong to want America to be righteous, but equating its political objectives with God's is jihadism. We are taken aback when a Christian leader calls for the assassination of a standing president who does not align with U.S. interests. The United States has a moral role in the world, but is it destined to save the world? If so, it makes sense to impose the American way of life onto the world for its own redemption.

The war on terror was declared not in the name of Christianity but for moral purposes, such as national security, global stability, and so on. Yet, to judge from Christian media in the United States that never tire of demonizing Islam (not just al-Qaeda) as the enemy, Christianity is once again at risk of turning a political objective into a heavenly purpose. Underlying this is the hope that in a skeptical age the empirical demonstration of religion on the world stage can turn back the tide of those who say that the monkey and not God is the origin of humanity. In this sense, the perception among some Christians is that the White House has the role of demonstrating the truth of Christianity to those who deny it. It is tempting to believe that utopia, perfection, heaven can be achieved here on earth. This is not to deny that the hope for the kingdom to come can inspire believers to great acts of service and charity. The eschatological promise should have some effect here and now. But this promise remains primarily a hope to be anticipated in a world to come. Hanging that hope on the affairs of this world invariably requires division of humanity into two camps—God's friends and God's foes, Christ and Antichrist.

The spiritual masters of Islam, like their Christian counterparts, have long noted the fickle nature of the human soul, likening it to a wild horse in need of bridling. Here, it is the soul—not Satan—that is true enemy. Muhammad reportedly asked his companions their view of a friend whom you serve and honor and afterwards casts you into hell. This, they reply, would be a false friend. He then asked their view of a person whom you oppose, whose wishes you refuse, but who, after all that, leads you to paradise. They reply that this would be a true friend. Such, the prophet says, is the nature of your soul. Give in to it, it leads to hell. Deny its inclinations, it leads to heaven.

The deceptive nature of the soul led Muslim scholars to posit a preliminary jihad against the soul as necessary precondition for armed jihad. Only by first mortifying one's passions and desires, ensuring that one is not under the influence of worldly ambitions, can one hope to enter into war with a godly end in mind rather than one's own ambitions. That is, war-making cannot be pursued in the name of religion without first ordering the soul to God rather than worldly ends. War-making that makes supremacy its goal rather than a moral purpose has no religious sanction, since its goal is worldly domination.

This is hardly to deny religion a role in public life. Leaving ethics entirely to the state (i.e., to secular authorities) is problematic, because the state sometimes needs to be checked, a role religion continues to play, sometimes with dramatic success—one thinks of the contribution of John Paul II to the demise of communism. Moreover, state institutions, we know, do not alone guarantee the moral life of the nation, and so religion does have a place in helping the state achieve its purpose, namely, the public good, even, perhaps especially, in democratic societies where individuals enjoy great freedom to pursue their private ambitions sometimes recklessly. All the same, religion is in danger when it equates heavenly purposes with state purposes. Why does it sometimes do so?

If, as the Qur'an proposes, monotheism is key to the eradication of injustice that comes about when people set themselves up as lords, it is not difficult to see how Muslims would conclude that a just society can be achieved only if governed by Islam, a kind of religious governance by shari'a ensuring that all people get their due as equal servants of God. The idea that justice is served only under Islam seems a bit odd, given that human societies have achieved a measure of justice without Islam and even without revealed guidance, a point admitted by Muslim scholars, most famously by Ibn Khaldun, who concluded in the fourteenth century that although religion can serve a worldly purpose, rule, if just, can last without it. However, for Islam at its beginnings, in the tribal context into which it was born, monotheism was the most effective guarantor of justice for all, and so it was felt that prayer to the one God was not enough. A polity in which Islam held sway was also needed to ensure justice.

From this departure point, Islam, while remaining true to monotheistic morality, also took on political and territorial dimensions, something akin to European Christendom. Religion was no longer simply the morality of monotheism but civilization as well: the abode of Islam which, despite internal fragmentation, was a more or less clearly demarcated territory under caliphs and sultans governing in the name of Islam. The abode of Islam (*dar al-islam*) was set against lands where Islam did not hold sway, designated as the abode of war (*dar al-harb*), that is, not yet subordinate to the monotheistic justice of Islam. It is worth noting, however, just as the concept of Christendom is not to be found in the New Testament, so too the phrases *abode of Islam* and *abode of war* do not exist in Qur'an and Sunna.

The reality of rule in the name of Islam did not mean that Islam became a state affair. Rulers were not the mediators of religion. That was the role of shari'a scholars, guardians of morality as heirs to the teaching authority of the prophet. The law-making capacity of the ruler was limited to worldly governance (*siyasa*), including tax collection, the organization of the army, and so on. The ruler was also subject to God's ways as embodied in shari'a, understood in this sense as the rule of law.

Jihad took on diverse meanings in response to these shifting historical circumstances. In principle, to defend or extend shari'a was seen as ample cause for jihad, but it is important to remember that the classical doctrine of jihad was formulated in a context of empire. The religious scholars generally worked to ensure the moral purpose of jihad, setting out rules for military conduct in battle that limited the use of force to those elements of the enemy's populace that constituted a threat to the Muslims. Force could not be used against the populace entire, only its combatants. At the same time, within the political culture of the premodern past, the concept of jihad was shaped in light of the imperial dynamic, that is, defending and extending territorial dominion. It is in this sense that Islam took on a territorial character as one abode in opposition to another, when, in fact, the morality of monotheism, as Islam's scholars themselves insist, does not depend on location. Were Muslims who lived or did business outside the abode of Islam relieved of religiously defined morals?

This division of the world into two abodes, even if not revealed by God, has become a familiar part of Muslim consciousness. But it is worth asking whether such a division of human existence is viable in this age where Muslims live in virtually every part of the globe. There is now no line—if there ever was—to distinguish where the abode of Islam ends and the abode of war begins. It would be all too easy to globalize jihad, to make it an individual duty simply to fight the enemy on all global fronts without a clear sense of the moral purpose of defending a particular territory and protecting the legitimate interests of its people. Traditionally, jihad did become an individual duty when the Muslim army was unable to repel the enemy. However, even as individual duty, the goal was moral, not ritual display of piety. Jihadism, linked to a global identity rather than a moral purpose, actually ends by killing Muslims whose lives and properties jihad in its original meaning is supposed to protect.

The combination of religion and empire was also the norm in Christian lands before and even after the rise of the nation state. The ruling houses of Europe, the Hapsburgs, Bourbons, and Windsors, to say nothing of Ferdinand and Isabella, *los reyes catolicos* of the Iberian peninsula and its many overseas dominions, were not too different in this respect from their Muslim counterparts: Umayyads, Abbasids, Ottomans, and so on. Christianity too went hand in hand with empire extension, and let us not forget Pope Urban II. In a speech at Clermont, France, in 1095 he called Christendom to a crusade to liberate the holy land. His speech wove pious devotion together with political and territorial goals, arguing that infidels had occupied Christian land. What does it mean to say that land has a religious character? Identifying worldly goals with the purpose of religion, Urban II linked warfare with salvation, promising forgiveness of sins to those who answered the call to crusade. This logic, where warfare becomes worship, is jihadism par excellence.

It did not go unnoticed that caliphs and sultans rose and fell and fought one another. Even if Muslims have a strong sense of belonging to a single *umma*, the abode of Islam never achieved political unity. Some Muslim potentates made alliances with infidel powers—even with Crusaders. For a time in the thirteenth century, the greater part of the abode of Islam fell to the Mongols, yet Islam survived and even flourished despite the loss of imperial sway. That politics was incapable of representing the purposes of religion was never a source of anxiety because worldly power was not seen as guarantor of the religious integrity of the community. That was the work of shari'a scholars and spiritual masters who taught people the ways of God and inspired them to journey to his throne. When it came to caliphs and sultans, the abode of Islam was hopelessly fragmented. Its unity lay in a realm of shared morality and spirituality as led by scholarly and saintly authorities who themselves sometimes bickered but always recognized where heavenly truth lay—with God. The political order was not irrelevant to the purposes of Islam, but it did not have to be perfectly religious itself. It was not the mediator of religious truth.

All this underwent dramatic change with colonial rule. Many blamed the preference for moral and spiritual concerns over politics as the reason for the weakness (some said backwardness) of the abode of Islam in the face of Europe. The independent movements were partly conceived as a drive to restore true Islam, that is, the Islam of the past that had put Muslims at the top of human civilization. Religious revival was increasingly understood to have a political purpose. Jihad was recast as a patriotic struggle, not on behalf of God or even the caliphal leader theoretically at the helm of a single abode of Islam, but now on behalf of the nation. Islam in general—and jihad along with it—was welded to the quest for national strength.

This story, the story of Islam as expression of national identity, is still unfolding and is the subject of the next chapter. The rise of jihadism is part of this story, whereby Islam became recast as a political project. How has jihad come to serve the purposes of terrorism? How has jihad for supremacy replaced jihad for morality, the jihad of al-Qaeda dislodging the jihad of the Qur'an? This development has been harmful to Muslims and, indeed, to Islam and has required tremendous global resources and energies to combat.

The easy answer is that the more extreme brands of Islamism became frustrated. Secular dictators remained in power, hindering the hope for political liberalization that would allow Islamist parties to come to power through elections. This, combined with a misplaced pride in having repulsed a superpower from Afghanistan, an accomplishment that would have been impossible without U.S. support, led some Islamists to look to the global rather than national stage as site of spiritual warfare. The pharaoh to be fought was not the ruler of a nation, such as the president of Egypt, but the ruler of the world, that is, the United

States and its various allies. This, of course, is only to talk of beginnings. Jihadism today has moved in so many directions, but it is worth
emphasizing the shift from national to global stage. It became logical
to think of jihad as a battle for a religious identity, a virtual *umma*
with no boundaries, rather than a struggle for a moral purpose. And
Wahhabism, as noted earlier, helped set the stage, especially its idea
of condemning Muslims who seem to associate partners with God.
This condemnation of associating partners with God was originally
aimed at those Muslims who invoked saints and revered imams. However, jihadism recast Wahhabism in political terms, claiming that the
ruler who fails to represent divine sovereignty is a tyrannical idol
(*taghut*): The scriptural narrative is mapped onto political affairs. Thus
Muslims, whether soldier or civilian, who recognize the authority of
secular rule become legitimate objects of attack, making it entirely
logical to see conflict as the place where God's final judgment is determined. It is for this reason that the jihadist mindset sees violence
against fellow Muslims, now God's enemies, as a way to render oneself
pleasing to God. Indeed, death in battle, one's own death, becomes
the highest mark of piety. Death is often considered the ultimate sign
of devotion to a cause. We revere soldiers who die in battle in defense
of the nation even if in hindsight we recognize the cause was not
entirely true. But here, the battle is a heavenly one and therefore knows
no bounds.

The reduction of religion, originally a call to God, to a worldly battle
can be illustrated by a series of apostasy cases in Egypt in the 1980s and
1990s.[16] In Islam, the apostate can be forced to divorce his wife if she is
Muslim, because it is not permitted for a Muslim woman to be married
to a non-Muslim man. The apostate could face death for having be-
trayed the religion of God, although this punishment does not apply
to the female apostate. These cases, which put on trial a number of
intellectuals, were remarkable in that state officials—not shari'a scholars—were made arbiters of beliefs. They were to decide the orthodoxy
of these intellectuals on the basis of their writings even when these
intellectuals professed their belief in Islam.

In the past apostasy in Islam was not determined by state inquisition and assessment of interior convictions but by the declarations of the accused. Moreover, even if declaring himself not to be a Muslim, he might be ostracized by the community but could not be punished by the state unless his unbelief was accompanied by a declaration of war on Muslim society—in other words, only if his unbelief constituted a danger to a public order that was based in Islam and ensured (but not defined) by the state.

In contrast, in these recent cases, what mattered was not the defendants' self-understanding but examination of writings that the ideologically minded Muslim plaintiffs wanted the state to define as unorthodox. These cases, then, amounted to proxy battle. The ultimate concern for the Islamist plaintiffs was the nature of the state's orientation—secular or religious. In other words, the intellectuals accused of apostasy were simply collateral damage in a much larger—now global—battle in which jihad has become the vehicle for realizing the purposes of religion in a quest for supremacy over the secular state. In the premodern past, morality had been the affair of religion, but the modern state, once it came into being, claimed all authority for itself, including realms that had once been left to religion to define. Thus, in seeking revenge for the state's usurpation of its moral authority, religion risks overstepping the limits of its jurisdiction. As such, it risks recreating itself in the secular image of the state. That is, religion, as in these apostasy cases, can unwittingly accept the secularist assumption that religion is the state's to define and that it is at the state level that identity, religious or secular, is to be contested.

In this sense, al-Qaeda is no example of God breaking out, as if representing the wrath of God against a world bereft of capacity for him. Rather, it is a case of the secularization of the religious imagination, religiosity operating on secular rather than on religious terms. The point is that religion is now contesting secularism, and sometimes beating it, on its own terms. Once modernity discarded the public relevancy of religion, making science, not religion, the guide to human society, piety, to show its credibility, had to demonstrate its meaning in worldly form. As the Enlightenment posited, the only reality is that which can be empirically verified, a secular principle that some believers have accepted. As a result, the only way to demonstrate the empirical verifiability of the kingdom to come is to act it out on the world stage in spiritual warfare now thoroughly identified with global affairs. Jihad is the struggle to manifest God's word and to elevate it above all, but this is based on the recognition that God's word can never be adequately represented as political project. Jihadism, by contrast, accepts the principle of modern secularism that only this world matters. Thus, with al-Qaeda, religion ironically aspires to modernist heights, assuming that only political institutions can represent God's word, and if they fail to do that, they and those who recognize their authority are to be fought.

This is the secular dilemma that religion faces. The premodern state, the dynasty, had no organic relation to its subjects. It ruled, collected taxes, and was expected to preserve order, but it did not define people's moral character. That was generally left to one's cultural and religious heritage. The modern nation state, in contrast, claims an organic (i.e., total) relation to its people, now defined as citizens, no longer subjects. As representative of the people rather than only the dynasty, the modern state sometimes claims the authority to define all aspects of national life, including the moral character of society as represented in its educational programs. In other words, with modernity, morality often turns into a state affair, defined by national legislation, a state project to which religion itself is to conform. As a result, belief can itself become secularized, looking to worldly projects to justify itself in the face of the Enlightenment's denial of nonempirical existence, such as the world to come.[17] The state, then, became touchstone of religious legitimacy, (though, of course, many Christians and Muslims continued to tie religious legitimacy to spiritual authority or individual reading of scripture). Indeed, the state was looked to as primary representative of the transcendent.[18] It is in this world and not the other that the kingdom of God is to be realized.

There is some echo of this in the witch hunts that peaked in Europe, not during the Middle Ages, as many assume, but in the sixteenth and seventeenth centuries, when the Renaissance and Reformation were in full swing and when the first signs appeared of a Christian interest in making state authority the arbiter of true religion. One sees this equation of church and state authority in Calvin's Geneva, whereas previously the state had been understood to enforce religion but not define it. Witch-hunting, as argued by Rodney Stark, was not as widespread or bloody as commonly imagined today.[19] The accused often confessed their sins and went home. His central point, however, is that witch-hunts did not exist in isolation but formed part of a larger battle for Christian truth that took on decidedly political, even military, overtones.

Witches were not viewed as witches so much as heretics. It was not a matter of a single predominant faith and a bit of black-magic sorcery on the margin of society. What sorcery there might have been in the past was marginal. But much more was now at stake, because a single faith no longer held sway over Europe but instead multiple Christianities. And these varied Christianities not only had followings and institutional holdings but also increasingly looked to state authorities, kings and princes, for legitimacy, whereas formerly it had generally been the state that looked to religion, church authorities, for legitimacy. Witch-hunts, like the apostasy cases mentioned earlier, were collateral damage in a larger battle involving religion, not only religion but religion that increasingly looked to political dominion as mark, and thus mediation, of the truth of its claims. It is easy to deceive ourselves into thinking that a belief must be true simply because it prevails politically.

Jihadism, that is, terrorism in the name of religion, can be understood similarly. The victims of jihadism are collateral damage in a much larger battle that is ideological rather than moral. Who is to be supreme master of the political realm, now global and not simply national in scope? Will it be secular or religious authority? And in this postmodern moment, when secularism has been exposed to be—quite like religion—not scientifically neutral but simply another point of view with its own values and principles, it can no longer claim uncontested mastery over the public sphere, but must demonstrate its worth in the face of religion. Islam as well as Christianity and other religions in some of their forms have locked horns with secularism at the state level as the place where moral authority is located and thus legitimated. Are morals to be secular or religious? Conceiving of the public sphere in such either-or categories is, however, to think of things not in terms of the good of all but rather in terms of the identity that is to be supreme in the public sphere. The myths are not false in themselves: belief over unbelief, good over evil, God over Pharaoh. What makes them false is the assumption that their legitimacy can be secured only through supremacy. The fear is that religion, if reduced to spirituality, will have no relevancy for society, and so the spiritual dimension of religion, its very heart, is easily discarded. Our discussion of character in chapter 3 shows that both Christianity and Islam recognize the ethical impact of spirituality. Religion need not be politically supreme for it to be relevant to the world.

Jihadism deploys violence of the most dramatic kind to make a pointed statement, to challenge the assumption that the world's authorities are masters of this realm. If they were, they would be able to control jihadism. Jihadists are therefore making it known in perverse fashion that they, self-proclaimed representatives of God's word, will not submit to the secular powers of this world. The jihadist use of worldly force to manifest God's power, however, makes them very much like the secular authorities they disdain. Furthermore, the victims of terrorism, like the witches of the past, are simply convenient targets used by jihadists to prove that they decide who lives and who dies, that truth is in their hands, that they are the ones in control of the world, and that they too—not only modern states that claim a monopoly on the legitimate use of force—can brandish power in this world.

Jihadism shows that violence can be expressed in religious no less than in secular terms. But violence in religious attire only clothes deeper anxieties about the place of religion in today's world. Witch-hunts were only an extreme form of struggle for Christian truth. The struggle between different forms of Christianity was largely pursued by other means: theological debate, polemics, and political maneuvering short of killing and maiming. Similarly, jihadism is only an extreme form of the struggle today to find space for religion in the world. The public manifestation of religion is not generally expressed through terrorism but rather through media channels, political lobbying, grassroots organization, charitable endeavors, development initiatives, and debate with secularists as well as with other believers.

The question, then, is not whether religion should be permitted to express itself publicly but how? How is jihad to be understood today? Terrorism, which in the recent past was secular rather than religious, is only one among many options. It is worth considering one example of jihad that holds to the moral implications of beliefs and refuses to reduce beliefs to identity. Here, utopia in this world is rejected and therefore recourse to violence to bring it about is denied. Here, the orientation of religion remains a kingdom to come, always in the future, certainly not irrelevant for human purposes in this world, but never quite completely here and now. Here, religion is not group identity but consciousness of the transcendent.

The example comes from nineteenth-century Algeria. The populace had been brutally pacified by the French military to subject them to purportedly civilized rule. The true threat to Algeria was not French military might but the attempt to remake Algerian society in the French image. The aim was not only to conquer Algerian lands but also Algerian souls, stripping them of a native character that had been nurtured by local customs and Muslim beliefs. The goal, then, was to liberate them from their Muslim capacity for God. Many Algerians did assume European ways, convinced that only by becoming like the French would they be able to resist them. In other words, Algerian nationalists came to see jihad as a struggle for the nation in and of itself, apart from other considerations. This is not to trivialize the patriotic struggle. To equate it with jihad as struggle for God without referencing the moral and spiritual heritage that has long informed jihad, however, makes violence for the nation ordinary rather than extraordinary, familiar and common rather than limited to a specific time, place, and purpose.

This has been the tragic outcome in Algeria, especially in the 1990s but still today. By playing the game according to French rules, the

Algerian soul has come to resemble its past master, willingly using violence so that identity, rather than morality, might be supreme. It doesn't matter whether identity is religious or secular, the result is the same. Both secular authorities and Islamist militants in Algeria have adopted the methods of the former colonial overlords, namely brutal violence. This parallels al-Qaeda and the global response to it, where power is deployed on various sides to assert identity without referencing morality or spirituality.

There were extraordinary exceptions to the nationalization of jihad in Algeria, notably a spiritual figure of great influence by the name of Shaykh 'Alawi.[20] He did advise his disciples, numbering in the thousands, not to accept French citizenship, because he felt that adoption of French law would undermine their moral character as Muslims. He also did not oppose the struggle for independence per se. He was not at all pleased, however, by the disdain resistance leaders showed for the spiritual heritage of Algeria, which they viewed as an obstacle to nationalist goals, casting it aside for a secularized version of religion. For Shaykh 'Alawi, the greatest threat to Islam and its moral character was not the French colonial project but rather Muslims who saw fit to reduce Islam to a secular, that is, political, struggle. This, he foresaw, would lay the groundwork for the dismissal of God as true sovereign, leading Muslims to set themselves up as masters over others for the sake of identity apart from other moral considerations, effectively replacing God as purported masters of this world—the very sin the Qur'an warns against. For 'Alawi, the nationalists had essentially worldified their outlook on life, unable to see God in the world to come, only their own glory in this one.

'Alawi, in contrast, adhered to the message of the Qur'an: "The true way to hurt the enemy is to be occupied with the love of the [divine] Friend; on the one hand, if you engage in war with the enemy, he will have obtained what he wanted from you [i.e., he will have made you like him], and at the same time you will have lost the opportunity of loving the Friend [i.e., you will lose sight of God by turning religion into a secular affair]."[21] For 'Alawi, battling the French on their terms would keep Muslims from their true purposes, namely consideration of God. This would be the victory the French sought, secularization of the Muslim soul, disposing it to politics of the most violent kind.

'Alawi offers insight into the struggle with evil and therefore the religious mission in this world. It may be necessary to struggle with evil amidst the realities of the world, but evil may be compounded by the realities of a soul that is not ordered to a purpose beyond politics alone. 'Alawi certainly viewed French annexation of Algeria as a great injustice—a failure on the part of the French to appreciate the moral point of the Qur'an's monotheistic message. But the greatest error in his view was the Algerian response in kind: It was driven not by monotheistic morality but by the same motives that drove the French. The Algerian resistance had dangerously opened itself to take on aspects of the very evil that it sought to repel.

In the end, it is necessary to return to the Qur'an and its conception of *shirk* (polytheism) as an evil to be battled against. It is certainly debatable whether action that is not ordered to God (i.e., that does not involve a proper ordering of the soul) can be truly just, because some would say justice does not depend on the disclosure of the one God. But the Qur'an—and Shaykh 'Alawi—would have an ally in Saint Augustine, key architect of Christian thinking on just war. Augustine claimed that the earthly city glories only in itself whereas the heavenly city glories in God.[22] Moreover, he argued, in the earthly city, the lust for domination lords it over its princes, as over the nations it subjugates. And so, one city, the earthly city, loves its own strengths as displayed by powerful leaders, whereas the other city, the heavenly city, says to God, "I will love you, my Lord, my strength."[23] For Augustine, Christians, even if dwelling in the earthly city, were still to order their souls not to its purposes but to those of the heavenly one.

It is not possible to ask secular authorities, whose mission is to ensure law and order in the earthly city, to make contemplation of God a policy objective in the war on terror, but all of us, regardless of our beliefs, must guard against lending our souls to the ideological tendencies of global politics today, lest we become like the evil we seek to repel. The state is a good within the earthly city and is constrained to operate according to its secular principles. But believers, though they acknowledge the legitimacy of the state, have another mission to pursue. They do not want to be deprived of God's presence. Ironically, this is the result when religion is reduced to ideology apart from moral considerations. A common Christian-Muslim jihad to counter jihadism can be undertaken, drawing on the moral vigor of Paul and Muhammad. Its main occupation, to echo Shaykh 'Alawi, would be the divine friend, or, in echo of Saint Augustine, the proper ordering of the soul to the heavenly city. Ultimately, a state-led war against religious terrorism is not going to be enough to contain it and may even prolong it by treating religion in state-like terms. No one seems interested in Islam as a religious consciousness any longer, and some are surprised to learn that Islam is in fact a religion. In other words, we have all fallen into the trap of viewing religion as a political category.

Serious, widespread, and sustained discussion is needed about the public expression of religion and the jihad proper to it. The discussion needs to include Christian-Muslim recognition of God whose reign, even if anticipated, is beyond human history. It can be contemplated as inspiration in the struggle for moral righteousness in communities and societies and not only individual life, but it cannot be realized as political goal. As Augustine noted, there is no point in a nation going to war if it "seeks to be victorious over other nations, though it is itself the slave of [its own] base passions."[24] A hadith puts it another way: "God the Blessed and Exalted grants rewards according to intention." The question, then, at least for believers, is whether our intention is truly monotheistic, truly oriented to God as source of truth or to something else. Crusades can be moral or ideological. The same is true of jihad.

NOTES

1. On the idea of Christian ethics as societal in outlook, see Michael J. Schuck, *That They Be One: The Social Teachings of the Papal Encyclicals, 1740–1989* (Washington, DC: Georgetown University Press, 1991).

2. On diverse notions of jihad in classical Islam, see Paul L. Heck, "Jihad Revisited," *Journal of Religious Ethics* 32 (2004): 95–128.

3. See, for example, al-Sharif's 2007 manifesto *Tarshid al-Jihad fi Misr wa-l-'Alam*, http://egyig.com (Arabic).

4. The well-known Syrian scholar, Muhammad Sa'id Ramadan al-Buti, stated this very idea—that force can be used not to convert but to spread the rule of Islam as representative of God's order—on a television program (*Fiqh al-Sira*, on the Saudi television channel Iqra') broadcast on November 25, 2008.

5. For an overview of the rise of terrorism during the last century and a half, see David C. Rapoport, "The Four Waves of Modern Terrorism," in *Attacking Terrorism: Elements of a Grand Strategy*, eds. A. K. Cronin and J. M. Ludes (Washington, DC: Georgetown University Press, 2004), 46–73.

6. This clearly stands out in the biographies of the early Moroccan Islamists, many of whom had been devotees of socialism or communism or heavily influenced by them. It was not a huge leap, then, to give religious clothing to global visions of perfect dominion. See Bilal al-Talidi, *Dhakirat al-Harakat al-Islamiyya al-Maghribiyya*, 2 vols. (Rabat: Top Press, 2008).

7. Some jihadists are aware of being the successors to the likes of Mao Zedong and Che Guevara. See, for example, Brynjar Lia, *Architect of Global Jihad. The Life of al-Qaida Strategist Abu Mus'ab al-Suri* (New York: Columbia University Press, 2008), 373.

8. Eugene Rice Jr., *The Foundations of Early Modern Europe, 1460–1559*, 2nd ed. (New York: W. W. Norton, 1994), 165–66.

9. That is, Wahhabism does not have a problem with human rule but with doctrinal deviation. Ibn 'Abd al-Wahhab (died 1792), the progenitor of Wahhabism, called for endurance in the face of political injustice (*jawr al-wulat*). See Ibn 'Abd al-Wahhab, "Masa'il al-Jahiliyya," in *Kashf al-Shubuhat fi-l-Tawhid* (Cairo: al-Matba'at al-Salafiyya AH, 1390), 21. In other words, the idea that divine sovereignty (*hakimiyya*) can be realized in this world, an idea advanced by Sayyid Qutb (died 1966), is not at play in the thought of Ibn 'Abd al-Wahhab. This is one reason why Wahhabism is useful to the Saudi dynasty, giving them free rein to rule as they please so long as they promote the doctrine of Wahhabism at home and abroad.

10. Ibn Taymiyya, *Risalat al-Ulfa bayn al-Muslimin* (Aleppo: Maktabat al-Matbu'at al-Islamiyya, 1996).

11. Sadly, extraordinary expressions of identity-driven hatred are known in scholarly circles in Saudi Arabia. The claim that the trinity is a form of paganism encourages hostility toward Christians on the basis of belief apart from any recognizable moral criteria. Similar arguments are made against Judaism and Shi'ism. See for example, the MEMRI report on 'Abd al-'Aziz al-Fawzan, available at www.memri.net/bin/articles.cgi?Page=countries&Area=saudiarabia&ID=SP1069

06. Of course, Saudi officials seek to counter this religious hatred, especially in their recent attempts to overhaul the national religious establishment. This struggle within Saudi Islam holds tremendous consequences for the rest of the world.

12. See Ahmad Dallal, "The Origins and Objectives of Islamic Revivalist Thought, 1750–1850," *Journal of the American Oriental Society* 113, no. 3 (1993): 341–59.

13. See, for example, Isaac Hasson, "Les Ši'ites vus par les néo-Wahhabites," *Arabica* 53, no. 3 (2006): 299–330.

14. See Stuart A. Wright, ed., *Armageddon in Waco: Critical Perspectives on the Branch Davidian Conflict* (Chicago: University of Chicago Press, 1995).

15. See David P. Gushee and Justin Phillips, "Moral Formation and the Evangelical Voter: A Report from the Red States," *Journal of the Society of Christian Ethics* 26, no. 2 (2006): 23–60.

16. See Baber Johansen, "Apostasy as Objective and Depersonalized Fact: Two Recent Egyptian Court Judgments," *Social Research* 79, no. 3 (2003): 687–710.

17. This outlook drives the emerging Muslim study of the scientific incomparability of the Qur'an (*i'jaz al-qur'an al-'ilmi*), whereby the Qur'an is understood to have revealed what modern science is now only discovering. In this sense, worldly criteria, namely modern science, become the touchstone for the truth of Islam, reversing centuries of thinking that make the world to come the criterion for religious truth.

18. See Mark Lilla, *The Stillborn God: Religion, Politics, and the Modern West* (New York: Alfred A. Knopf, 2007).

19. See Rodney Stark, *For the Glory of God: How Monotheisms Led to Reformations, Science, Witch-Hunts, and the End of Slavery* (Princeton, NJ: Princeton University Press, 2003).

20. See Reza Shah-Kazemi, "From Sufism to Terrorism: The Distortion of Islam in the Political Culture of Algeria," in Reza Shah-Kazemi, ed., *Algeria: Revolution Revisited* (London: Islamic World Report, 1997), 160–92.

21. Ibid.

22. St. Augustine, *De civitate Dei*, XIV, 28.

23. Ibid.

24. St. Augustine, *De civitate Dei*, XV, 4.

CHAPTER FIVE

ISLAM

More or Less Democratic than Christianity?

I N THE QUR'AN, God delegates care of the world not to a single individual but to Adam and his progeny, making all people his representatives (caliphs) on earth. Is this a divine mandate for democracy? The Qur'an is not a political tract. The point, rather, is the human responsibility to live morally. Echoing this, a hadith stipulates obedience to rulers as long as they do not command disobedience to God. In other words, public life is to be governed according to ethical principles, not the law of the jungle where the powerful dominate the weak. At the very least, rulers are not to prevent people from fulfilling religious duties that stand at the heart of a pious society. But God's delegation of power to humans raises questions about the nature and purpose of rule in Islam. Is it a religious contract binding society to the ways of God? Or is it a social contract whereby rulers govern in the interests of the people? Does this make democracy irrelevant so long as the common good is served? What happens when rule fails its purpose? Are Muslims to create a parallel society governed by the laws of Islam or quietly pray for better days?

Such questions are not unknown in Christianity. To make salvation available to all nations, Saint Paul tied it to faith in Christ apart from a particular body of religious laws. This does not mean that Christians have no legal concerns but rather that the grace of God is not limited to a cultural way of life and its attendant legal norms. Indeed, the Gospel states that Christ's kingdom is not of this world. Even if inaugurated by the work of God in Jesus, it is not translatable into a political project. The second letter of Peter exhorts believers "to honor the ruler." That is, earthly power has its own purpose and differs fundamentally from the kingdom of God. Yet the Christian message is not free of political import. Loyalty ultimately belongs to God. This created tensions for early Christians who were soldiers in the Roman army. It continues to create tensions for contemporary Christians who challenge regimes that beget economic injustice, neglect the poor, or fail to defend the family. This is particularly troubling when such failings occur under democratic rule. Are Christians to resist or simply wait for the kingdom to come? How are believers to participate in God's victory over sin?[1]

Polls show a high level of Muslim support for both democracy and public respect for Islam.[2] Muslims combine secular and religious ideas in thinking about national life. Does this mean they cannot be democratic? Democracy was not revealed by God. It arose to limit tyranny, but religion can support democracy.[3] Believers who hold that God is the sole, unchallengeable authority look askance at rulers who set themselves above the law. The Qur'an is clear: God alone is Lord. The authority of religion can be abused, but it also questions abusive power, the prototype being Moses' challenge of Pharaoh as recounted in both Bible and Qur'an. It is therefore wrong to make secularization a precondition for democracy. Some say that only by removing religious ideas from the public sphere can people vote their conscience free of ideological hindrance. Democracy in this sense is impossible: The conscience is always informed by a set of beliefs, religious or secular, and people do not discount them when voting. Democracy is the ability of all members of a nation to contest public office, especially the highest, through free and fair elections. It does not demand moral neutrality. It is rule by the people but it is not relativism. In this sense it has something in common with religion.

There are varied understandings of democracy. A key issue is equality. All Muslims acknowledge that only God is God. This, in principle, levels the playing field: No one has a privileged right to rule. At the same time, there is a sense that rule should reflect the divine will in some fashion. But God shows no sign of descending from his heavenly throne to rule his creatures directly. In Islam, a messianic figure known as the *mahdi* has occasionally emerged to rule directly on God's behalf, but this has always coincided with unusual circumstances in which Islam is felt to be under grave threat, making direct divine intervention vital to its well-being, and rule by the *mahdi* never lasts. It is a kind of politics that serves a specific moment but is unsustainable over the long term.

For this reason, Islam does not make politics the testing ground for the religious integrity of the *umma*. Islam's religious authorities sometimes act as counselors to rulers, and do call them to rule justly, but do not see government as the primary agent in the struggle for belief over unbelief. It is in the mosque, on pilgrimage, in the spiritual company of the prophet Muhammad, and, ultimately, on judgment day, where divine favor is won, not in royal courts or national assemblies. Politics is to be guided by ethics but is not the place where beliefs are fulfilled. The idea of a religious state, which has its adherents, has always been rejected, not simply because it is politically ineffective, but more so because it is theologically flawed.

This helps explain Muslim support for democracy in the sense of political equality. Only God is God. No one has a special right to rule. All are entitled to hold power if they merit it. However, political equality is one thing, moral equality is another. Although democracy has yet to take hold in many a Muslim society, Muslims do call for government accountability and fuller representation of the interests of the people in national decision making. But this does not mean that all lifestyles have equal space in the public sphere. In some Muslim societies the vote has not been given to all (or to any), but these are the exceptions (notably Saudi Arabia). In most places where Islam prevails, everyone has the right to vote regardless of beliefs, and Islam enshrines certain general principles that Muslims and non-Muslims alike embrace: justice, protection of the weak, punishment of crime, fair business practices, equal treatment before the law, and so on. Islam, however, also has specific teachings on the nature of marriage, the beginning and end of life, modest dress, financial transactions (based on profit-sharing rather than predetermined interest), the place of religion in national education, and curbs on some kinds of expression (slander, hate speech, or blasphemy) when harmful to public interests; this could include public consumption of food during Ramadan. In a nation with a Muslim majority, popular sentiment may favor public commitment to these norms to ensure that the polity as a whole enjoys God's favor.

All nations give greater weight to certain voices. In the United States, everyone has a vote, and the law does not discriminate between one group and another, at least not since the 1960s, but the nation does not judge all points of view equally. The capitalist is preferred to the socialist. In some places the atheist must speak discretely, whereas in others it is the believer who needs to be on guard. Every nation strikes a balance between the political equality of all and the nation's values, which may not represent all ways of life. In the United States, some religious groups vigorously defend the family against court efforts to devalue it in the name of equality. It is not that such voices oppose equality or the civil rights of all citizens. Rather, they recognize a hierarchy of truths that may limit equality of individual choice. For others, of course, individual choice is the touchstone of moral truth. The point, then, is that democracy is a form of politics but also a way a nation expresses its values in law. Is democracy, then, the right of all to aspire to political office or is it the right of all to determine moral values? The concept of equality that began as a political notion has now moved into the arena of morals, and this is the point of contention.

How, then, is a secular state to rule democratically over a believing nation? A democratic government cannot ignore the values of its people in the name of political equality. Here, however, we are asking a different question. Do Muslim and Christian beliefs encourage or discourage democracy? Does religion make the world safer for democracy? God did not command one political system over another but instead worship and good works. There must be specific reasons, political and theological, that make democracy the choice of believers. Christianity and

Islam, each in its own way, recognize that freedom is best for religion, to protect it from state control and to allow believers to live its message without hindrance. But to demand freedom for religion means granting it to all, including those who publicly attack religion. Is liberty a conundrum for believers? In many Muslim lands, the state controls religion and many religious figures would like greater independence from the state but would still want the values of Islam to be affirmed at a national level. Moreover, believers generally do not advocate anarchy but instead affirm a set of truths. Freedom, then, is not an end in itself but instead has a moral purpose. This may also be true for nonbelievers whose truths are philosophical rather than religious. Is there an objective moral order? If so, is it something humans aspire to freely or something the state is to impose by force?

It may be tempting for believers to hope for a pious dictator to enforce God's will by political decree, as occurred in Pakistan under the military rule of Zia-ul-Haqq (1977–1988). But the close association of religion with rule invariably compromises religion, turning it into a coercive tool of political power. Religion is a moral guide for society but is no longer effective as such once made into a state project. Islam has long worked to protect societies from political tyranny by defending moral principles that originate in God. It can no longer do so once religious authority is ceded to the state, as witnessed in Iran and the Sudan.

The challenge for believers in this age is to win public representation of their values by democratic processes. This requires a willingness to abide by unfavorable results. Riots broke out in Jos, Nigeria, with much loss of life when the Muslim-backed party lost state elections in November 2008. The followers of Muqtada al-Sadr made threatening comments when the Iraqi parliament approved the security agreement with the United States in November 2008. Hezbollah of Lebanon and Hamas of Palestine have effectively participated in elections but have also used violence against fellow citizens, making it unclear whether they are democratically oriented parties or ideological movements with militant propensities. There are counter examples. From Malaysia to

Morocco, Islamist parties generally seek not to dominate but rather to participate in political processes that do not always yield desired results.[4] It is, then, possible to speak of jihad as a democratic struggle in which all Adam's progeny are recognized as God's caliphs on earth even when they do not vote for the Islamist project. Moral relativism is certainly a slippery slope for believers and nonbelievers alike, and religious relativism is a challenge for believers. Can a framework of truth be preserved at a time when respect for the individual conscience is widely acknowledged? This balancing act is noticeable in *Dignitatis humanae*, the Vatican II document on religious liberty, which affirms the dignity of the individual conscience even when failing to affirm the truth. In this fashion, a framework of religious and moral truth is retained but dissent is not cause to devalue the worth of a human being.

Why do believers opt for democracy even when affirming a hierarchy of moral truths? Political repression, especially when directed at religion, demonstrates the need for liberty—not as an end in itself but to protect the religion. Undemocratic contexts alone, however, do not always persuade believers of the benefits of democracy. There also has to be a sense that the will of God, at least in some areas of national life, has not been determined in advance (i.e., revealed). Can the will of God be squared with the will of the people? Is God's will for the nation known in advance, simply needing implementation? Do people intuitively know God's designs for the nation apart from explicit religious instruction? Has God left space for people to determine his will? The Muslim Brotherhood of Egypt, for example, opposes the appointment of women judges and the possibility of non-Muslims running for president, though not for lower offices. At the same time it acknowledges that alternate viewpoints exist within Islam. The people, then, are to decide where exactly the will of God lies in these and other matters.[5]

The resistance to power-sharing, of course, comes from authoritarian rulers, not Muslim peoples. Jordan and Morocco are technically constitutional monarchies, ruling in the name of Islam, but effective power lies with the court and the prime minister is appointed by the king, not parliament. Saudi Arabia is a dynastic monarchy under which leading members of the ruling clan hold key positions of state. The Saudis cede moral supervision of society to a cadre of religious authorities who in turn leave policy matters to the monarchy apart from popular input. Iran, Pakistan, and the Sudan are Islamic republics, but limiting republican government to religious teachings has made it easy for charismatic figures—whether clerics or generals—to claim a divine mandate and ignore the will of the people. Muslim society also knows secular republics ruled by life-term presidents: Algeria, Egypt, Syria, and Tunisia. Oddly, in such secular states, the constitution defines Islam as official religion of the state or requires the president to be Muslim, and a state ministry of religious affairs supervises mosque appointments, religious curriculum, and so on. In such undemocratic contexts, Islamist groups act as important channels of popular opposition. They also seek to wrest religious authority from state control. But they are not clearly prodemocratic. They seek to displace the secular monopoly on religious authority, but some would replace the secular dictatorship with a religious one. What is the point of religious liberty? Is it freedom for the sake of religious supremacy? Or freedom for all whether or not they accept Islam? Can freedom be demanded for Islam without granting it to all?

One cannot ignore economic realities. Most people today embrace a democratic discourse. Still, in poorer areas of the world, the need to work out a viable democracy may take second place to more pressing concerns. In both Morocco and Jordan, there is unofficial competition between the monarchy and political parties in meeting the people's needs. Who can deliver the goods more effectively? This competition has a democratic element in that both monarchy and political parties seek to win the hearts of the people, but it is impossible to compete with the king's resources. As a result, for the time being, the people affirm monarchy over the institutionalization of democracy as a more effective way to meet their basic needs. Moreover, a host of other issues that have nothing to do with Islam can make democracy appear suspicious or irrelevant to personal and national welfare: high levels of cronyism in the political parties, alternative sources of representation (such as tribe or religious brotherhood), and so on.

In Islam, religious authority is generally not the privilege of political power, but political power is expected to adhere to certain principles in governing society. The legitimacy of sultans or shahs rested on their willingness to back shari'a as the moral order of society, but political power itself was not a religious affair. The reason for this is simple. God is silent on the matter. The Qur'an speaks of righteous prosperity as the way of believers but does not specify the political order to achieve it. As a result, Muslims over the centuries have been open to all political systems, from monarchy to democracy, as long as they are responsive to the moral values of Islam, understood as best guarantor of righteous prosperity. Indeed, when it came to the constitution of rule in Islam, Muslims have long drawn on secular knowledge: Greco-Hellenistic philosophy, Persian counsel for rulers, Byzantine forms of administration, Turkic-Mongol military prowess, and, today, Euro-American ideas about nationhood. Muslims look to human civilization at large to understand the purpose of rule as well as effective means of governance (i.e., tax collection, military organization, security, public works, and the like). In this sense, religion and rule are not one and the same. They occupy distinct spheres, operating in a complementary fashion for the greater good of Muslim society. An ancient saying with circulation in classical Islam expresses the idea this way: "Religion and rule are twins. Rule without religion has no foundation, and religion without rule has no guardian." Mitt Romney could not have put it better.[6]

Alongside rulers, religious scholars, the keepers of shari'a, have acted as custodians of the moral order. No potentate, even a descendant of the prophet Muhammad, could ignore the religious teachings that these scholars transmitted from one generation to the next. In this sense, the good of Muslim society operated through division of labor. A dynastic house exercised political power through a variety of administrative and military offices. It was expected to rule justly for the sake of stability and order, but such earthly power was transitory. The Qur'an speaks of God giving rule and taking it away as he wishes. Worldly potentates may come and go, but Islam ensures continuity through a set of moral expectations to which all are subject. Religious scholars were always in the employ of sultans and shahs, but many kept their distance from politics. At the same time, religion has had a relation to political power in Islam, but views on the matter differed. To contextualize the discussion, it will be worth mentioning three in brief.

Ibn Taymiyya (died 1328), who lived during the Mongol conquests, showed little interest in restoring the Abbasid caliphate and did not encourage Muslims to revolt against rulers who failed to implement shari'a perfectly. He did, however, have strong words for rulers who did not at least recognize the moral authority of Islam, specifically the Mongols who by his time had become Muslim but ruled according to their own legal heritage. In his famous treatise on politics, *Shari'a Governance*, he gave political power a good deal of leeway when God's will is unspecified as long as it enforces what God has clearly revealed, including penalties for theft, adultery, brigandage, slander, alcohol use, and so on. The polity has a contract with God, and all—rulers and ruled—have duties to one another and to God. The state, though not a revealed entity, is to defend the teachings of Islam, but these teachings are not unlimited.

In contrast, Ibn Khaldun (died 1406), a scholar from North Africa, saw rule in Islam in much broader terms. Muslims have religious obligations to perform to ensure good standing in the next world, and religion helps cement the bonds holding a nation together, but rule in Islam involves much more than political commitment to religious teachings. Indeed, there is a natural order to the world that explains the rise and fall of nations. Ibn Khaldun identified it as God's way of dealing with his creation. A nation inevitably declines, regardless of its religious identity, if it ignores the socioeconomic conditions that make for prosperous rule.

Farabi (died 950), one of Islam's greatest philosophers, brought another perspective to the question. Noting how religious claims can divide a polity, he called for a system of governance in which the teachings of religion have their place, though not to the point of undermining political harmony. For this reason, he awarded a central role to reason in determining the good of the nation. Rule in Islam, though responsive to shari'a, is more fundamentally geared to the well-being of the polity as a whole. Politics according to Farabi includes religious language, because religion embodies the beliefs by which people live. But religious language, when publicly deployed, is to meet rational criteria to ensure that rule not become sectarian, jeopardizing the common good.

These varied outlooks continue today. Like Ibn Taymiyya, the Muslim Brotherhood, although it acknowledges the rules of democracy, views the state as defender of religion. This can have the effect of conflating the political platform of the Brotherhood with the will of God, national citizenship with religious loyalty. There is also anxiety over the nation's standing before God because, as the Qur'an suggests, a threat hangs over those who implement his revealed order selectively (2:85). Additionally, some elements in the Brotherhood view democracy as tyrannical: People, when allowed to rule themselves, will seek to dominate one another and will even use democratic means to do so. Thus, true justice exists only under divine rule when the Qur'an is the constitution, shari'a the national law, and God the head of state.

At the same time, there is a sense that Islam is under attack by national and international forces that seek to exploit the nation for partisan interests. Thus, as spelled out in the Egyptian Brotherhood's 2005 election program, it is Islam that will best preserve the greater interests of the *umma*. For this reason, the Brotherhood advances a religious narrative in which political empowerment, obtained gradually rather than by revolution, becomes the goal of faith.[7] This, of course, is where the Brotherhood diverges from classical Islam. It has always been felt that the state is to be responsive to God's rulings (*ahkam*), but by equating them with rule (*hukuma*), the Brotherhood makes politics essential to Islam, as if Muslims are not pleasing to God if not holding the reins of power. Thus, for the Brotherhood, the state is ultimately a transcendent entity. Traditional religious voices criticize this outlook. For them, the good standing of the *umma* does not depend on the character of the state but rather on the moral tenor of the believing community.[8]

Like Ibn Khaldun, Morocco's Party of Justice and Development (PJD) does not reduce rule to particular religious teachings. In contrast to the Brotherhood, they distinguish their political program from questions of religious identity, emphasizing justice and socioeconomic development. For this reason, they draw attention to the dual character of the prophet's mission. On the one hand, as a prophet, Muhammad issued timeless instructions for rituals and morals. On the other, as a political leader, he gave directives that are not eternally valid. The politics of the prophet, though embodying wise principles, is historically limited in its details. For this reason, PJD rhetoric, though not free of religious language, also does not descend into religious sloganeering as in the Brotherhood's perennial cry, Islam is the solution. Its opponents do accuse it of doublespeak, cloaking its real goal of rule by Islam behind the rhetoric of justice and socioeconomic development. If really committed to the secular character of politics, why refer to Islam at all, because religion, explicit or implicit, is about advice giving and not policy planning?[9] PJD activity, however, is geared not to religious specifics but to religious principles, which the party leadership refers to as political universals.[10] Traditionally, these universals are known as the five necessities: religion, life, intellect, progeny, and property. If these basic principles were not defended, it is held, society would descend into chaos. They are thus necessary to preserve the common good. Moreover, in a postprophetic age, no human can claim to be backed by heaven, making it the right of the people to choose their political representatives. Indeed, the detailed program issued in advance of the 2007 elections indicates that the PJD is a unique form of Islamism.[11] In contrast to the Brotherhood, there is no demand for greater freedom to promote the mission of Islam. The focus is the general purposes of politics as understood by Islam, that is, justice and development. No special religious training is needed to pursue such goals. Islam is one but its politicians and missionaries have distinct roles. As a result, the state is not the place where the religious integrity of Islam is to be tested, even if it has a purpose that the religion recognizes, namely human prosperity.[12] Ambiguities notwithstanding, the PJD has formulated a framework for democracy that also aspires to represent the values of Islam.

Finally, echoing Farabi, Abdolkarim Soroush, an Iranian intellectual who has challenged the religious character of the Islamic Republic of Iran for three decades, seeks not to expel religious language from public life but rather to align it with the needs of the polity. He balks at secularist notions of equality that associate it with moral freedom, but does maintain that public affairs, including beliefs, are to be adjudicated by reasoned argument and not simple reference to unexamined creeds. In this way, he questions the religious legitimacy of a state that equates its interests with Islam, turning political dissent into disobedience to God.[13] Soroush gives a modern tone to Farabi's ideas, defining freedom as a universal good at the heart of a virtuous polity. He thus seeks to save Islam from being compromised by its now intimate association with authoritarian rule. His fear is that this association makes religion appear hostile to freedom, and this in turn would create a situation where agnosticism is a necessary precondition for democracy—a situation he ascribes, perhaps not quite precisely, to the West. Like Farabi, he puts religious reasoning before religious rule: Islam is not to be implemented simply because it is Islam. Thus the introduction of religion into public life cannot violate the theological freedom of the nation. Islam is eternal insofar as it originates in God, but human knowledge of it expands and contracts according to historical circumstances. Religious knowledge is never fixed. Those who claim to rule in the name of religious knowledge as unchanging body of norms have therefore misunderstood the nature of religious knowledge. Without the freedom to inquire, including the freedom to question and dissent, believers will not be able to know how Islam applies to contemporary circumstances, and this ignorance will lead to the demise of religion. Thus a religious state, even one ruling in the name of Islam, becomes the enemy of religion when it imposes a single interpretation of Islam on the nation.

A religious society, however, is not the enemy of freedom because religion is part of the process of public reasoning that guides a society's morals. Indeed, the free discussion of beliefs is a way to ensure that they do not get manipulated by the state, whether religious or secular. Freedom does not require disbelief but rather the liberty to engage beliefs publicly. This means that beliefs have to be comprehensible. When addressed to the public sphere, beliefs cannot appear obscure to nonbelievers. Believers must be able to speak cogently to the issues of the day. Soroush's view of religion is individualistic, but he is not defending moral autonomy. He is instead advocating the rationality of religion in public life at a time when the Iranian state has made it a partisan interest. If the values of religion are to have place in public life, they must reflect an objective moral order that believers and nonbelievers alike recognize.

Once freed of Saddam Hussein, Iraqis raced to the polls, but they did not see democracy as a pretext to free themselves from a cultural heritage and its moral principles. Only recently have political circumstances allowed for greater Muslim engagement with democracy. Following the 1998 fall of Soeharto's New Order in Indonesia, the first president to be democratically elected in the nation's history was Abdurrahman Wahid, leader of the country's largest Muslim organization. In Indonesia, there is strong support for democracy, including free and fair contestation of rule by political parties, equality before the law, and freedom of the media from state control. There is also strong support for Islam in public life, including closing restaurants during Ramadan and monitoring sexual relations in public.[14] In Islam, then, human autonomy is grounded in politics (*siyasa*) not in morals (shari'a)—democracy with modesty. One enjoys autonomy in the face of state tyranny but not before God. Liberty is thus a political category, not a moral one. There is, of course, considerable diversity of opinion on Islam's morals. Democracy in Indonesia, as elsewhere, works together with communal values, including the values of Islam.

But does this apply to non-Muslim minorities or to Muslim dissenters? Is the political community equal to the believing community? In the United States, many would be uncomfortable with a non-Christian president even though the Constitution allows it. Pat Robertson claims that only Christians are qualified to rule. But the Constitution protects minorities, a position Christians uphold. In Islam, a long-standing principle allows for shari'a to be suspended if applying it would lead to civil strife (*fitna*). This is not simply a nice idea. In 2002 a proposal in the Indonesian parliament to implement shari'a as the law of the land was defeated because it was opposed by the nation's two largest Muslim organizations, Nahdlatul Ulama and Muhammadiyah, which placed the welfare of a pluralistic nation above religious hegemony.[15] Some groups aspire to religious supremacy at all costs, but for the vast majority, as indicated, politics is a moral venture, not an ideological one: The political integrity of Indonesia's religious minorities is not to be trampled on by the Muslim majority.

The Muslim hope for public decency includes both government accountability and respect for the values of Islam. High levels of government corruption have led some Muslims to form separate communities: alternative societies, networks of piety, which live according to Islam in a kind of religiously oriented civil society. Why entrust oneself to a political system that exists only for its own survival? These groups also offer services to society that the state fails to provide. As a result, they have earned a political mandate in certain segments of society—not to end democracy for religious supremacy but to further it by participating in power civilly for the welfare of the nation.

In the United States, where democratic institutions are well established, religious groups still call the nation to moral norms. Alongside constitutionalism, the Gospel is at play in national life. James Dobson advances the moral teachings of the Gospel, calling Christians to break with the culture of individualism and live the culture of the family. Promise Keepers calls the nation's men to a godly mission as head and protector of the family. Rick Warren of the Saddleback Church promotes the social teachings of the Gospel, seeking to care for those in most need, including AIDS victims. Catholic Charities USA also plays a noticeable role in this regard. There are others who seek to translate Christianity into a political project, asserting that believers are best suited to rule the nation. Concerned that the religious character of the nation would be lost to secularizing forces, a cadre of preachers, notably Jerry Falwell and Pat Robertson, helped birth the Religious Right.

For Christianity no less than Islam, there is a temptation to map the religious community onto the nation. The idea that the United States has a Christian character is particularly strong in evangelical communities.[16] But even if disturbed by secularization, these communities are committed to freedom as a religious value and not simply a political one. Choice is part and parcel of religious truth because evangelicals see salvation as an individual and voluntary process, making it counterintuitive to want to impose it. The commitment of evangelicals to democracy is, then, partly the result of the need for freedom to share the Gospel. This commitment holds even when national life lacks righteousness. The struggle for public morality can therefore coexist harmoniously with the commitment to political liberty for all, that is, equal citizenship regardless of piety.[17]

Beliefs can be at home with freedom. In the United States, beliefs of all kinds, secular and religious, are at play in public life. One sees this in elections, where Christian groups distribute voter education guides; in courts of law, where judgments are handed down, sometimes favorably, on the constitutionality of faith-based initiatives; and in the lobbying efforts of faith-based interest groups.[18] Religious reasoning is not hostile to open inquiry and may even require it. When it comes to the affairs of this world as opposed to the next, truth—believers would concur—is never a forgone conclusion.

That it is not has long been recognized by Islam. Prayer is a duty that God has set for all time, and certain moral teachings, such as the prohibition of alcohol and adultery, are similarly fixed. But the way the common good is achieved in the polity has not been predetermined by revelation and therefore requires open inquiry. To claim truth for this world is to reduce human existence to utopian ideologies. Believers themselves admit that history is not over, truth not yet made fully manifest. What has been problematic for many Muslims is not secularism per se but the secularist marginalization of religious reasoning, as occurred under Kemalism, Nasserism, or Ba'thism. These ideologies assumed that moral truth is a secularist monopoly and that Muslims simply need to accept what purportedly enlightened state authorities tell them about the truths of the world. The Muslim desire for public decency does not mean that politically involved Muslims are antidemocratic. The complaint is not with democracy but the lack of public morality. The feeling is that the public trust is best served by the values of Islam along with democratic deliberation. Authoritarian regimes block both. Thus, if democratic politics were to replace authoritarian rule in many a Muslim society, shari'a would not suddenly become irrelevant. Religious values no less than secular ones can contribute to the common good without prejudice to democratic procedures. It is when religion is made into an ideology that it threatens democracy. The same is true of secularism.

This is not to suggest that religious communities ought to be democratic in their internal workings. We vote for our political leaders but our core beliefs are too sacred to leave to a simple majority. Some groups are democratic in their internal governance and even in matters pertaining to God. In general, however, believers acknowledge religious authority. Those more versed in Scripture, ordained into the priestly order, or filled with the spirit, are awarded a privileged—though not uncontested—authority to speak for religion. We do not vote on God but worship him as Supreme Being as he reveals himself. Religion follows the guiding presence of God. It cannot be denied, disobeyed, or voted upon. Jesus said that all sin will be forgiven except sin against the Holy Spirit.

There is potential tension, then, between a community's contract with God (the religious contract) and its contract with the political order in which it lives (the social contract). How to negotiate the divide between what is eternal and what is transitory? Is the religious community to withdraw from the wider society to pursue its contract with God? Fight it until it too submits to divine authority? Enter into dialogue with it to reach some balance between heavenly and earthly concerns? Can believers be responsive to both a religious and a social contract? The invocation of God is a way to counter political and religious tyranny, but it can collide with democratic sentiment. Stanley

Hauerwas, an American theologian, has lambasted Christianity's love affair with liberal democracy, which, he claims, kills Christianity by domesticating its strongest truth claims. In contrast, John Courtney Murray, a key architect of the Vatican II document on religious liberty, saw liberal democracy as a source of divine wisdom. The New England Puritans were known for their resistance to British tyranny, both political and religious, but once established in their biblical commonwealth, they were highly intolerant of nonconformists. Roger Williams finally had enough, founding Rhode Island as a haven where one might enjoy political rights regardless of creedal commitments. In the parlance of Islam, Williams' insight amounts to the irrevocable truth that governance (*siyasa*) has no final jurisdiction over shari'a—the state does not mediate beliefs even if it is to enforce a public morality.

Religion is a complex affair. Jesus said his kingdom is not of this world, but his message posed a serious challenge to worldliness. Prophets, including Muhammad, were sent not to lord it over others but to scrutinize the failings, even arrogance, of worldly power vis-à-vis the poor and dispossessed. They too, however humbly, bear the image of God no less than the powerful, as the Qur'an notes (17:70): "We have honored the children of Adam" (i.e., all humanity and not only believers).

Religion is liberation from the standards of this world, ennobling and dignifying in the face of those who elevate themselves over others. And yet religion also calls for public morality. Can this be left to individuals to determine? A religion may claim a privileged authority when it comes to its own beliefs and values, but how does it evaluate the authority of those who do not share them? Were the New England Puritans consistent in limiting both religious and political authority to the saints, those chosen by God to be vessels of Christian grace, that is, the regenerated, as opposed to those who had not shown signs of a full conversion? Political authority is not subjective, dependent on the state of one's soul, but objective, common to all, and thus necessarily geared to the common good of all. This would imply that the human mind, whether assenting to religious authority or not, is still capable of recognizing public interests.

In contrast, all do not enjoy the same capacity for religious authority. In the end, it is God's exclusively, making it the preserve of a religious community and not of outsiders. But believers also recognize that all enjoy a right to protection and care whether professing belief in God or not because all are made in the image of God. Still, despite long-standing commitment to the common good as the will of God here on earth, both Christianity and Islam have not always favored democratic processes. There is a paternalistic side to religion. Do people at large, uneducated and undisciplined, know what is best even when it comes to worldly affairs? Human nature, though not evil, is weak. Is the will of a corruptible humanity to be trusted in judging affairs on earth (i.e., public morality, justice, prosperity), to say nothing of affairs in heaven (i.e., salvation)?

Christian democracy in Europe got started as a people's movement, blessed by Pope Leo XIII in his 1901 encyclical *Graves de communi*, which described democracy not so much as mass participation in rule but as popular Catholic action, especially on behalf of laborers who in the immediate aftermath of the Industrial Revolution lived and worked in deplorable conditions. The church has always called for care of others, especially the poor and marginalized, advocating, since its beginnings, a concept of human rule ordered to the well-being of all. This is clearly set out by Thomas Aquinas. However, even with the rise of Christian democracy in Europe, fueled in large part by Catholic activism, the Catholic hierarchy of Europe remained suspicious of parliamentary democracy and religious pluralism. After all, governance by people at large, those unlearned in the faith or even hostile to it, could lead to laws at odds with Christian values. The lesson was learned only during the last century, when the church witnessed the devastating threat to freedom, including religious freedom, posed by secularist ideologies, such as Nazism and communism. Freedom for Catholic beliefs, it was seen, cannot be secured without securing it for all. This lesson was underscored by the experience of American Catholics who did not see democracy as a threat to the authority of religion and its teachings, even though it did not guarantee state enforcement of them.[19] A commitment to religious truths and the dignity of those who believe differently can be simultaneously maintained.

A similar process has unfolded in Muslim society over the last century. Democracy is no longer seen as a threat to Islam but has been embraced as the best way to ensure space for shari'a in public life. This process is often referred to as the awakening (*al-sahwa*), where piety and freedom from authoritarianism—first colonial and then postcolonial—go together. This is not to be confused with the tribal movement in Iraq, also known as the awakening, which worked with the United States to eradicate terrorism. The course has by no means been smooth. The awakening can take on the hue of ideological battle—between secular states and Islamist movements. What is emerging, though, is the recognition that the kind of statehood best for Islam is the civil state (*al-dawla al-madaniyya*) in which no ideology dominates and both secular and religious reasoning are afforded space in public life. Such a state needs democracy to be what it is meant to be—a public entity that does not define truth as forgone conclusion but continually tests all ideas against the greater good of Muslim society. The state alone is not arbiter of moral life but is to facilitate the process by which society collectively strives to bring about God's purposes for society: public morality, justice, and prosperity. In addition, shari'a alone cannot guarantee political success. Other sources of wisdom are also needed. A religious state is therefore, and ironically, unacceptable in Islam. Islam has place in politics but is not reducible to politics.

The verdict is still out on Islamism (i.e., political action inspired by Islam). It is neither uniform nor static but has yet to work out the relation of Islam to national life. Over the last century, Islamism responded to changing realities but Islamist groups are not chameleons. They have a vision of the way the world works and the place of Islam in it. They are not all alike, however. A key issue is the scope of religious knowledge. Does it cover all things? Is it limited to rituals and morals or does it apply to economics and politics as well, and is such knowledge predetermined in advance, that is, revealed? If religious knowledge is a matter of rituals and morals, Muslims can pray, avoid adultery, and so on, and hope for a favorable judgment in the world to come. However, believers and nonbelievers expect ethical standards of public life. How are those standards formulated? Is it the task of religious specialists who derive principles from holy texts and apply them to life's circumstances? Do only believers have a say in determining these standards? Or do all people have a natural sense for the ethics of public life irrespective of religious convictions?

For example, Hezbollah of Lebanon participates in national and local elections and even builds coalitions with Christian politicians.[20] At its founding, it called for a religious state but realized that partial gains could be made by participating in a political system that it does not accept in principle.[21] The question, of course, is why it rejects the Lebanese political system. Hezbollah is a complex group. It is apparently bent on the destruction of Israel.[22] It acts as something of a nation within a nation, equipped with its own military, but it also claims to be committed to the Lebanese nation as a whole. It rejects the current political system because that system unfairly distributes power according to confessional interests rather than popular representation. But it is also inspired by the thought of an Iraqi intellectual, Muhammad Baqr al-Sadr, killed by Saddam Hussein in 1980, who left a deep mark on contemporary Shi'ism by greatly expanding the scope of religious knowledge.[23] He aimed to show that Islam has a global perspective capable of competing with both communism and capitalism. Although revelation ended, he argued, the religious heritage contains ethical concepts that apply to all issues. In other words, Islam has the resources to beget a modern state. In contrast, Shi'ism traditionally recognizes the limited nature of religious knowledge, allowing believers to participate in political power that does not represent Shi'i religious aspirations, provided they are able to maintain their individual ethical integrity while doing so.[24]

Hezbollah and other Shi'i groups have taken up the mantle of Ayatollah Khomeini (died 1989), who argued that justice could be obtained only under religious rule.[25] Political authority thus belongs to the religious scholar. For this reason, Hezbollah's first loyalty lies beyond Lebanon with Khomeini's successor, Ayatollah Khamenei, supreme leader of the Islamic Republic of Iran. However, at a deeper level, Hezbollah reflects the thought of Muhammad Baqr al-Sadr, who claimed that no aspect of life is free of divine decree. No issue, even those that religion does not explicitly address, is devoid of ethical import: urban planning, hedge funds, the use of weapons of mass destruction, tax collection, zoning laws, water consumption, organ transplants, sex-change operations, democracy, and so on.[26] The question, again, is how to determine the ethical status of such issues. If one says that ethics is entirely a function of religious teachings, then all national policies take on religious value. The nation itself becomes a religious aspiration. Believers will have to do more than just pray and avoid adultery to please God. Thus, though participating in Lebanese politics democratically, Hezbollah is also tempted to dominate, claiming to do so for the nation's own good. Its leaders speak of liberation, the liberation of the dispossessed, but do not trust secular processes to achieve it. Only Islam can liberate. But what is the purpose of liberation? Is the goal democracy unhindered by powerful interests or religious rule that defines all aspects of national life, including politics and economics? Hezbollah's commitment to democracy remains ambiguous. It calls for full liberation from corrupt politics but also espouses a belief system in which religious knowledge is unlimited. It is not religion per se but a religious vision that knows no bounds that is at odds with democracy.

In contrast, the AK Party of Turkey, now governing the nation, has a strong reverence for secularity. It calls for economic and political liberalization but not in explicitly religious language. Liberalization, of course, is good for Islam in a country where a secularist ideology, Kemalism, has long controlled the religious spirit of the nation, defining secular modernism as the purpose of life. Some of the AK Party's predecessors, notably former Prime Minister Necmettin Erbakan, viewed liberation from Kemalism as the first step toward establishing a religious state, leading secularist forces to topple his government in 1997.

This coup triggered a transformation in Turkish Islamism. Previously, Islamists had supported economic liberalization. They would henceforth back political liberalization too: human rights, democracy, civil liberties, things once viewed negatively as products of the West. Kemalist repression of nonstate expressions of Islam, climaxing in the removal of Erbakan from power, led Muslim leaders to link Islam to political freedom, seeing it as a necessary precondition for the well-being of Islam. This development, however, is not simply a response to repressive action. It has also been captured in religious language, a message of love and tolerance without loss of Islam's unique call.

A key figure in this regard is Fethullah Gülen, leader of a movement numbering in the millions with interests in education, business, and the mass media. Its activities are international in scope, with top schools in Central Asia and interfaith initiatives in the West. Gülen seeks to accommodate the Kemalist state. He is a deeply spiritual figure with roots in Sufism. He is committed to the secular state but also to the teachings of Islam. His followers are socially diverse and morally conservative, and some elements in Turkish society view them with caution. In general, they reject Erbakan's antagonistic approach to the state but support the AK Party, especially its goal of freeing society from state ideology.[27] The leadership of the AK Party, once associated with Erbakan, drew on Gülen's ideas to forge a new (post-1997) approach to national politics: religiosity that is dynamically Muslim but also positively engaged with secular realities themselves worthy of reverence as part of God's created order.[28] The aim of Islam, then, is ethical, not political, seeking to restore the character of a nation disfigured by the materialist ideology of the state. Renewal of national character, however, is not reducible to philosophical abstracts but depends on a message that speaks to the cultural particularities and ethical loyalties of the people, including Islam, yet also resonates with a national and global whole.[29] Gülen is thus not addressing Kemalism but Turkish society, shaping a national framework where the ideological secularism of the state is discredited as a partisan interest.

Gülen was a disciple of Sa'id Nursi (died 1960) whose voluminous commentary on the Qur'an, *The Treaty of Light* (*Risale-ye Nur*), widely studied in Turkey, weaves together questions of modern science with a spiritual vision of the cosmos, leaving the impression that secularity is itself part of Islam's sacred narrative. Gülen, in turn, has added civic activism to Nursi's legacy, inspiring his followers to bring piety to life in the form of service to the nation. Indeed, the movement calls itself service (*hizmet*). Its promotion of piety operates not by preaching (*teblig*) but by representing (*temsil*) the ethics of Islam: truthfulness, honesty, generosity, humility, altruism, love, and so on. Islam still has its particular norms to which Gülen is committed, but more profoundly interacts harmoniously with secular realities through the prism of such universal values.

Many factors have gone into the Turkish transition to democracy, including the hope for EU candidacy, but consolidation of a religious vision of democracy is vital in a nation committed to Islam. Gülen sees civil society as part of God's plan. It is therefore unnecessary to define it in explicitly religious categories. Turkey, like Lebanon, has known democratic shortcomings, but Islamism in Turkey has responded in a very different way. Both Hezbollah and the AK Party participate in democratic processes but they have contrasting understandings of the nature and scope of religious knowledge. As a result, they do not see the relation of religion to democratic liberty in the same light. For the AK Party, democracy, albeit a modern phenomenon based on a social rather than a religious contract, has religious worth as a political system. This is not merely because it serves the common good but also because it represents the ethics of God by challenging ideological rule that limits the spiritual potential of the human being. For Muslims to be Muslims, a civil society free of state control is necessary. This means, of course, that all citizens are free. Are they, then, to be led to live according to the dictates of religious knowledge as defining mark of Turkish ethics? The values of Islam, to be sure, will not be barred from public life, and the AK Party has attempted to promote them (and risked closure by the state in 2008 when it sought to lift the headscarf ban on university students). Still, democracy in Turkey now has religious force. It is seen as best for Islam, backed by a powerful religious vision that recognizes the integrity of secular processes as part of God's creation. Citizens who do not accept Islam, in whole or in part, are still fully citizens. Civil society is not free of ethical considerations to which Islam can contribute. Still, the nation need not be totally Islamized for Muslims to be Muslims. God is at work in the nation's commitment to democracy and civil liberties.

Does Islam call for rule by God or rule for God? The former, rule by God, would turn politics into a religious affair. Can the Qur'an serve as a national constitution? Do state officials rather than religious scholars determine Islam? Such thinking is new among Muslims, emerging in response to European rule in the nineteenth and twentieth centuries. Many accepted colonial power as long as it did not suppress Islam, but others called for reform to strengthen the Muslim spirit against Europe.[30] A key element of this reformism was a growing appreciation for national identity.[31] The people and not only traditional authorities were to determine the affairs of the *umma*, as citizens, not subjects.

This development transformed classical notions of the relation of religion to rule.[32] Previously, a specialization of roles had been imagined, religion guiding society's morals and rule governing its politics. Dynastic rulers had always acknowledged the moral authority of religion in public life. In turn, religious scholars supported the political order of the day. There were, then, two sets of laws. But modern statehood meant that all authority would belong to the nation. The people were to be masters of their own destiny, both political and moral. How was Islam to factor into this new formula for Muslim society? Could the people and their representatives be trusted to respect the ways of God? Would it be necessary to enthrone God over the nation to ensure the continuity of Islam? And what was to be done with non-Muslim citizens? Did they have equal voice in determining the affairs of a Muslim nation?[33]

Muslims still have a strong appreciation for traditional religious authorities, who themselves have had to adapt to modern realities, but a measure of democratic sentiment has left its mark on the beliefs of the *umma* no less than its politics.[34] Are the people now also to determine the morals of society no less than its public policies? If religion is the source of morals, does this not mean that the people have the responsibility of ensuring Islam's national representation?[35]

How is Islam to exist alongside democracy? In theory, it should have been a simple reformulation of power in democratic as opposed to dynastic categories—the nation as a whole now in power, not a single family. For example, in the Iranian constitutional revolution of the early twentieth century, the goal in general was not to do away with religion but to defend its mandate for this world—justice and prosperity in addition to public morality. The shahs were selling off the nation's resources to foreigners for their own gain. It was clear that if dynastic rule were not checked by popular representation, the welfare of the nation would be harmed.

But some saw it otherwise. Representative government meant that popularly elected officials would have the authority to legislate in accordance with public sentiment. Would this not lead to disregard for shari'a? Could the people be trusted to bring about God's will? Some ayatollahs supported constitutionalism, others opposed it. How was governance to be transferred to the people without prejudice to Islam? Was religious authority also to be democratized? In the end, it did not matter for Iran, because the shah (Mohammad 'Ali Shah Qajar), with British backing, bombed the national assembly on June 23, 1908, bringing the constitutional movement to a sudden end.

A variety of Islamist thinkers sought to work out the relation of Islam to nationhood over the course of the twentieth century. At least initially, they tended to see Islam not simply as the benchmark of national morality but as source of nationhood; only an explicitly religious state could rule an Islamic nation. This view, which can justify authoritarian rule in the name of Islam, originated with Abu-l-A'la Mawdudi (died 1979), a South Asian Muslim who first coined the concept of divine sovereignty (*hakimiyya*), conflating God's purposes with political power.[36] Mawdudi had deep anxieties about secularism. If not checked, it would spell the end of Islam. Rule by God was therefore the only way to save Muslims.[37] As a first step, he founded the Islamic Group (*Jama'at-i Islami*) in 1941, several years before the partition of India, with the goal of educating Muslims in the teachings of Islam. With the establishment of Pakistan in 1947, it turned its attention to politics, advancing the idea of Pakistan as a nation under divine sovereignty. It has enjoyed limited success at the polls but encourages expectations of rule in the image of God, blurring the lines between religion and power (even military power).[38] The Islamic Group exists throughout South Asia but in Pakistan oscillates between political participation as means to power and withdrawal from democratic processes to preserve its religious integrity from compromise by secular ways. It judges the failure of the nation to implement shari'a as offensive to God.

Mawdudi's writings spread the central Islamist idea of rule as essential to the religious integrity of the *umma*. Hasan al-Banna (died 1949), founder of the Muslim Brotherhood, shared the aversion to secular rule. He did not spell out a political system as precisely as Mawdudi but still assumed the religious character of government. Together, Mawdudi and al-Banna have had tremendous impact on Islamist thinking. For example, Hasan Turabi (born 1932), Sudanese affiliate of the Brotherhood, built his Islamist program on previous efforts to Islamize national law under President Ja'far Numayri (ruled 1969–1985), which took place incoherently at the hands of state officials inadequately trained in shari'a.[39] That is, the state acted as chief religious authority, a complete reversal of the classical heritage, paving the way for greater Islamization of the nation by military rule, a project that Turabi engineered, describing it as Islam's form of liberal representative democracy.[40]

The architects of Islamism did think of Islam in democratic terms.[41] It was not, however, democracy in the service of God's ways but democracy as revealed by God. Mawdudi called it a theo-democracy, and Turabi equated traditional concepts of legal reasoning, such as interpretation (*ijtihad*) and consensus (*ijma'*), with democratic principles of voting and popular will.[42] When formulated as such, democracy becomes a single option for God's will as known in advance.

Islamism has failed as a political project because it equates Islam with nationhood, neglecting the long-standing distinction in Islam between religious knowledge and political power. This recast the politics of Islam into a specifically religious endeavor, making rule part and parcel of the revealed order rather than autonomous entity serviceable to the public goals of religion (public morality, justice, and prosperity). This greatly contributed to the idea that Islam is primarily a political identity. Breaking with tradition, Islamists speak of Islam as religion (*din*) and state (*dawla*), equating religious devotion with political allegiance, a formula that dictators have exploited in suppressing alternative points of view.[43] In contrast, traditional scholars note that the allegiance (*al-bay'a*) that the prophet received from his companions was allegiance not to a form of political rule, not even a caliphate, but to Islam and its morals: prayer, fasting, no stealing, no adultery, and exclusive worship of God.

Indeed, making the details of the prophet's rule essential to the religious mission of Islam would require Muslims to live according to the sociopolitical norms of seventh-century Arabia, casting doubt on Islam's validity for all times and places.[44] This is the consequence of making politics a revealed phenomenon. It fixes religion in time, but the tradition never viewed rule as such. The towering scholar of the classical period, al-Mawardi (died 1058), discussed norms for governance in Islam but never equated rule with religion. Leadership, he wrote in his well-known political tract, *The Rules of Power*, exists to protect religion (*hirasat al-din*) and govern the world (*siyasat al-dunya*). He did not say that rule is the purpose of religion. Indeed, he was very conscious that rule is dynastic—it comes and it goes. Only Islam remains.

The refrain that Islam is both religion and state, still common in Islamist circles, has been nuanced. There are many reasons for this. Islamists have always demanded freedom to advance the cause of God, but they increasingly realize that to secure freedom for their own purposes they must grant it to all. Change by force yields no benefits. This is not to overlook Islamist propensities to violence. But there are essential differences between Islamism and Jihadism. Islamists do not condemn the idea of nationhood in principle. They do not define jihad as rising up against apostate rulers.[45] Furthermore, the morals of Islam

generally apply whether dealing with friend or foe.[46] Both Islamism and
Jihadism came out of the awakening that sometimes cast Islam in the
role of global dissident, locked in a struggle against colonial and now
postcolonial powers perceived to be intent on suppressing Islam. But
Islamists do not seek to eradicate all that is not explicitly Islam. Indeed,
they recognized that the enemy is authoritarian rule, not secular realities
per se.

Ambiguity of purpose remains. Opposition to authoritarian rule is
one thing. Commitment to democracy is another. Hamas won a majority of the Palestinian parliament in 2006, but its violent conquest of
Gaza in 2007, which it compared to the prophet's peaceful conquest of
Mecca, confirmed suspicions about Islamist commitments to democracy. In contrast, over recent decades, the Brotherhood in Egypt has
engaged a political process that is not defined by Islam from the outset.
One way it has done so is by de-divinizing its concept of the state: The
state proper to Islam is not a religious state but a civil one. It is, then, a
worldly phenomenon and not subject to predetermined notions of what
best serves the common good of Muslim society.[47] In that sense, it
can accommodate a plurality of viewpoints, both religious and secular,
provided they serve the common good and reflect the will of the people.
When allowed to participate in Egypt's elections, the Brotherhood
plays by democratic rules. Its members in parliament act pragmatically,
advocating for the common good in light of Islam's broader intentions.

Still, the Brotherhood aspires to ground the national constitution
in Islam. Egypt's constitution recognizes the principles of shari'a as
chief—but not exclusive—source of national law, and the Supreme
Constitutional Court has the task of ensuring that no law contradicts
it.[48] But this is not enough for the Brotherhood. In the 2007 draft of its
political platform, the Brotherhood only thinly veiled its desire for a
national constitution wholly defined by Islam. Is the Brotherhood re-
verting to the religious state where Islam encompasses all? Or is it seeking a way to guarantee Islam's independence from civil institutions such
as the Supreme Constitutional Court?[49] As noted earlier, the Catholic
Church, in the face of secularist ideologies such as Nazism and communism, more fully committed itself to political freedom as a religious

good. It has not ceased its call to God, including its moral teachings, but it recognizes popular sovereignty as the basis of constitutional legitimacy.[50] It does not seek to control national governments or define national constitutions in religious terms. In contrast, the Islamism of the Brotherhood shows that the relation of Islam to democracy has not yet been fully worked out.

Why, though, should a Muslim society embrace a secular constitution if not representing the will of the people or the aspirations of its most active movements? Democracy comes in different forms. In the United States, religion is strongly at play in shaping the moral sentiments of the nation, but the U.S. Constitution is not defined in religious terms. Islam is committed to nonauthoritarian rule, as argued earlier. It also seeks public respect for the values of Islam, even if not demanding that all follow them. The force of Islamism in today's world, however, raises questions about constitutional outlook. Democracy, of course, is bound to the common good of the nation. It is not simply a venture in individualism but works to check the monopolization of power. This idea resonates with Islamist groups too, but Islamist aspirations for religious constitutionalism pose a conundrum: How exactly is Islam to prevail as national identity in a democratic society? Can the religious concept of covenant be aligned with the political concept of democracy?

As noted, Islam is not to be simplistically implemented when detrimental to the common good. A constitution defined by Islam does not necessarily mean that all policy is defined in advance. Rather, it could require policymaking to heed certain principles that all affirm. Again, it depends on one's understanding of religious knowledge. Does it cover all things, politics included, or is it limited? Still, a constitution defined by Islam makes political power a religious affair. For Islamists, then, the idea of nationhood as rule by the people is still in question. They are able to win the hearts of many who are disgusted with corrupt governments. And in the authoritarian contexts in which many Muslims live, it is common to see rule by Islam as the ideal of justice. This fosters ideas of nationhood that look to Islam as a bulwark against injustice, whereas in a nonauthoritarian context such a connection is not evident. But this is the Islamist dilemma. It is a strong voice against authoritarian power. But what happens when it comes to power? Is the goal rule that is responsive to Islam, as traditionally defined, or rule by Islam, as constitutionally defined?

Islamism is a work in project. The Brotherhood's discourse has been penetrated by democratic language. It has partly moved away from a vision of religious supremacy in favor of religiously backed democracy. It has not, though, fully defined its constitutional aspirations—rule by God or rule for God, divine sovereignty or popular sovereignty that includes respect for Islam's values. Indeed, the Brotherhood's double-speak shows where religion ceases to be compatible with the democratic outlook. The Brotherhood stands at a crossroads. It has nuanced its view of the relation of the state to the divine enterprise. Its younger members increasingly recognize that the state, though important, is not revealed by God. Indeed, the concept of a moral covenant may feature in future democratic politics, but in today's pluralistic age, it will not work if limited to a particular set of believers. Can a covenant with God, serving as a basis for a national constitution, recognize all, believer and dissenter alike, as equal? The answer to this depends in part on the religious value given to dissent. It also depends on a society's understanding of objective morals that all are to recognize.

The idea that it is not the religious state but the civil state that best matches Islam reflects the failings of the secularist state, which, to judge from its track record in Muslim society, does not rule either by the people or for the people. In short, religion may not be enough to govern, but neither is secularism. Islamism is more responsive to—and confident in—the popular will no less than the divine will as source of its mandate. The notion of popular will is now integral to Islamist logic. Even if advocating shari'a as the vehicle by which true justice is to be achieved, Islamist groups do not seek to limit the democratic process in advance to a predetermined agenda. There are gray areas, including the capacity of women and non-Muslims to hold highest offices, but Islamists are increasingly comfortable at democratic contestation.

There is now visible Islamist synergy between religion and democracy as the best way to achieve the common good. And again, more significantly, Islamist groups now generally recognize that shari'a alone cannot determine the common good in advance because that would reduce religion to politics, to the detriment of Islam. The Islamist embrace of multiparty democracy is a lesson learned only with great pain: Limiting politics to one viewpoint, even if divine, is a ready formula for dictatorship, which contradicts God's purposes for human society. Only God is absolute. Islam, like Christianity, has realized that democracy is the best way to preserve not only public morality but also religious freedom. God's voice will not be lost when the people rule.

The struggle for democracy in Islam continues to move in diverse directions. Democracy is not always viewed as religious ideal in Islamist circles, but Islamists do connect democracy to religious freedom. Some Islamists, insisting on a religious definition of nationhood, do raise questions about Islam's relation to democracy. What can be said is that Muslims and Christians in their own ways distinguish between rule and religion. Religion is not all in all. It does not have all the answers, but it does have something to offer. The common good, determined by local societies through democratic deliberations and shared values, remains a human venture that religion can support.

NOTES

1. For one example of this in nineteenth-century America, see Mark A. Noll, *America's God: From Jonathan Edwards to Abraham Lincoln* (Oxford: Oxford University Press, 2002), especially 293–329.

2. For one example, see Katherine Meyer et al., "Changed Political Attitudes in the Middle East: The Case of Kuwait," *International Sociology* 22, no. 3 (2007): 289–324.

3. See Graham Maddox, *Religion and the Rise of Democracy* (London: Routledge 1996).

4. The example from Malaysia is the Pan-Malaysian Islamic Party (Parti Islam SeMalaysia). Despite negative attitudes toward other groups, it has adhered

to the rules of democracy since 1955 (i.e., before national independence in 1957) with limited success, mainly in the provinces of Kelantan and Terenagganu. See Farish Noor, "Blood, Sweat and Jihad: The Radicalisation of the Discourse of the Pan-Malaysian Islamic Party (PAS) from the 1980s to the Present," *Journal of the Centre for Southeast Asian Studies* 25, no. 2 (2003): 200–232.

5. Such thinking was expressed in the wake of the controversial release of the draft of the Muslim Brotherhood's first political platform in August 2007. The most controversial part of the draft was the call for a council of religious scholars to oversee the legislative process to ensure compliance with shari'a. Considerable ambiguity continues to mark the rhetoric of the Brotherhood in Egypt and elsewhere. For example, it speaks of the right of private belief (*i'tiqad khass*) for all, but only Islam has place in public life. See "Ru'yat Jama'at al-Ikhwan al-Muslimin fi Suriyya," www.jimsyr.com.

6. The reference is to his December 2007 speech in which he responded to evangelical concerns that he, as a Mormon, was unfit to hold the highest office of the land. Defending religious freedom, he also argued that religion, all religion, has a place in national life.

7. See the June 30, 2008, article of 'Ali Jarisha, advisor to Egypt's Muslim Brotherhood, "al-Mustashar 'Ali Jarisha Yaktub: al-Harakat al-Islamiyya, ila Ayna?" www.ikhwanonline.com/Article.asp?ArtID = 38497&SecID = 391. In this article, Jarisha assessed the Islamist movement in view of the tripartite nature of the prophet's mission: his communication of the call to God, his education of his followers, and emigration to Medina and political empowerment (*tamkin*). This also captures the vision of Hasan al-Banna, founder of the Brotherhood, who spoke of instruction, formation, and, finally, execution. Islamists have achieved success in the first two areas, Jarisha wrote, and are now making progress in the third. He went on to detail the needed reforms: democracy, development, and the protection of public morals and family life. This requires the total implementation of Islam, but current realities permit only partial gains. The Brotherhood should therefore cooperate with others, including secularists, but not to the point of compromising its ideals. The prophet himself pursued a gradualist approach, and Jarisha cited verses from the Qur'an to justify this strategy. In the long term, however, Islamists must strive for total implementation of God's ways to escape the threat (*al-wa'id*) hanging over those who believe in scripture selectively, as indicated in the Qur'an (2:85).

8. For example, Farid al-Ansari, *al-Bayan al-Da'wi wa-Zahirat al-Tadakhkhum al-Siyasi* (Meknes: Matba'at al-Najah al-Jadida, 2003).

9. For an example of Moroccan secularist opposition to Islamism, see al-Husayn Wafiq, "al-'Amal al-Islami bayna l-Waqi' wa-l-Sarab," *al-Ayyam*, no. 257 December 2–8, 2006, 7.

10. On religious principles, see "al-Birnamij al-Intikhabi: Jami'an nabni Magh-rib al-'Adala," http://www.pjd.ma. On political universals, see, for example, Sa'd al-Din al-'Uthmani, *Tasarrufat al-Rusul bi-l-Imama* (Casablanca: Manshurat al-Zaman 2002); "al-Islam wa-l-Dawlat al-Madaniyya: Izalat al-Tanaqud," www.pjd.ma.

11. See "al-Birnamij al-Intikhabi: Jami'an nabni Maghrib al-'Adala," www.pjd.ma.

12. Of course, one reason the PJD does not make such a fuss about the religious character of the state is the fact that Morocco's monarchy is a religious state, headed by a descendent of the prophet.

13. For a selection of Soroush's writings, see *Reason, Freedom, and Democracy in Islam: Essential Writings of 'Abdolkarim Soroush*, trans. Mahmoud and Ahmad Sadri (Oxford: Oxford University Press, 2000). Shi'ism, of course, has long recognized diversity of religious opinion within circles of authorized religious scholars. Now, however, Islamist identification of religious authority with state power makes alternative religious viewpoints, even those of authorized scholars, a threat to God. A special court was established in 1987 to try religious scholars for opinions that challenge the state's monopolization of religious interpretation. See Charles Kurzman, "Critics Within: Islamic Scholars' Protests against the Islamic State in Iran," *International Journal of Politics, Culture and Society* 15, no. 2 (2001): 341–69.

14. Robert W. Hefner, "Constitutionalism and Democratization in Islam," (conference paper, Religion and the Global Politics of Human Rights, Georgetown University, March 16–17, 2007).

15. Robert W. Hefner, "Muslim Democrats and Islamist Violence in Post-Soeharto Indonesia," in *Remaking Muslim Politics* (Princeton, NJ: Princeton University Press, 2004), 273–301.

16. David Little, "Religious Freedom and American Protestantism," in *Politics and Religion in France and the United States*, eds. Alec G. Hargreaves et al. (Lanham, MD: Rowman & Littlefield, 2007), 29–48.

17. Christian Smith, *Christian America? What Evangelicals Really Want* (Berkeley: University of California Press, 2000).

18. Judgments on faith-based initiatives are not always favorable, however. See Winnifred Fallers Sullivan, *The Impossibility of Religious Freedom* (Princeton, NJ: Princeton University Press, 2005). On lobbying efforts, see, for example, David Yamane, *The Catholic Church in State Politics* (Lanham, MD: Rowman & Littlefield, 2005).

19. The international spirit of the European Union is a direct legacy of twenti-eth-century Christian democracy, which effectively countered, if not always checked, excessive claims to power by nation states that sought to centralize all authority under state control. See Peter Pulzer, "Nationalism and Internationalism

in European Christian Democracy," in *Christian Democracy in Europe since 1945*, eds. Michael Gehler and Wolfram Kaiser (London: Routledge 2004), 10–24.

20. For two of the better treatments of Hezbollah, see Amal Saad Ghorayeb, *Hizbullah: Politics and Religion* (London: Pluto Press, 2002); Ahmad Nizar Hamzeh, *In the Path of Hizbullah* (Syracuse, NY: Syracuse University Press, 2004).

21. As reported by Na'im Qasim, *Hizbullah: al-Manhaj, al-Tajriba, al-Mustaqbil* (Beirut: Dar al-Hadi, 2002), 267.

22. Of course, such a position could change. For one study that claims ideological flexibility for Hezbollah, see Joseph Elie Alagha, "The Shifts in Hizbullah's Ideology: Religious Ideology, Political Ideology, and Political Program," PhD diss. (Leiden: ISIM Dissertations, Amsterdam University Press, 2006).

23. On al-Sadr in general, see T. M. Aziz, "The Role of Muhammad Baqir al-Sadr in Shi'i Political Activism in Iraq from 1958–1980," *International Journal of Middle East Studies* 25 (1993): 207–22. Muhammad Baqr al-Sadr based his thinking on what he called the region of the void (*mantiqat al-faragh*). See his *Iqtisaduna*, 20th ed. (Beirut: Dar al-Ta'aruf lil-Matbu'at, 1987), 378–90. The concept goes back to classical Islam. What to do in situations where revelation offers no certain ruling? The question applied to many areas (the revealed texts, after all, are limited, whereas life situations are not), including the domain of governance. That God is silent on various aspects of life did not mean that ethical considerations did not apply. How to know those ethical considerations? Some said that the human mind is free to determine moral norms where God has not clearly specified a ruling. Others said that the intentions of shari'a can be extended to all areas of life by a jurisprudential process that accounts for interests both worldly and heavenly. There has been and continues to be wide disagreement over definitions of worldly and heavenly interests. Some claim that heavenly interests are limited to the rewards one is to receive in the next life for performing religious obligations clearly specified by revelation. Others say that heavenly interests extend to all domains of worldly reality, making it incumbent on religious scholars to discover the rulings of God for all situations. The intentions of shari'a are known, it has been argued, and therefore can be applied to situations where no specific ruling exists. Islamists use the concept in their own ways, but it has long been part of Islam. See Felicitas Opwis, "*Maslaha* in Contemporary Legal Theory," *Islamic Law and Society* 12, no. 2 (2005): 182–223.

24. See Norman Calder, "Accommodation and Revolution in Imami Shi'i Jurisprudence: Khumayni and the Classical Tradition," *Middle Eastern Studies* 18 (1982): 3–20. For texts that speak to traditional Shi'i accommodation of religiously illegitimate states, see Muhammad Mahdi Shams al-Din, *Fi l-Ijtima' al-Siyasi al-Islami* (Beirut: al-Mu'assat al-Jami'yya lil-Dirasat wa-l-Nashr wa-l-Tawzi', 1992), 327.

25. Ruhollah Khomeini, *Islam and Revolution: Writings and Declarations of Imam Khomeini*, trans. Hamid Algar (Berkeley: Mizan Press, 1981). Khomeini's claim for religious rule has been widely contested within Shi'i circles. For example, Abdolkarim Soroush and Mohammed Mojtahed al-Shabestari have argued for the limits of religious knowledge from a philosophical and theological perspective, making it impossible for religion to be used as a basis of rule even if having a vital role in informing a nation's ethics. Mohsen Kadivar has demonstrated that Khomeini's particular understanding of religious authority (*wilayat al-faqih*) is a distortion of the tradition. See Mahmood T. Davari, *The Political Thought of Ayatullah Murtaza Mutahhari: An Iranian Theoretician of the Islamic State* (London: RoutledgeCurzon, 2005), 121–60. Two of the most influential Shi'i authorities today, Hussein 'Ali Montazeri and 'Ali al-Sistani, maintain that the *faqih* is to guide but not govern. The *faqih* is to advise and can be activist in his advisory role, but the state is not a religious entity and thus not the place for religious scholars.

26. For example, on how to fill the legislative void (areas of life not explicitly addressed by revelation), see the Lebanese Shi'i authority, Muhammad Mahdi Shams al-Din, "Majal al-Ijtihad wa-Manatiq al-Faragh al-Tashri'i," www .balagh.com//mosoa/feqh/u512by60.htm. This does not mean that Shi'i authorities in Lebanon (and elsewhere) are not modern in the way they apply the religious heritage to contemporary life. For example, Muhammad Hussein Fadlallah represents Shi'a at large in Lebanon but has greatly influenced Hizbullah, notably its post-1989 maturation. As early as 1988, he recast the political goals of Shi'ism in Lebanon, speaking of the human state (*dawlat al-insan*), embracing all confessions while defending national independence and social justice, rather than a specifically Islamic state (*dawlat al-islam*). Fadlallah has forged his own unique vision of Shi'ism, one that is rational and modern, calling—in the name of Islam—for recognition of pluralism, human rights including equal rights for women, democracy, Shi'i–Sunni reconciliation, and even a more diffuse conception of religious authority that includes women. His language is hostile to Israel and the United States but also condemns al-Qaeda. See Jamal Sankari, *Fadlallah: The Making of a Radical Shi'ite Leader* (London: Saqi, 2005).

27. To be sure, demographic factors have played a role, such as the rise of a middle class with pious sentiments, as well as sociological ones, such as the ability of faith-based groups to mobilize people for sociopolitical goals with familiar language, that is, in synch with their values. See Jenny B. White, *Islamist Mobilization in Turkey: A Study in Vernacular Politics* (Seattle: University of Washington Press, 2002). Still, in explaining the success of Islam in a political context dominated by a secularist ideology, one must also take into account the kind of Islam that prevails in Turkey, one with the resources to coexist relatively peaceably with an essentially antireligious ideology—and still challenge it by means short of revolution.

28. The idea that a religious group can accommodate a state that is hostile to it, even aggressively so, features in Berna Turam, *Between Islam and the State: The Politics of Engagement* (Stanford, CA: Stanford University Press, 2007). This is an excellent study. My only reservation is that in documenting the various kinds of engagement between the Gülen movement and the Kemalist state, it does not consider the belief system that makes this engagement possible in the first place. It is not just a matter of creating channels of interaction between a religious movement and a state with a secularist ideology but also of having a belief system that makes sense of such interaction. The Gülen movement has been able to incorporate the discourse of modernity, including secularism, into the sacred narrative of Islam by means of Sufism. See "Muslim World in Transition: Contributions of the Gülen Movement" (proceedings of conference, London, October 2007); M. Hakan Yavuz, *Islamic Political Identity in Turkey* (Oxford: Oxford University Press, 2003).

29. Serif Mardin, "Turkish Islamic Exceptionalism Yesterday and Today: Continuity, Rupture and Reconstruction in Operational Codes," in *Religion and Politics in Turkey*, eds. Ali Çarkoglu and Barry Rubin (London: Routledge, 2006), 3–23.

30. For religious accommodation with colonial rule in British South Asia, see Francis Robinson, *The 'Ulama of Farangi Mahall and Islamic Culture in South Asia* (London: Hurst, 2001). The idea of strengthening the Muslim spirit continues today. For example, Muhammad Sa'id Ramadan al-Buti on a television program (*al-Jadid fi I'jaz l-Qur'an*, broadcast July 8, 2007, on the Egyptian al-Resala TV) explained that the *umma* is no longer faithful to its covenant with God. They have exchanged their religion for worldliness and so God has given up on them. In other words, there is a basic qur'anic law (*sunna qur'aniyya*), extending to all peoples, whereby efforts are rewarded, even efforts made for this world and not for the next. This is al-Buti's explanation for the worldly success of western peoples who do make efforts, bringing them success according to God's qur'anic law even if not (in his view) believers in God.

31. For the impact on religious thinking, see, for example, David Johnston, "A Turn in the Epistemology and Hermeneutics of Twentieth Century *Usul al-Fiqh*," *Islamic Law and Society* 11, no. 2 (2004): 233–82; Ahmad Dallal, "Appropriating the Past: Twentieth-Century Reconstruction of Pre-Modern Islamic Thought," *Islamic Law and Society* 7, no. 1 (2000): 325–58; Mahmoud Haddad, "Arab Religious Nationalism in the Colonial Era: Rereading Rashid Rida's Ideas on the Caliphate," *Journal of the American Oriental Society* 117, no. 2 (1997): 253–77.

32. Much has also been made of the impact of colonizing Europe on the conceptualization of shari'a, which underwent codification as state law, giving state officials unprecedented jurisdiction over shari'a as legal code, where in the past it had been more of a corpus of diverse precedents over which religious scholars alone

had the authority. See, for example, Murteza Bedir, "Fikih to Law: Secularization through Curriculum," *Islamic Law and* Society 11, no. 3 (2004): 378–401; Aharon Layish, "The Transformation of the Shari'a from Jurists' Law to Statutory Law in the Contemporary Muslim World," *Die Welt des Islams* 44 (2004): 85–113. Care, however, must be taken not to posit such a radical break between classical past and emergent modernity in Islam's legal processes. In the end, shari'a was the purview of religious authorities, but there was endless contestation between religious authorities and state officials over spheres of influence from very early on. For continuity in legal processes between the pre-colonial and colonial periods, see Khalid Fahmy and Rudolph Peters, "The Legal History of Ottoman Egypt," *Islamic Law and Society* 6, no. 2 (1999): 129–35.

33. Muslim and non-Muslim communities did not, of course, live in mutual isolation. Indeed, non-Muslims, though they had a secondary legal status under Islam, did at times avail themselves of Islamic courts when it served their interests. See Najwa al-Qattan, "*Dhimmis* in Muslim Courts: Legal Autonomy and Religious Discrimination," *International Journal of Middle Eastern Studies* 31, no. 3 (1999): 429–44.

34. For an example of Muslim appreciation of traditional religious authority, see Brinkley Messick, *The Calligraphic State: Textual Domination and History in a Muslim Society* (Berkeley: University of California Press, 1993). For examples of the adaptation of religious authorities to modern realities, see Malika Zeghal, *Gardiens de l'Islam: Les oulémas d'Al Azhar dans l'Égypte contemporaine* (Paris: Sciences Politiques, 1996); Muhammad Qasim Zaman, *The Ulama in Contemporary Islam: Custodians of Change* (Princeton, NJ: Princeton University Press, 2002).

35. For examples, see R. Michael Feener, "Indonesian Movements for the Creation of a 'National Madhhab'," *Islamic Law and Society* 9, no. 1 (2001): 83–115; David Dean Commins, *Islamic Reform: Politics and Social Chance in Late Ottoman Syria* (Oxford: Oxford University Press, 1990).

36. See, for example, Seyyed Vali Riza Nasr, *Mawdudi and the Making of Islamic Revivalism* (New York: Oxford University Press, 1996).

37. For Mawdudi's political thought, see Charles J. Adams, "Mawdudi and the Islamic State," in *Voices of Resurgent Islam*, ed. John L. Esposito (New York: Oxford University Press, 1983), 99–133. See also Khurshid Ahmad and Zafar Ishaq Ansari, *Mawdudi: An Introduction to His Life and Thought* (Leicester: The Islamic Foundation, 1986).

38. See Omar Khalidi, "Mawlana Mawdudi and the Future Political Order in British India," *Muslim World* 93, nos. 3 and 4 (2004): 415–27; Abdul Rashid Moten, "Mawdudi and the Transformation of Jama'at-e-Islami in Pakistan," *Muslim World* 93, nos. 3 and 4 (2004): 391–413; and Frédéric Grare, "Islam, Militarism, and the 2007–2008 Elections in Pakistan," *Carnegie Papers* No. 70 (Washington, DC: Carnegie Endowment for International Peace, 2006).

39. J. Millard Burr and Robert O. Collins, *Revolutionary Sudan: Hasan Turabi and the Islamist State, 1989–2000* (Leiden: Brill, 2003). See Aharon Layish and Gabriel R. Warburg, *The Reinstatement of Islamic Law in Sudan under Numayri: An Evaluation of a Legal Experiment in the Light of Its Historical Context, Methodology, and Repercussions* (Leiden: Brill, 2002).

40. See Hasan Turabi, "The Islamic State," in *Voices of Resurgent Islam*, ed. John L. Esposito (New York: Oxford University Press, 1983), 241–51.

41. al-Banna actually aspired to political office, setting a precedent for the Brotherhood to participate in democratic processes. But like Mawdudi, he rejected the idea of political parties (*ahzab*), given that the nation should have one orientation, namely Islam. This may partly explain the Brotherhood's reluctance to create a political party of its own or even outline a political agenda. That is, with no party, there is no need to articulate a political vision in addition to the religious mission. Elsewhere too, the Brotherhood has looked favorably on democracy as antidote to authoritarian rule and potential means of bringing about rule by Islam. One sees openness to democracy, but ambiguity about its purpose, in the writings of Sa'id Hawwa, spiritual guide of the Muslim Brotherhood in Syria. See his *Jund Allah Takhtitan* (Cairo: Maktabat Wahba, 1988), 105–11. On the Brotherhood's early participation in elections in Syria, see Joshua Teitelbaum, "The Muslim Brotherhood and the 'Struggle for Syria,' 1947–1958: Between Accommodation and Ideology," *Middle Eastern Studies* 40, no. 3 (2004): 134–58.

42. For Turabi's Islamist vision, see *Tajdid Usul al-Fiqh al-Islami* (Khartoum: Maktabat Dar al-Fikr, 1980); *Tajdid al-Fikr al-Islami* (Rabat: Dar al-Qarafi, 1993); *Qadaya al-Tajdid nahwa Manhaj Usuli* (Beirut: Dar al-Haji, 2000); *al-Siyasa wa-l-Hukm: al-Nuzum al-Sultaniyya bayn al-Usul wa-Sunan al-Waqi'*, 2nd ed. (London: Dar al-Saqi, 2004).

43. For example, see Mohamed Mahmoud, "When Shari'a Governs: The Impasse of Religious Relation in Sudan," *Islam and Christian-Muslim Relations* 18, no. 2 (2007): 275–86.

44. Jihadists would claim that the historical aspect of the prophet's mission in its literal details is the truth of Islam and thus must be reenacted in all times and places. This would denude the politics of Islam of morals for the sake of rituals, that is, reenactment of a ritual narrative regardless of other considerations.

45. The Islamist notion of jihad is expressed in religious categories but is tied to national honor. One could call it religio-national honor, which is defended by the resistance against all threats to the nation's political and territorial integrity. In contrast, jihad for jihadists is not a question of national pride, and the resistance is therefore not the term that describes it. Al-Qaeda and its affiliates dwell on a pair of qur'anic terms: *khuruj* (to go out, to fight) and *qu'ud* (to sit, to avoid fighting). Jihadism is understood not in terms of the resistance but rather in terms of *khuruj*,

namely going out to fight all rulers (*hukkam*) who do not apply God's decrees, making them agents of idolatry (*taghut*). Jihadists, then, do not have a political strategy in mind but seek rather to live out a sacred narrative as recounted in the Qur'an. They thus make offensive and not only defensive jihad a religious obligation; *khuruj* against religiously unacceptable rulers in general is incumbent on all individual believers. It is the highest duty of Islam, with the goal of defending and avenging religio-global honor. Similarities can be found in Islamist and Jihadist tactics and strategies, but there are also striking differences. Islamists and Jihadists castigate one another while competing for the allegiance of Muslim youth.

46. The one exception is Israel, which Islamists see as threat to the nation as much as to Islam. Israeli society as a whole thus constitutes a legitimate battleground, whereas the United States may be foe but is still not object of attack for Islamists, in contrast to Jihadists, for whom it is. Islamist détente with Israel is possible in principle because Islamism acknowledges worldly interests in decision-making processes, but at the moment this is unlikely.

47. De-divinization of the state does not mean removing religion from the public realm but rather recognizing that the political order is not divine and that the ruler has no divine right. The way this process occurs is historically unpredictable. For example, the Glorious Revolution of 1688, a contestation involving religion, the right of kings to rule by divine mandate, and the emergent powers of Parliament to limit royal authority, had the unintended consequence of sealing the fate of British politics as a decisively pragmatic affair. James II, a Catholic, sought to level the religious playing field of his realm by repealing laws that forbade Catholic worship and education and kept Catholics from office and Parliament. To do so, he had to manipulate law-making processes, unacceptably extending his prerogatives and threatening the legislative power and independence of Parliament. Whigs and Tories alike turned against him, setting the stage for William of Orange to invade England and eventually be enthroned along with his wife, Mary, James's daughter and a Protestant. A king had been deposed (even if officially he abdicated) and a new king and queen enthroned, ostensibly to protect a Protestant nation from Catholic influence. The long-term impact, however, was much more significant. Shortly thereafter John Locke penned his *Two Treatises of Government*, in which he claimed that governance depends on the consent of the governed, making a ruler's failure to govern in the people's interest and heed their advice grounds for his removal. Although viewed as potentially anarchic, Locke's ideas signaled an important shift in political thinking triggered by the Glorious Revolution. The underpinnings of governance in England were no longer thought of in terms of divine providence but simply as a matter of human decision making—expediency, common sense, and the public welfare. But this de-divinization of politics did not mean removal of religious thinking from public reasoning, as is clear in Locke's writings. See John Miller, *The Glorious Revolution*, 2nd ed. (London: Longman, 1997), 31.

48. For background on the source of national law, see Clark Benner Lombardi, "Islamic Law as a Source of Constitutional Law in Egypt: The Constitutionalization of the Shari'a in a Modern Arab State," *Columbia Journal of Transnational Law* 37 (1998–1999): 81–123.

49. It could be asked whether the proposal is at odds with the religious character of the Brotherhood. There is synergy at times between the Brotherhood and traditional religious authorities, but the Brotherhood has long taught that all believers are responsible for Islam, making it strange for the Brotherhood to look to traditional religious authorities to guarantee the religious identity of the nation. In this sense, the draft aligns the Brotherhood more with the politics of Shi'ism than those of Sunnism, especially the form of rule in place in Iran where legislation is controlled by religious authorities.

50. See the 2002 publication of the Congregation for the Doctrine of the Faith, "Doctrinal Note Regarding the Participation of Catholics in Public Life." See www .vatican.va/roman_curia/congregations/cfaith/documents/rc_con_cfaith_doc_2002 1124_politica_en.html.

CHAPTER SIX

GOD'S RIGHTS

A Threat to Human Rights?

NEITHER THE BIBLE nor the Qur'an decisively condemns slavery. In the past, most Christians and Muslims saw slavery as part of God's order. Today, human trafficking is big business, but no credible religious authority backs it. It is considered an offense to the dignity and equality of all peoples. In contrast, although gender equality in public life is now the norm in many places, the largest branches of Christianity and Islam do not recognize women as leaders of formal prayer. Priest, preacher, and imam are religious offices. They are not bound, it is argued, by the same rules that apply to political office or educational opportunity or employment compensation. It is not a question of equality per se. Both Bible and Qur'an speak of the equality of men and women before God, and Christians of all kinds recognize the political and civic rights of women. Rather, when it comes to the sacred, there has to be a precedent in scripture or tradition. Certainly, women can pray no less than men. They love God no less than men. They play significant roles in all religious communities—as administrators, educators, and missionaries. For many groups, though, the office of prayer leader is ordered not to this world but to the next, making it a divine invitation, not individual right. Many, of course, argue that God extends this invitation to both genders equally.

Religious teachings, then, respond to some but not all developments that touch on questions of human rights. Many Christians and Muslims do support women as formal prayer leaders, but when it comes to Catholics, most Evangelicals, and all branches of Islam, this is not the official teaching. To be sure, not allowing women to be formal prayer leaders, although to some a sign of resistance to changing times, is not a violation of human rights.[1] However, asking the government to discriminate against religious communities that do allow women to be formal prayer leaders would constitute such a violation. Catholics and Evangelicals do not do that. Thus it is recognized that, as long as people have a choice, religious communities are free to govern their own affairs.

Other issues, abortion and gay marriage, are more controversial. U.S. law currently defines abortion as a basic constitutional right. Many believe that gay marriage should be similarly defined. Thus, for some, Catholic and Evangelical opposition to such issues amounts to an attack on rights, whereas for many Catholics and Evangelicals abortion is an attack on the right to life of the unborn and gay marriage is an attack on the natural order of society. Who defines such issues: God, the state, the individual?

Muslims, like Christians, are committed to the dignity of human life. They are also sensitive to insults against the prophet and to conversion out of Islam. A liberal society is one that celebrates individual expression of conscience. A person can openly insult the prophet if so moved. Muslim societies in general emphasize common virtues. Some things are sacred, religion being one of them. One may not like Islam, but one does not say so publicly. This does not mean that Muslim society is opposed to human rights, only that it balances them against a sense of sacred duty. What one does in the privacy of one's own home is another matter. Eating in public during Ramadan is discouraged if not forbidden. Many happily fast as the religion teaches, but many, behind closed doors, do not. Reservations about the teachings of Islam are best kept to oneself. In Europe, not having the right to insult the prophet or any other holy person is felt to be a constraint on freedom of expression, but in Muslim societies it is not. However, state discrimination against minority communities who follow a prophet the Muslim majority considers a false prophet does constitute such a violation. In Iran, for example, there is official persecution of the Baha'i community, which emerged in the nineteenth century to announce a new age of religious truth where shari'a no longer has a place. In Malaysia, the nation's top religious authority, the National Fatwa Council, recently issued an edict prohibiting non-Muslims from using the word *Allah*, affirming that the god of Islam is not the god of others. It also prohibited Muslims from practicing yoga. What is most sacred in the eyes of God? Where does his glory lie? The global commitment to human rights has encouraged new religious thinking on such matters. The Catholic Church, for example, emphasizes the sanctity of human conscience. Even when it errs, it retains its dignity. For this reason, the Catholic Church has become a great defender of human rights. But not all human rights talk is the same, and this is where the confusion lies.

The protection of human rights is often cast in terms of the right to dissent from the majority. This is the hallmark of a liberal society. Muslim societies do sometimes struggle with freedom of expression. But a liberal society can also harm individuals when it awards individual conscience final authority. It can, for example, rationalize moral depravity: "It's my body and I can do whatever I want with it." Or the concentration of wealth alongside poverty: "It's my money, I made it." Or predatory contracts—technically legal but still unjust: "She signed the loan." As heirs of Adam Smith, we think that the unencumbered pursuit of individual interests leads to the good of all. The invisible hand is guiding society, making it right to trust market forces to determine and achieve not only a prosperous society but also the moral good. But how much can we trust the invisible hand to protect the rights and interests of all?

Indeed, a focus on protecting individuals, though important, can blind us to other kinds of human abuse. All agree on certain violations of human rights. The human image is not to be defaced by authoritarian regimes that detain, torture, and execute their citizens arbitrarily or restrict their political liberties. But is it a violation of human rights to send soldiers to a war that lacks a clear moral purpose? Is government cronyism a violation of human rights in depriving the public of competent rule, threatening national resources, and jeopardizing the welfare of society? Is it a transgression of human rights to demand that health care workers perform services that violate their moral conscience when such services, such as abortion, are deemed a constitutional right?

The Qur'an says that Muhammad's community is the best God has created; it commands the right and forbids the wrong. In this sense, Islam, like Christianity, is a force against moral permissiveness. One is to live according to the spirit of God and not the spirit of the world, as Saint Paul urges. This works fine on the individual level, but humans are creatures of society. Do those who live according to the spirit of the world pose a threat to God's desire to sanctify the world with his spirit and build it up in his image? One is to be free of the world's ways, not enslaved to them. Still, those who have not willingly made themselves slaves of God are free to live as they wish, no? Many believers, including Muslims, are committed to freedom as a religious goal. God makes human rights a condition of true religion. One is not to be coerced. Faith would have no point if not grounded in freedom. But events of recent years—from suicide bombings to sectarian conflict—make it seem that religious goals in Islam take priority over human rights. State enforcement of Islam in some countries acts to violate freedom of religious conscience. Calls for the death of novelists, cartoonists, and filmmakers raise questions about Islam's commitment to free speech. Some wonder about Islam's teachings on women. Do they exist simply to birth the next generation or do they have a life outside the home?

Such perceptions obscure the fact that Muslims are often the victims of human rights abuse. States that claim to rule in the name of Islam are not the best advocates of human rights. Is this the fault of Islam? Or has the confusion over religious authority in today's world made Islam more susceptible to state machinations? Is Islam itself an opponent of human rights, making it right to want to free Muslims from Islam? Or does the problem lie in the politicization of Islam? Do Muslims long for greater freedom from the political abuse of Islam? The influence of Muslim culture has a statistically insignificant relationship to a government's commitment to human rights.[2] Thus, on a purely empirical level, Muslims are generally like the rest of us, despite our use of Islam to reassure ourselves of our moral superiority. We're good, so they must be bad.

There are contradictions. The 2004 murder of the Dutch filmmaker Theo Van Gogh by a Muslim born and raised in Holland was a defining moment in shifting attitudes towards Islam in Europe. At the core of Islamophobia is the idea that Islam has no positive values in common with other peoples. The Dutch politician, Geert Wilders, pushes this line: Muslims, if they take Islam seriously, will inevitably be hostile toward Europe's way of life. Either Muslims in Europe must be Europeanized or Europe will be Islamized. In contrast, in a 2008 speech, Rowan Williams, archbishop of Canterbury, suggested a rapprochement between shari'a and British national law—interactive pluralism. Do Muslims need special representation in British law, for example, when it comes to marriage, divorce, inheritance? State recognition of Islam's family law could make Muslims more at home as British nationals, mitigating conflict between religious and political allegiances. At the moment, some think of themselves as citizens of Islam rather than Muslim citizens of Britain. To be sure, people always define themselves through a prism of differences as well as of similarities, and this is compounded by the historical moment, in which some seek to divide the world into two camps, Islam and the West, forcing Muslims in Europe to take sides, rather than combine religious and national convictions into a single whole. And yet the British public decried the archbishop's suggestion. Was this Islamophobia? Or healthy resistance to the idea that religion is the affair of particular communities and not national society as a whole? Some have decried the appearance of mosques in Europe and the demands of some Muslims for separate treatment in public schools (e.g., physical education expectations). In the United States, by contrast, police have monitored Muslim communities more aggressively since 9/11, but assimilation of Muslims into mainstream American life has been much smoother than in Europe.

Indeed, in Europe, the challenge is not the presence of Muslims, but the need to develop religious forms that harmonize with long-standing cultural particularities. In the United States, where pluralism is quasi-sacred, there is no demand that Muslims fit in culturally, only politically.[3]

In Quebec, Muslim women who wear the face veil in addition to the head covering have been kept from voting. Of Quebec's 7 million residents apparently only thirty-odd women wear the face veil, and Canadian law has long accommodated personal circumstances at polling stations. The Egyptian Ministry of Religious Affairs forbids women to wear the face veil while on pilgrimage to Mecca. Islam does not require women to veil the face but only to cover the head, and the Egyptian state is concerned that some women wear the veil as a subversive tactic; government officials need to identify people by face, and the face veil challenges the authority of the state to control society. But God has rights too, and some Muslims today link their devotion to God to human rights, that is, religious freedom. For some Muslim women, modesty, including the veiling of the face, is a duty to God. Are God's rights as lived by Muslims worthy of equal protection? The tension arises when the rights of God to which a particular person is committed are not seen as part of a nation's heritage. At least one Muslim woman in France has been stripped of her citizenship for not assimilating enough to French cultural standards.

In April 2007, a group of Muslims in Texas went to the state capitol to learn more about state government. All went smoothly except that Dan Patrick, Texas state senator, stepped off the senate floor when a local imam offered the daily prayer, the first Muslim to do so in the Texas senate. Patrick explained that he did not want to appear to be endorsing the prayer but later praised American tolerance in allowing all to pray as they wish. In Britain, the leader of the Conservative Party, David Cameron, stirred controversy by claiming that Muslims plan to create a separate nation within Britain, governed by their own laws, but he has also criticized British tendencies to scapegoat Muslims for society's problems, which, he says, are socioeconomic and cannot be attributed to a religious community.

In Bangladesh, a group of Muslims has pressured the government to define the country's Ahmadiyya minority as apostate for recognizing a prophet after the prophet Muhammad. The government chose instead to ban the publication of Ahmadiyya literature, stopping short of a constitutional article condemning the Ahmadiyya, as exists in Pakistan. Shortly thereafter, Bangladesh's high court halted the ban. In Islamabad, a group of women connected to the Red Mosque raided a brothel, the prelude to the mosque's bloody standoff with police in 2007. They claimed the right as individual citizens to put an end to immoral activity, although Islam traditionally awards that right to government authorities exclusively. In some places in Pakistan's North-West Frontier Province, video shops are attacked for carrying immoral films and nonreligious music is prohibited. The return of the Taliban has not been good for women. In some places in Indonesia, the law permits police to jail women for being on the street at night without a headscarf. After many years, British Airways now allows all staff to wear religious symbols, including the Muslim headscarf, after a Christian employee claimed the right to wear a cross at work. Imaan, a support group for gay Muslims in Britain, entered a float in the 2006 Euro-Pride Parade in London with the placard Gay Muslims Unveiled. The previous year they wore rainbow burqas. Such a display of gay pride could not happen in Muslim society. The principal of the King Fahd Academy in London, which is funded by Saudi Arabia, defended the school's use of books that describe Jews as pigs and Christians as monkeys but had the offensive chapters removed as inconsistent with the prophet's teachings.

The former leader of Australia's Muslim community, the Egyptian-born Taj al-Din al-Hilali, referred to Australian women as uncovered meat. They do not dress modestly in public, inviting sexual harassment. Prime Minister John Howard criticized other Muslim leaders for failing to oust him as their chief mufti. Al-Hilali, who has not learned English after twenty years in Australia, was eventually forced to resign. He had called for the formation of a political party for Australia's 300,000 Muslims. Other Muslim leaders fly the Australian flag outside mosques to affirm loyalty to the nation. Jewish leaders in Australia distanced themselves from an Israeli academic who called on the Australian government to cap Muslim immigration, arguing that a rise in the Muslim population would lead to sectarian violence. Israel's 1 million Muslim citizens (i.e., those in Israel since its founding in 1948, not the Palestinians of the occupied territories) continue to face discrimination in land ownership rights and access to public services; some Israeli lawmakers would strip some of them of citizenship.

In 2007, Jewish and Christian leaders in Detroit condemned an attack on a city mosque motivated by anti-Muslim bigotry. The same year, France fired the head of the school board in Lyon for refusing to allow local Muslims to open a high school. They had planned to operate the school with private funding in full conformity with the national curriculum. One in five high schools in France are Catholic and often receive state funding, and Muslims are often more comfortable in Catholic schools, which, unlike government schools, appreciate religion and permit Muslim girls to wear the headscarf. FIFA, the rule makers of international soccer, almost banned the Muslim headscarf but finally left it to individual referees to decide whether it poses a danger to play. Egypt named its first female judges in 2007 with the backing of the rector of al-Azhar, Muhammad Tantawi, who stated that nothing in the Qur'an bars a female from being a judge, even chief judge. By contrast, the powerful Islamist group the Muslim Brotherhood strongly condemned the appointments. In a separate issue, Tantawi issued a 1988 fatwa permitting sex-change operations, not as the choice of individuals, but as a doctor-recommended cure for a pathological condition.

'Ali Gom'a, Egypt's grand mufti, has stated that in Islam women can be heads of state. The idea that Islam prevents women from exercising the highest levels of public authority, he argues, made sense in a past age when caliphs combined secular authority and religious leadership, but does not apply to the modern nation. In 2006, he signed a resolution of Muslim scholars outlawing female genital mutilation. No revealed or prophetic precedent exists in Islam for such a practice, the resolution reads, and it calls on Muslims to end this deplorable practice. In 2007, on a *Washington Post* website, Gom'a stated that Muslims are free to change their religion. They will be accountable to God in the next life but are not subject to punishment in this one. In Egypt, this claim was roundly rejected by leading religious voices. Also in 2007, the Egyptian state orchestrated a plebiscite to legitimize a ban on all faith-based politics. The goal was to counter the 2005 electoral successes of the Muslim Brotherhood. In the process the state claimed sweeping security powers in what Amnesty International called the greatest erosion of human rights in the country since the reinstatement of emergency laws after the 1981 assassination of Anwar Sadat.

A new English translation of the Qur'an seeks to disassociate Islam from violence against women. The translation, by the Iranian-American Laleh Bakhtiar, questions a particular verse of the Qur'an that at face value permits husbands to beat rebellious wives (4:34). Bakhtiar, who carefully researched the linguistic background of the disputed word, translates it not as *hit* but as *send away*. In Turkey, the Ministry of Religious Affairs has begun a project to reconsider the authenticity of prophetic traditions that demean women because the prophet would have never supported such teachings. Prince Naif, interior minister of Saudi Arabia, a country where women are not permitted to drive a car, has stated that gender segregation is not right. In Saudi society, the female presence is generally viewed as offensive to public morals. Professional women are now able to spend a night in a hotel (i.e., outside the family home) when business takes them to other cities, though they must register with local authorities. 'Abd al-Rahman al-Lahim, a Saudi human rights lawyer, has challenged the nation's laws against promiscuity. They are meant to protect women but are sometimes misused by the police, as well as by the women's own families, to intimidate and abuse them. Islam does prohibit promiscuity, but these laws fail to meet the intentions of Islam, which is to instruct, not intimidate. The result, according to al-Lahim, is jungle shari'a as opposed to shari'a justice. He defended a chemistry teacher sentenced to forty months in prison and 750 lashes for "trying to sow doubt" among his students by speaking positively about Judaism and Christianity; the teacher was pardoned by the king. Al-Lahim also defended a journalist arrested for what were referred to as "destructive thoughts" by suggesting on the Internet that homosexuality is a genetic predisposition; the case was thrown out of court. Al-Lahim sees the rule of law and protection of human rights as a key concern of Islam, and what makes him effective in Saudi Arabia's shariʿa courts is his own shariʿa expertise.

The point is that religion can be terribly mismanaged when it comes to human rights, and nowhere is that more striking than in a 2007 case in Germany in which a Moroccan woman, resident in Germany, sought protection from an abusive husband. The judge, Christa Datz-Winter, a non-Muslim woman, ruled against the Moroccan woman, citing the qurʾanic verse that at face value allows husbands to beat rebellious wives. Ironically, the plaintiff would have received greater protection from Moroccan law. How is it that in Europe a non-Muslim judge, untrained in shariʿa, can use it to reach a verdict that fails to protect a woman's human rights in opposition to German law, whereas in Saudi Arabia a Muslim lawyer can use shariʿa to protect human rights abuses that conform to the letter but not the intention of Saudi law? Datz-Winter was removed, but the case caused concern among Germany's Muslims that state officials with no training in shariʿa might use it against them.

Islam calls not simply for the application of shariʿa but its just application. Scholars heavily nuance the verse that appears to permit husbands to beat rebellious wives. The goal of marital dissension is reconciliation, not violence. Scholars also note that the prophet Muhammad, ultimate standard of Muslim behavior, never hit his wives and actually stated that whoever does so is ignoble (*laʾim*). Furthermore, the verse does not specify the means of beating, which scholars have limited to a *siwak*, a stick no bigger than a small twig that Muslims sometimes use to clean between the teeth. Datz-Winter was ignorant not only of the shariʿa reasoning but also of family law in Islam and the duties it imposes on both spouses. Had the husband in this case fulfilled those duties, such as care and maintenance of the family? Had the woman failed to fulfill hers, including her duty to make herself sexually available if physically and psychologically able? If not, the verse notwithstanding, punishment would have no support from shariʿa. This is not to say that the verse is not problematic, but it is also necessary to appreciate how Muslims deal with it.

We are faced with a field of conundrums when it comes to religion and human rights. Does the fact that human rights are spelled out by international conventions make them superfluous for believers? After all, religious traditions emphasize respect and care for others. Muslim esteem for human life is grounded in the Qur'an, which in one verse says that God has honored all humans, in another that all humans come from a single soul, and in another that killing a single soul is equivalent to killing humanity entire and saving a single soul to saving all humanity. A key concept in Islam is inviolability (*hurma*). Certain things have been made inviolable by God. Religion is one of those things, but so are life, progeny, dignity, and property. A key notion at play in Muslim society is mutual respect (*ihtiram*). Scripture, both Bible and Qur'an, may not speak of human rights explicitly, but it is not difficult to find texts that call for compassion toward others: the parable of the Good Samaritan in the New Testament and the verse in the Qur'an (4:36) that ties true belief to kindness—not only to parents and family but also to the needy and neighbors, whether blood relatives or not. Why, then, do believers need international conventions to inform them of standards of human rights?

The religious concept of human dignity does not mean indiscriminate freedom to do as one pleases. Similarly, the protection of human rights means more than individual liberties. People have rights and freedoms but also need a public order to realize them. Thus religious concepts of dignity and secular concepts of human rights both assume a set of moral constraints but differ in the way they name them. Islam is clear about the right to be free from the tyranny of the powerful but would also say that God has rights—above all the right to be worshipped. Blasphemy would therefore violate God's rights. His rights also limit certain kinds of behavior: alcohol consumption, extramarital sex, false accusation, theft, and so on. God has rights, but he has also specified rights for his servants, that is, humans. These human rights give further direction to legitimate behavior: no exploitation of the weak, no homicide, no unjust contracts.

This system of divinely ordained rights exists to protect society, preserve life, and foster decency. Why would one want to be liberated from the rights of God? The atrocities suffered by Jewish and other peoples in World War II tragically demonstrated the need for a document such as the 1948 Universal Declaration of Human Rights. No one, however, suggested the Jews need to be protected from Judaism. Rather, they, like everyone, need to be protected from barbaric states. Muslims too want to be protected, and it would sound odd that such protection is to be achieved by liberation from Islam.

There is, to be sure, slippage when it comes to religion and human rights. Does one forfeit human rights, such as the right to life, if one fails to respect God's rights? The key issue here is the relation of state power to the rights of God. Some states see their rule as part of God's rights and define infractions against God's rights as a challenge to their rule. Some nonstate actors equate justice exclusively with the rights of God and take God's law into their own hands, attacking secular society indiscriminately as abominable to God. In many places, religion and its moral guidelines are a communal performance and not the choice of individuals. This is not inherently problematic (one can simply leave the community) but becomes problematic when the communal way of life—Islam in this case—is tied to national loyalty. Religious dissenters become public enemies, and what is religiously prohibited becomes punishable by national law.

There are serious punishments for offending the rights of God— stoning for adultery, amputation for theft, lashing for alcohol consump- tion. But the shari'a heritage goes out of its way to keep enforcement of God's rights from state power. For example, throughout the Otto- man period, roughly 700 years, there is no record that the state ever put anyone to death for adultery. It could be said that Islam traditionally places the duty of enforcing God's rights on the individual who violates them as a form of penance to expiate for sins. The sinner could request to be lashed for alcohol consumption or stoned to death for adultery to face God on judgment day with a clean slate, but the state is not to go out of its way to enforce God's rights.

Of course, God's rights sometimes overlap with state concerns for public order—crime and theft. What should be punished by law and enforced by the state and what should be punished by individual penance? And what is the purpose of applying shari'a punishments? It depends on who is doing the punishing. If applied by individuals and communities, the goal might be expiation of sins or religious reform. If applied by the state, the goal might be public order, depending on the offense against God's rights in question. When the state begins to punish offenses that are more relevant to individual and communal reform than to public order, however, it is likely seeking to distract attention from its political failures by displaying its willingness to enforce the rights of God.

One should not overstate the case for religious freedom apart from legitimate political concerns. Political oversight of religion is not a unique product of the modern state. In the past, however, it was limited to the state's duty to preserve public order. Nizam al-Mulk, the great vizier of the Seljuk dynasty, struck down by Isma'ili assassins in 1092, remarked in a celebrated treatise on politics that disorder in religious affairs produces chaos in the land. When heresy grows rife, rebels appear. Political authorities therefore need to monitor beliefs, and this the viziers of past Islam did, sponsoring debates on all matters of creed to test them against humanistic reflection. But Nizam al-Mulk's call for political supervision of beliefs did not mean inquisition of souls. People could believe what they wanted in the private forum, but beliefs in public could not disturb the tranquility of society.[4] The state had a duty to ensure that religion not descend into confessional factionalism. Today, state management of belief includes secular no less than religious beliefs. It is a balancing act.

Public order was not only the interest of rulers. It also mattered to religion. The scholarly custodians of shari'a affirmed the importance of public order and the duty of the ruler to ensure it. Abu Yusuf (died 798), a prominent legal scholar of his day, addressed a treatise to the Abbasid Caliph Harun al-Rashid (ruled 786–809). In it, echoing the Qur'an, Abu Yusuf emphasized the ruler's responsibility for the common good (*salah*). He maintained that the ruler's political judgment could override prophetic precedent if doing so furthered the public interests of Muslim society. Abu Yusuf identified the purpose of rule as protection of the common good. It therefore has a religious claim on the obedience of believers. Thus, though scholars have always defended the independence of Islam, they also recognize that politics has its own legitimate purposes that cannot be undermined by claims to religious freedom.

Past concerns continue today. Beliefs in Islam sometimes become cacophonous to the point of endangering public order, one group attacking another for its particular creed, its veneration of saints, or its manner of praying. To be sure, rulers can exaggerate this danger to justify heavy-handed treatment of political dissent, but the chaos of beliefs can be destabilizing when beliefs translate into political positions. Fatwas, traditionally confined to ritual and moral life, were in the past occasionally issued in support of dynastic interests. But today fatwa-givers increasingly address political issues much more broadly on their own initiative and with complete lack of coherency: for and against U.S. policies in Iraq, for and against suicide attacks, for and against democracy, for and against peace with Israel, for and against honor killing, and so on. This challenges the policymaking powers of political authorities, fostering turmoil in society where individual citizens take their political positions from fatwas not geared to the common good of a nation but to a particular set of beliefs.[5] Today, the question is not heresy as potential cause of rebellion, as Nizam al-Mulk feared. But beliefs are diverse and divisive, and when they shape political attitudes they undermine a state's ability to hold a nation together. This, as scholars of past Islam recognized, justifies political oversight of religion—not its ritual and moral teachings but its place in public life.

For this reason, many nations in Muslim lands, including those ruled by secular states, refer to religion in their constitutions. Article 29 of the Indonesian constitution says that the state is based on the belief in the One and Only God. Article 116 of the Malaysian constitution defines ethnic Malays as Muslim. Article 2 of the Algerian constitution says that Islam is the religion of the state, and article 76 calls the president to glorify Islam. Article 3 of the Syrian constitution says that Islam is the religion of the president and also a principal source of national law. All these nations are secular republics, unlike, for example, the Islamic republics of Pakistan and Iran, which themselves have very different notions of the relation of the state to Islam. But the close relation these secular states have to Islam raises questions of identity. Indeed, these nations all have well-staffed ministries of religion within the state structure, charged with the task of managing beliefs: A state ministry appoints mosque preachers and monitors the content of sermons and national religious education. Even Turkey and Uzbekistan, which make no constitutional reference to Islam, have such ministries.

The religious authorities employed in these ministries are sometimes referred to as the sultan's clergy (*shuyukh al-sultan*); their credibility among believers, especially those who dislike the state, is suspect. This situation, however, does not make Islam completely subservient to state policies. The state-aligned religious authorities do recognize the duty of the state to manage national affairs but they also make use of their positions to give the morals of Islam greater play in public discourse. And they do not always capitulate to state requests. Their willingness to bless state policies depends on shifting political circumstances, but the point is that the political management of Islam is not a modern phenomenon that appeared with the rise of the nation state.[6]

What is new is the demand on states to respond to international standards of human rights that some Muslims see as offensive to Islam. Some Muslims ascribe double standards to the intentions of international organizations, and there may be reason to doubt the way international conventions are applied at a local level. Indeed, some states can exploit secular principles to justify authoritarian rule over believers who, as believers, are deemed rationally unfit to know what is best for the nation in the modern age. In addition to managing beliefs at home, states are also under pressure to bring the beliefs of the nation into line with international expectations. The ability of the state to do this depends on a number of factors—including the willingness of religious authorities to commit Islam to new realities. Some believers see this as a way to secularize Muslim society. Is the international community to determine God's religion?

At the same time, state management of beliefs sometimes implicates religion in human rights abuse. Why? Religion, after all, can be a great defender of human rights. Some states ignore the moral purposes of shari'a, subordinating it to the logic of politics. The result can be a very narrow application of shari'a that targets women. In places like Nigeria, Pakistan, and Saudi Arabia, punishment of unwed mothers, even when the cause of pregnancy is unclear, becomes the litmus test for the Islamic identity of the state irrespective of other considerations. These cases are not, then, about shari'a per se but the subversion of its moral vision to political interests or tribal honor. Honor killings in Muslim societies are often justified in the name of shari'a, but the practice originates in tribal law. Adultery does carry the death penalty, but there are conditions that make it almost impossible to prosecute.[7] For example, there must be four witnesses to the act of penetration, which is highly unlikely. And prudence traditionally guides all *hudud* cases, that is, those that could result in corporal punishment. A shari'a principle states that judges should avoid *hudud* punishments whenever there are doubts (*idra' al-hudud bi-l-shubuhat*); circumstantial evidence is not enough to apply *hudud*.

Targeting women and minorities is an easy way for a state to pretend to Islamic legitimacy without having to subject itself to the demands of shari'a justice. State authorities sometimes uphold shari'a rulings (*ahkam*) without regard to their greater aims and intentions (*maqasid*). To make it seem that it is committed to Islam, a state declares its readiness to execute homosexuals; stone an unmarried woman for a rape-induced pregnancy; or deny a divorced woman financial support from her husband beyond what shari'a stipulates, even if it results in her impoverishment.[8] The sad irony is that these states fail to meet shari'a standards when it comes to public life in general—rule of law, national prosperity, basic rights that Islam would protect, such as rights against state torture. The Qur'an is very clear about the fate of hypocrites.

This is where human rights have a role in Islam, not to replace shari'a but to ensure that its purposes are not subverted. When not co-opted by political actors, shari'a can be, as it has been in the past, a great bulwark against state tyranny. Public morality is important but not at the cost of human rights that shari'a itself enshrines, above all the right not to be subject to political oppression. Islam may not recognize autonomy from shari'a, that is, the rights of God, though it may postpone punishment for transgressing his rights to judgment day, but it does recognize autonomy from political oppression, that is, from tyranny and terrorism in the name of worldly goals. Autonomy in Islam, as noted in chapter 5, is affirmed in relation to political power, not shari'a. Political liberties are fully consonant with Islam even if moral liberties are not. There are some gray areas. For example, do women and non-Muslims enjoy full political rights in Muslim society, such as the right to exercise political authority at the highest level? One could ask a similar question of other societies. Is the French public comfortable with a citizen of Arab origin exercising political authority at the highest level?

Muslims do need to be protected—not from God and his ways but from the ungodly ways in which his will is implemented. There is, of course, the question of moral autonomy. Some Muslims may want to be free of God and his rights. This is a controversial issue in societies that emphasize common virtues. But the long-standing consensus in Islam is that apostates are not to be killed if their apostasy is not treasonous, that is, does not threaten the moral fabric of Muslim society. This would, of course, limit atheism to the closets of Muslim society, but the same is true, apparently, of atheism in the U.S. military. Many Muslim women in France, for example, are grateful for the national ban on the headscarf in the national schools because it relieves them of communal pressure to wear one against their will. At the same time, there are those who feel the ban violates the rights of the Muslim community in France to fulfill the rights of God. The emergent sense among Muslims is that shari'a functions best, its purposes most effectively served, when it works hand in hand with international standards of human rights as a check against politically motivated applications of shari'a.[9] Women should be protected from wearing the headscarf against their will but should also not be prevented from wearing it if they choose to do so. Human rights do not replace shari'a but help it protect Muslims and even Islam from politicized distortions of its purposes. The former president of Iran, Muhammad Khatami, is a leading example of this type of thinking.

Religion greatly values human dignity but does not necessarily celebrate the individual above all else. It may affirm the value of individual conscience but at the same time does not abandon the idea of an objective moral order. Some formulations of human rights are radically individualistic, defining the human as autonomous and unencumbered by any duties whatsoever, whether to God or to others. Some feel that human rights are simply the latest chapter in the West's attempt to colonize other peoples: The modern formulation of human rights, though European in origin, is promoted as universal norm. In this view, human rights become a neocolonial tool to impose a secularized definition of human life on societies that hold religion dear. Are human rights just a way for European powers to get the rest of the world to be atheist too and embrace individualism as the climax of human civilization? Many nations—China comes to mind—have used this line of reasoning to justify noncompliance with human rights standards in the name of cultural specificity. The United States sometimes ignores human rights standards in the name of national interests. Indeed, under the administration of George W. Bush, the U.S. government committed actions that the Founding Fathers gave as reasons for declaring independence from the British Crown (e.g., transporting combatants overseas to be tried for pretended offences). State authorities find all sorts of loopholes to get around human rights standards. Our concern here, however, is with religion. Does it have a unique conception of human existence with implications for human rights? Does religion itself obstruct human rights?

Robert Kraynak, author of *Christian Faith and Modern Democracy: God and Politics in the Fallen World*, has argued that modern definitions of human rights are traceable to the Enlightenment, not to Christianity. Thus, Christianity, though not necessarily opposed to human rights, does not see them as the end and purpose of human existence but as a way to ensure the common good. Christian groups of various sorts do

act as great defenders of human rights today. They bring global attention to the plight of the poor, decry state tyranny against citizens, and
make social justice a pillar of the Christian mission.

Still, the Christian affirmation of human rights does not mean that
Christians view humans as morally autonomous with no purpose other
than doing what they please irrespective of God's rights. Christianity—
like Islam—affirms freedom from tyranny and oppression but not freedom from God. This does not mean that people lose their human rights
if they commit moral infractions (or even crimes) at odds with the Holy
Spirit. Rather, society is to protect and build up human life in the image
of God. It is this that makes human dignity God-given—and therefore
inalienable—and gives humanity an unparalleled stature in the created
order. But it does not mean individual rights without consideration of
the common good of all. The right to be free, politically, from state
tyranny is sometimes conflated with the right to be free, morally, from
duties to others. Human rights cannot offer a pretext to ignore the
connection and duty humans have to one another as common children
of God.

Freedom in Christianity, Kraynak argued, is about rights granted by
God to humans, but these rights are not absolute or unconditional.
They must be balanced by God-given duties to care for the needs of
others and society as a whole, including economic justice for all. Human
rights in Christianity would not include the right to abortion or same-
sex marriage or the right to neglect the poor and uneducated or the
right to make a contract that is technically legal but clearly immoral.
Such rights would conflict with the rights of God, glorifying (even dei-
fying) individual autonomy over the purpose of society, namely the
good of all as set forth in natural and divine law. Freedom for Christianity, as for Islam, is not absolute but exists for a moral purpose.

This does not mean that religion devalues personal experience, even
subjectivity, especially when it comes to human encounter with God,
but it can diverge from liberalism in the modernist sense. Kraynak has
posited that modernist liberalism amounts to a call to protect individual
liberties not only in the political realm but also in the moral one, the

right to determine one's own moral way of life without reference to the moral way of life set down by God as known from the natural order of the universe and divine revelation. Of course, God's mercy extends even to those considered morally profligate, who are created in the image of God no less than others and who have a dignity that must be respected regardless of moral stature or political standing. And there are religious arguments for protecting moral liberties no less than political liberties. Religion, though, cannot overlook the rights of God. Similarly, with Islam, there is liberty—political liberty but not to the detriment of religious morality.

Islam is a tightly regulated economy of rights (*huquq*) owed to God, to fellow humans, and even to oneself. God has the right to be worshipped, as embodied in various ritual duties, but has also revealed sanctions against harmful behavior, as noted above. Believers who commit offenses will have to pay the penalty either in this world or the next. But God, if he chooses, can cover over (*satr*) the sins of people in his mercy (*rahma*). The prophet Muhammad embodied this godly character as model ruler, ensuring justice and righteousness but also willingly foregoing retribution for a greater moral purpose, such as peace in society.

Members of society also have duties to one another, and God has forbidden Muslims from transgressing the life, property, and dignity of others without cause (e.g., if the person is a murderer and judged to deserve death or is an unrepentant blasphemer who also works against the common good of Muslim society). Spouses have duties to one another and to their children. In this sense, adultery is seen as a crime against the rights of others. Society as a whole has a duty to care for the weak and poor, and relations between individuals are to be guided by justice, that is, everyone getting their due, especially when it comes to commerce. Islam places great emphasis on keeping promises and fulfilling contracts. When obligations are not met, justice can be sought, but there is also the option to be merciful towards others in imitation of the prophet. Rulers are to be obeyed as long as they do not transgress the rights of God and his servants (i.e., humans). This could imply just rule or rule that does not offend Islam's morality or, at a minimum, rule that does not prevent believers from performing their ritual duties (e.g., praying, fasting, and so on).

This does not mean that such infractions of God's rights, such as adultery and neglect of the poor, do not exist in Muslim society, but the point of shari'a is to protect individuals. This is done by establishing a moral society in which people exist not as a collection of individuals but are bound together in right relations under God through a web of rights and duties. Islam views society not as a random sample of disconnected individuals, affirmed in their rights and unencumbered by others, but as a complex of persons with duties no less than rights. That is the goal of Islam: to build religious communities respectful of modest living, not religious states, for that would put religious authority in the hands of state officials rather than communal leaders. The state, *siyasa* governance, is tasked with the preservation of public order, including enforcement of duties people owe to one another, but there have always been restrictions, affirmed by shari'a, on the scope of *siyasa* supervision of the moral life of society.[10] A concept of privacy, the inviolability of the family home and personal conscience, is strongly affirmed in Islam, even if public display of one's private life is discouraged. The history of Islam is relatively free of inquisitorial tendencies. People's morals have traditionally been judged by their public conduct rather than their beliefs, and hypocrites were left to God to deal with in the next life and not to humans in this one.

Muslim scholars realized long ago that Islam had not been revealed without a purpose. God is not playing a game with humans. Rather, Islam had been revealed for the good of society. As a result, although specific precedents are important, they cannot be applied if the result undermines public interests (*masalih*), and long-standing principles speak to this. For example, no harm to self or others (*la darar wa-la dirar*) means that a shari'a precedent is not to be applied if doing so causes harm to oneself or to others or, especially, to society as a whole. Another principle states that repelling evil takes precedence over procuring good (*dar' al-sharr muqaddam 'ala jalb al-khayr)*, meaning that shari'a, understood as the good in Islam, cannot be applied if it would produce harm such as civil strife. A hierarchy of principles thus inform shariʻa processes, the highest of which are called the five necessities. They are called necessities because the failure to preserve them would result in chaos in society, undermining the very purpose of shariʻa. These five interests, understood as universal interests, that is, as common to all, are the preservation of religion, life, progeny, dignity, and property.

These principles are conceived as duties owed to individuals rather than individual rights, but they do reflect a Muslim understanding of basic rights, that is, things that cannot be violated—they enjoy inviolability (*hurma*). In premodern Islam, the term for right (*haqq*) had the same connotation as *ius* (right) in premodern Europe, that is, what is due a person. In this sense, it is the right of a criminal to be punished because that is his due. In Islam, it is held that one's moral duties to God and to others and to self cannot be fulfilled without a properly functioning intellect, and so it is the Muslim's right not to be intoxicated, given that intoxication would prevent one from fulfilling what is due God and due others.

Rights cannot be conceived apart from duties; in Islam, humans are both right-bearing and duty-owing. A couple has sexual rights over each other because that is what they owe each other when physically able to do so. Premodern conceptions of rights in Islam, however, increasingly coalesce with modern discourse on human rights. In other words, the possibility of synergy between shariʻa and human rights is in the works. The results are not unambiguous, but it does mean that Muslims are finding ways to combine universal concepts of human life with particular shariʻa norms.

Max Stackhouse argues that human rights necessarily involve both universal principles and particular expressions of them.[11] Universal principles of human rights are often abstract and make no sense unless expressed in the language of local culture and traditions, which often include religious sentiment. In the United States, affirmation of human liberties as well as calls for moral values are sometimes framed in religious language. Likewise, it is more accurate to consider shariʻa as a heritage of particular rulings (precedents) that must also be consistent with universal principles as defined by shari'a, that is, the five necessities, which, although abstract, enshrine core values of human existence. Thus particular precedents, if no longer in harmony with universal principles, need to be reconsidered if shari'a is going to be applied according to the intentions for which it was revealed, that is, the good of humanity. Such a process unfolds only gradually, and here it is illustrated in view of gender rights in Islam.

In the past, in Muslim society as elsewhere, women did not enjoy political and legal equality with men, nor did they hold public office. Their place was the home. In Islam, this did not mean that they could not leave the home or even pursue a trade. Rather, in light of the norms of the day, they were unfit to hold authority over others, public authority, such as caliph or judge, as in other premodern contexts. Elements from the religious heritage were used to legitimize what would today be considered restrictions on women. Many religious authorities, but by no means all, defined women as intellectually and religiously deficient. As such, they could not hold authority over others. Biblical verse has been used for similar purpose. All of that has today been challenged, in Muslim society as elsewhere. It is now generally assumed that women have rights in the public sphere—to vote, to hold political office, to be appointed or elected to judgeships, if they have appropriate credentials. Islam, which in the past was interpreted to uphold the secondary status of women, is capable of responding to current realities.

For example, the argument that women are not fit for public authority is based on a verse in the Qur'an that suggests that a woman's testimony in court is inferior to a man's. However, in issues specific to the female body, such as adultery and abortion, Islam has always recognized the full weight of female testimony. The operative principle in evaluating the weight of a person's testimony is thus not gender but competence. This makes it possible to reconsider past precedents limiting female testimony in light of a contemporary reality where women demonstrate competence in public life. Of course, despite scriptural acknowledgment of the equality of women and men before God, Islam, like traditional forms of Judaism and Christianity, bars women from the leading role in ritual life, that is, the community's liturgy, despite ancient examples of female excellence in shari'a learning and hadith teaching. The fifty-eighth chapter of the Qur'an, The Female Disputant (*al-Mujadila*), was revealed to vindicate a woman against the prophet Muhammad in a divorce case he had dismissed in favor of her husband. There are also verses in Scripture that speak of all, male and female, as equal in Christ, but Evangelicals do not recognize the religious authority of women, preferring other verses that seem to forbid the public voice of women, particularly Paul's First Letter to Timothy (2:9–15). Were such verses meant for all time? Our goal here is not to address gender roles within the religious community, which are not decisively linked to human rights, provided people have the option to leave the religious community, but rather the religion's view of women's rights in public life. Is she to be confined to the family home night and day on the basis of now outdated interpretations of God's will?

There are precedents but there are also principles that can work to overcome or renew past teachings. The Qur'an is understood by some to give public authority to men exclusively. Increasingly, albeit not without resistance, religious authorities recognize that such precedents no longer hold if Islam is to be true to its principles. There are certainly Muslim scholars who argue—and Muslim women who agree—that women exist solely to birth the next generation, but a shift is in the works where authority is not tied to gender but to competence. Illiteracy among women in Muslim societies is high, yet more and more women are being educated for professional work. Notably, what is earned by the married Muslim woman is hers to keep according to Islam because family support is the responsibility of the male, though if the woman chooses she can use the income for family needs. Of course, authorities maintain that a woman's family duties to spouse and children take precedence over public commitments. Once these duties are fulfilled, she is free to take a public role in building up Muslim society at large.

The pace of renewal is by no means uniform. In Saudi Arabia women are not seen as an acceptable presence—let alone authority—in public, whereas in Iran they are free to drive cars, vote, and hold office (though not as judges). In Egypt women received suffrage rights in 1956 despite the opposition of the religious establishment, but today the religious establishment recognizes that citizenship extends political rights to women, including the right to hold public office, and that these rights are not at odds with their duties as believers.[12] They now call on pious women to vote no less than they call on men, as a way to ensure respect for Islam in political processes, even if emphasizing the unique role of women in childrearing. Yet no one in the religious establishment would say that Muslim women have the right to be immodest in attire or sexual mores. In other words, shari'a is being renewed to ensure consistency with its own principles. As long as women, no less than men, adhere to the rights of God (i.e., Islam's morals), nothing in Islam prevents them from full enjoyment of political rights.

There are conundrums, because it could be argued that people enjoy political rights only insofar as they embrace shari'a duties. This was the case in the premodern past, when full legal capacity was enjoyed only by free Muslim males, leaving women, non-Muslims, and slaves, even if their basic rights to life and livelihood were protected, in a secondary position. History shows the difficulty people have had in separating creedal commitments from political rights, and yet the trend, in both Christianity and Islam, is recognition that God's bestowal of political rights does not depend on religious loyalties but on the willingness to exercise such rights in conformity to just laws that preserve public decency and justice, which the state is to guarantee.

That Muslim women need to be liberated from the headscarf to protect their human rights is a dubious claim, often advanced in the name of civilizing Muslims, itself a useful pretext to conduct warfare in the name of liberating women. There are many reasons why a Muslim woman wears the headscarf: personal piety, deterrent to harassment, respect for family morals, and so on. But the headscarf is not oppressive by definition, given that it does not necessarily keep women from participating in public life. In fact, in some cultures where a family's social standing is linked to female mores, the scarf is liberating, allowing females to venture into public life without compromising cultural attitudes about female modesty, attitudes which women themselves accept. Today, the scarf has been commoditized as a fashion industry: feminine beauty within moral parameters. The veil continues to be a highly contested issue in the battle between secularism and Islamism, turning the female body into an ideological battleground, but it is important to liberate ourselves from the notion that feminism is only western and secular, requiring sexual liberty along with political liberty. Indeed, women with and without headscarves increasingly interact in Muslim society alongside men without provoking a human rights crisis.[13]

Muslim feminists, then, are not struggling for the right to be immodest, to abandon the headscarf or pursue romance apart from marriage. Rather, they are struggling for political and legal equality: *siyasa* equality alongside shari'a morality. Even within the arena of shari'a, they have rights, which are seen not in terms of straightforward equality but complementarity whereby each gender enjoys equity within the framework of distinct roles; of course, the concept of complementarity can sometimes be used to keep women in traditional roles. It should be remembered that rights are never given by the powerful. Equality is achieved by struggle, as is well known from American history. This is no less true for Muslim women who join in the struggle for Islam. Muslim women have been actively participating in the so-called awakening of Islam—*al-sahwa*—especially the struggle to win respect for Islam in public life. They expect their male counterparts to acknowledge their contribution to the struggle by recognizing their liberties in the public sphere. Zaynab al-Ghazali of the Muslim Women's Association was a prime example of this, informing her husbands that her role in the struggle for Islam gave her full liberty in public life.[14] One can also point to the role of women in the Islamic Revolution in Iran and in the ongoing contestation over national identity in Turkey—between a secularist state and a Muslim society. Having struggled on behalf of

Islam in the public sphere, these women, in the name of Islam, do not intend to return to traditional definitions of womanhood and have been disappointed when their male counterparts expect them to do so.[15] One sees a similar trend in *Zanan*, the Iranian feminist journal,[16] and also in the teachings of Hidayat Tuksal, professor of theology at Ankara University. These women are not challenging Islam's morality but want political liberties as well as legal equality in the public sphere.

Legal equality, again, is more difficult within the scope of shari'a where the concept of equity is preferred. There are problems here, though, because it could imply that women have a secondary legal status when it comes to shari'a concerns that others would not view as specific to religion—divorce, court testimony, child custody, and the like; but even here, shari'a development is possible, as seen in Morocco's 2004 family law that gave women equal rights in family life. It should be noted, however, that the immediate results of this development have been very mixed. Attitudes about gender do not change simply because the law does.

Islam has its own internal logic of rights, which is not necessarily inconsistent with human rights. The challenge is not rights per se but rather a secularized conceptualization of human life that Muslims, like Christians, find troubling. Human rights discourse often emphasizes moral as well as political autonomy, the rights of individuals over the rights of communities. Humans have rights but so does God. Muslim women are claiming modernity in a unique way, not as arbiters of their own moral destiny but as political actors in modern society.

Some might posit that the communitarian vision of the human being is incompatible with individual rights. This would be true if a religious community were given state backing to punish those who offend its beliefs and values. It is not a community's values per se that pose a problem to those who dissent from them, but rather a state that in the name of national identity claims jurisdiction over a community's values, especially international communities—a state-defined national identity over against a community's extranational identity. The question, then, is not whether communal values result in human rights abuses, for example, when a community bans or ostracizes dissenters, but whether states have the right to enforce communal values. Does a state have jurisdiction over the rights of God? Is the state to be object of worship along with God? There have been heads of state who expected quasi-divine reverence, placing themselves above the law and formulating religion in highly nationalistic terms.

One of the most egregious contemporary examples is President Saparmurat Niyazov of Turkmenistan, who until his death in 2006 considered himself both president and prophet. He required citizens to accept his spiritual teaching, the *Ruhnama*, and forced Muslims to revere it alongside the Qur'an. Is it the state that claims loyalty on our core beliefs and values or a nonstate and even extraterritorial (i.e., extranational) authority? Catholics are dispersed in nations across the globe and are led by local bishops, but they also look to the Vatican as spiritual guide and moral authority. This does not poses challenges to national loyalties but can cause tensions when national laws contradict the moral teachings of the Church.

As noted earlier, some Muslims, especially in Europe, feel split between national and extranational (religious) identities. Are they destined for radicalization? Can a nation accommodate the religiosity of minorities, such as Muslims in Europe, within its cultural heritage? Will Europe have to be Islamized or Islam Europeanized? It most likely will not be so black or white. But European societies may reconsider ways religion is, or is not, recognized in the national heritage, to include space for Islam along with Christian symbols and secular principles. This is not to overlook Europe's welcome of large numbers of immigrants, including Muslims, but tensions arise when nations are blind to communal concerns for the rights of God. In other words, there is danger in establishing religion but also in establishing secularism whereby believers automatically become nonconformists.

State-defined national projects—whether religious or secular—often seek legitimacy by claiming the right to liberate or protect women, turning the female body into a battleground where national and extranational views of authority and identity clash. At this globalizing moment, which is transnationalizing, cross-nationalizing, denationalizing, the concept of the nation state is in crisis, and yet national courts remain the place where human rights questions are negotiated and acceptable religiosity within the parameters of national identity is defined.

This is strikingly obvious in the case of European Muslims, whose minority status poses a question about the relation between national (*siyasa*-defined) and religious (shari'a-defined) identity, with all kinds of confusion and conflation between the two.[17] A similar tension can be noticed elsewhere, making it worthwhile to think more expansively about national identities and their ability to accommodate the extranational identity of religious minorities. Certainly, extranational elements can become politicized, posing a threat to the security of the state and the continuation of national identity. The 2005 bombings in London, carried out by Muslim youth born and raised in Britain, demonstrates the seriousness of this dilemma, and Britain has moved to ban groups (such as Hizb ut-Tahrir) that foster religious radicalization. There are, then, security concerns, but we need to be careful about conflating them with religion in general. To what extent should a state regulate or inhibit the moral life of religious communities? The space accorded to Islam in public life is partly the result of culturally distinct understandings of the place of religion in national life but also reflects state management of public order.[18]

After fifteen years of controversy and debate, France decided in 2004 to forbid the ostensible display of all religious symbols in state institutions, that is, students in state schools and civil servants employed in government institutions: Jewish skullcaps, Sikh turbans, Christian crosses, as well as the Muslim headscarf. It has been argued that France's national self-understanding as *laïcité* warranted the ban on all display of religion. And yet some states in Germany, such as Baden-Württemberg or Bayern-Bavaria, also restrict the Muslim headscarf—but not Christian symbols—in state institutions.[19] In these cases, public identity is keyed not to *laïcité* but to a cultural heritage that acknowledges Christianity to the exclusion of other religions. In Italy, to cite another example, it was decided to keep crucifixes in state institutions, including courts, not for theological considerations but as part of the nation's cultural heritage. However, unlike the German states, Italy opted for accommodation alongside the public privileging of Christian symbols, allowing the Muslim headscarf in state institutions. That religion is not the issue per se in the headscarf controversy in Europe is evidenced by the support of Europe's Jewish and Christian leaders for the right of Muslim women to wear the headscarf in all circumstances. Other religions in Europe support the religious rights of Muslims because they too recognize the dilemma of making national identity arbiter of what is and what is not acceptable religion. Is God to be worshipped or the state? What does this say about the rights of God when limited by state policymaking?

This tension is at play in all nations, including Muslim lands. How do non-Muslims fit into a Sudanese or Iranian nationality that is defined in terms of Islam? The tension between state-defined national identity and other identities involves not only non-Muslim but also Muslim minorities who do not fit into the religiosity deemed acceptable by the state, such as Wahhabism in Saudi Arabia and Sunnism in Pakistan. This raises questions about the national belonging of Shi'i minorities, to say nothing of Christians.

The tension is also at play when a Muslim-majority nation has a state that defines its identity against Islam, such as in Turkey and Uzbekistan. Despite the religiosity of its citizens, the secularist state, through courts and state-controlled ministries of religious affairs, determines acceptable religiosity. Ironically, today, states—secular entities—claim jurisdiction over religious life. That the state in the modern context plays a key role in defining acceptable religiosity in the public sphere is a challenge to the rights of God from the Muslim perspective and to religious freedom from the human rights perspective. The Beckett Fund for Religious Liberty traces all kinds of state abuse of religious freedom. The victims are as often Muslims as not. What do we do in cases where the rights of religious minorities are left out of state definitions of acceptable religiosity? We still have a long way to go in dealing with this tension between national identity and attachment to extranational (that is, religious, even otherworldly) belonging, both of which show no signs of disappearing.

Religion faces a dilemma, both Christianity and Islam. What to make of a nation's law-making process that is blind to a religion's view of human existence, especially its moral outlook? In response, a religious community, perceiving the nation to be a threat to its values and way of life, may set itself in opposition to the national culture, emphasizing its group identity over national belonging. Religion affirms liberties but not without moralities, humans rights but also God's rights. Thus the debate over the nature of human rights raises a question that has been at play throughout this book. What is religion? Is it to be understood as group identity in the political sense, over and against other identities, or as a religious consciousness with an organic vision of its own, a God-consciousness, that can engage human society not to control it politically but to engage it morally? However important group identity is as departure point, if religion is reduced to group identity, then religions, Christianity and Islam, will have nothing to do with one another. But if religion is also about God-consciousness, then religions can find common motive and common purpose beyond group identity, a sense of being similarly even if uniquely moved toward God, religious friends with common ground, not enemies across an abyss of religious animosity. Oddly, the question of Christian-Muslim relations has a direct bearing on the relation of the extranational identity of religions to national identity. If Christians and Muslims promote in their mutual relation a fuller understanding of religion as not simply group identity but also and more profoundly God-consciousness, it would affect their view and way of relating to nations and political authorities: not as group identity over and against the nation but as God-consciousness that can embrace the nation in its worldview, creating positive rather than negative synergy between religious convictions and national goods. The nature of Christian-Muslim relations is important not only for the way these two sets of believers view each other but also for the challenges and possibilities of global politics today.

NOTES

1. At the same time, advocacy for female ordination often gets linked to support for homosexuality and abortion rights. Because of this, female ordination gets

tagged as part of a morally permissive culture that views all activity, including the divine office, in terms of individual rights. The issue, then, may not be female ordination per se but rather its association with a definition of human existence that many do not share. Decoupling female ordination from these issues, it has been argued, presenting it not as a right but as a calling from God, might allow for its acceptance. See Pamela D. H. Cochran, *Evangelical Feminism* (New York: New York University Press, 2005); and Mark Chaves, *Ordaining Women: Culture and Conflict in Religious Organizations* (Cambridge, MA: Harvard University Press, 1997).

2. Daniel Price, "Islam and Human Rights: A Case of Deceptive First Appearances," *Journal for the Scientific Study of Religion* 41, no. 2 (2002): 213–25.

3. For the different situations facing Muslim communities in the United States and Europe, see Philippa Strum and Danielle Tarantolo, eds., *Muslims in the United States* (Washington, DC: Woodrow Wilson International Center for Scholars, 2003); Marcel Maussen, "The Governance of Islam in Western Europe: A State of the Art Report," *IMISCOE Working Papers* No. 16 (Amsterdam: International Migration, Integration & Social Cohesion, June 2007).

4. This was a widely held notion in his day. See, for example, al-Juwayni, *Ghiyath al-Umam*, ed. 'Abd al-'Azim al-Dib, 2nd ed. (Cairo: al-Maktabat al-Kubra, 1981), 215–22. The idea of coercing people into communal harmony should not be seen as a contradiction to the qur'anic verse that forbids religious coercion (*la ikraha fi l-din*, 2:256) but as part of the logic of governance (i.e., achievement of a harmonious polity). The idea can be found in both al-Farabi, *Tahsil al-Sa'ada*, ed. Ja'far Al Yasin (Beirut: Dar al-Andalus, 1981), 79; and the Brethren of Purity, *Rasa'il Ikhwan al-Safa'*, ed. Khayr al-Din al-Zirikli, 4 vols. in 2 (Cairo: al-Matba'a al-'Arabiyya, 1928), section IV, letter 3, 83.

5. Mu'tazz al-Khatib, "Fiqh wa-l-Faqih wa-l-Dawlatu l-Haditha . . . Mashakil al-Tanafus bayna al-Quwwatayn: Fatwa wa-Qanun" *al-Hayat*, July, 21, 2007, 14.

6. See, for example, Moch Nur Ichwan, "'Ulama', State and Politics: Majalis Ulama Indonesia after Suharto," *Islamic Law and Society* 12, no. 1 (2005): 45–72. For an example of how state-aligned religious authorities negotiate Islam, see Ron Shaham, "State, Feminists and Islamists: The Debate over Stipulations in Marriage Contracts in Egypt," *Bulletin of the School of African and Oriental Studies* 62, no. 3 (1999): 462–83.

7. For fornication, that is, extramarital sex by unmarried people, the penalty is 100 lashes.

8. Bruce B. Lawrence, "Woman as Subject/Woman as Symbol: Islamic Fundamentalism and the Status of Women," *Journal of Religious Ethics* 22, no.1 (1994): 163–85.

9. Jumana Shehata, "Islam and Human Rights: Revisiting the Debate," *Arab Insight* 1, no. 1 (2007): 73–88.

10. For an example of how state-aligned religious authorities negotiate Islam, see Ron Shaham, "State, Feminists and Islamists."

11. Max L. Stackhouse, "Why Human Rights Need God: A Christian Perspective," in *Does Human Rights Need God*, eds. Elizabeth M. Bucar and Barbara Barnett (Grand Rapids, MI: William B. Eerdmans, 2005), 25–40.

12. Barbara Stowasser, "Old Shaykhs, Young Women, and the Internet: The Rewriting of Women's Political Rights in Islam," *The Muslim World* 91 (April 2001): 99–119.

13. Sema Genel and Kerem Karaosmanoglu, "A New Islamic Individualism in Turkey: Headscarved Women in the City," *Turkish Studies* 7, no. 3 (2006): 473–88.

14. Miriam Cooke, "Zaynab al-Ghazali: Saint or Subversive?" *Die Welt des Islams* 34, no. 1 (1994): 1–20; Burçak Keskin-Kozat, "Entangled in Secular Nationalism, Feminism, and Islamism: The Life of Konca Kuris," *Cultural Dynamics* 15, no. 2 (2003): 183–211. For broader perspective, see Lama Abu-Odeh, "Egyptian Feminism: Trapped in the Identity Debate," in *Islamic Law and the Challenges of Modernity*, eds. Yvonne Yazbeck Haddad and Barbara Freyer Stowasser (Walnut Creek, CA: AltaMira Press, 2004), 183–212.

15. Ersin Kalaycioglu, "The Mystery of the Türban: Participation or Revolt?" *Turkish Studies* 6, no. 2 (2005): 233–51.

16. Roza Eftekhari, "*Zanan*: Trials and Successes of a Feminist Magazine in Iran," in *Middle Eastern Women on the Move* (Washington, DC: Woodrow Wilson International Center for Scholars, Middle East Project, 2003), 15–22.

17. See, for example, Joel S. Fetzer and J. Christopher Soper, *Muslims and the State in Britain, France, and Germany* (Cambridge: Cambridge University Press, 2005).

18. See, for example, Louise Halper, "Disrupted Societies, Transformative States: Politics of Law and Gender in Republican Turkey and Iran," *Hawwa* 5, no. 1 (2007): 90–110. Halper rightly argues for popular attitudes towards state definitions of public life, but the role of the state is undeniable.

19. Dominic McGoldrick, *Human Rights and Religion: The Headscarf Debate in Europe* (Oxford: Hart Publishing, 2006).

CONCLUSION

ISLAM

Not a Separate Species

A MUSLIM cannot partake in the Eucharist. A Christian cannot go on pilgrimage to Mecca. A Muslim will always question the cross. A Christian will ask why the need for another prophet. Muslims refer to themselves as God's slaves, Christians as God's children. Theological differences are significant, but various aspirations are shared, in particular the desire to live in the presence of the one God. Christianity and Islam have unique forms of religious expression. A church is not a mosque. But there is resonance. Christians and Muslims both seek to get to God: Christians through remembrance of a person, Muslims through recitation of a book. In both cases, the experience occurs in the heart. Christians speak of Christ in the heart, Muslims of the Qur'an. The word of God, in both cases, aims to purify human hearts of all that would separate believers from God. Whether remembrance of a person or recitation of a book, one is speaking in both cases of God's redemptive action. God is the one who takes the initiative, sending his son, sending his book, to make it possible for humans to repent and turn back to him. Without his initiative, reassuring Christians of his love, Muslims of his mercy, one would despair of being with him. The point, then, is not only to live a particular kind of life but simply to live life in its various aspects with a sense of God-consciousness.

Religion is therefore not simply an identity marker. It is a set of beliefs with intellectual content that all peoples can discuss. People bring beliefs, both religious and secular, into public life. But once there, these beliefs are no longer the exclusive possession of the believing community. Do we know how to discuss beliefs? Do we know how to think about what moves us most deeply? Religious traditions have unique claims, but they also take shape across a range of issues that matter to all peoples. They offer a prism through which a society can explore ideas of real import and consider the values that most inspire it.

The study of religious pluralism is one way to reflect in this fashion. It pushes one to look at religion in a broader context and simultaneously pulls one back to the specifics of a particular tradition. The focus of this book has been Islam alongside Christianity. Islam is increasingly at home in a wide range of disciplines: literature, philosophy, political science, gender studies, and so on. Its prominence in global affairs encourages both Muslims and non-Muslims alike to examine their own beliefs more precisely. It features significantly in policymaking circles. Religion clearly does not exist in isolation. It is not agreeable to all, but it is an undeniable reference point.

In this sense, there is a point in studying not simply a plurality of religions but religious pluralism as well. The concern for religious pluralism is particular to U.S. society but has global dimensions. It is a key concern in Europe, India, China, Africa, now virtually everywhere. Religious pluralism is evaluated in different ways from one culture to another, but believers have always had to consider different kinds of belief. Since the birth of Islam, Muslims have been thinking about religion with others, and Christians have been a central interlocutor. This encounter is not just interreligious communication, one group of believers introducing themselves to another. There has been sustained interaction on common ground where the two traditions speak in tandem, sometimes with resonance and sometimes with dissonance. The other is always a reference point. In this book, the aim has been to direct attention to the study of religious pluralism by offering one approach to it—the study of two traditions through a single but refracted lens.

Christianity and Islam do share ground, but they can also exist without each other. Theologically, they do not need each other. Both look to a biblical past but also claim to have completed it on their own unique terms. Both have also been open to new insights and possibilities. The world, after all, did not end with the coming of Jesus or the appearance of the Qur'an. For Christians, Jesus Christ is not the end, but he is final in his uniqueness. Similarly, for Muslims, the Qur'an is incomparable. Christians see the message of the cross as liberation from patterns of sinfulness whereby humans inevitably fall short of pleasing God: God is love. Muslims see the message of the Qur'an as liberation from patterns of injustice whereby humans associate other interests with God to justify their own ambitions: God is mercifully one.

Christianity and Islam do not perfectly match. Christians see Islam as additional, not essential, to the sacred narrative of the biblical heritage. Muslims see Christianity as a partial distortion of it. Indeed, some religious leaders denigrate the other religion. The common ground is fragile, but it is there. What does this particular vantage point tell us about religion?

Despite distinct differences in wordings, especially in relation to Jesus Christ, Christianity and Islam share a common purpose. Both call people to live with God. That God, given the common biblical origins, is the one God. This common purpose is pursued by believers in concrete moments in history. But things change, and religious communities are faced with a challenge. The particulars of the religion may no longer make sense even if the purpose still does. Doubts encourage new ways of thinking about the religious tradition so that its purpose is not abandoned along with the elements that no longer make sense within a given historical moment. Skepticism is, then, essential to religion as a way to ensure that the religious message is never entirely reduced to a set of definitions, whether articles of faith or rules of behavior. Amidst the creeds and practices stands a relation that is known but still mysterious.

This relation is signaled by the face of God. Does this relation offer ethical insight for human society? It is a relation that can reduce the power of the ego. It tempers greed that undermines communal harmony. In that, the face of God can be seen as a socioeconomic good, vital for community sustainability. Indeed, study of the face of God in this sense may help us rethink whether a system driven by personal interest alone can guarantee prosperity. But the struggle for a godly society is not without its own problems, especially when the struggle fails to see that God's message, though worth living, is never fully realizable as a political project in this world. The face of God in this sense becomes a source of terror for a world that does not perfectly conform to its divinity. Great care, then, must be taken in locating evil in light of the face of God. The face of God is not source of evil but does sometimes become horribly distorted.

In addition to the disclosure of God, religion also emphasizes moral teachings, but this does not make it antidemocratic. Some believers understand moral life as part of a covenant with God. Others see it as part of a natural law that reflects divine law. A constitution based on representative democracy apart from divine sovereignty may create tension with the moral teachings of religion. Does democracy mean liberty from political tyranny or freedom from moral teachings, including care of the weak? Are the teachings of religion limited or unlimited? The way religion and democracy coexist depends on a number of factors, including definitions about the nature of democracy and the scope of religion.

Secularism is not a precondition for democracy, but religion, to be democratic, must acknowledge that the religiously untrained masses are able to determine God's will in some areas of life, to say nothing of their own interests. At the same time, religion also recognizes the corruptible side of human nature. Religious authorities may denounce aspects of public life under both authoritarian and democratic rule. Religion always runs into trouble when, in the hope of pleasing God, its representatives seek to limit freedom in the name of divine sovereignty. The moral authority of religion actually depends on its own freedom from political power. To enjoy this freedom, it must grant it to all.

Religion has come to learn that democracy is not a threat to religious authority. Indeed, democracy can be religion's friend. For religion, the purpose of rule is the common good, and in some societies, this may include the prevalence of religious values in public life. Still, even if democracy is not without its moral dilemmas, religion affirms that no one can claim to represent the sovereignty of God. Regular elections effectively work to check rule that fails to govern in the public interest, stifling the human spirit that religion seeks to promote.

At the same time, religion is a strongly communal phenomenon. It is especially when believers gather in prayer that they experience life in the presence of God. Religion, then, sometimes looks askance at the individualism that democratic sentiment can encourage. The extent to which religious symbols can be publicly ignored or devalued in the name of individual freedom depends on the society in question. Ultimately, as religion itself recognizes, beliefs cannot be controlled. Some societies are uncomfortable with religious freedom, however, and see it as a source of national instability. Others are uncomfortable with religion itself. This does not make religion a foe of human rights. Rather, although human rights are a universal phenomenon, there are different views on the way universal principles interact with local values, including religiously backed values.

Religion holds the human soul to be sacred. Religion also speaks of God as sacred. What exactly is the relation of the human soul to God? Does the human soul lose its dignity when it spurns the sanctity of God? Or is this dignity something intrinsic and indelible, whether or not it recognizes God's sanctity? This would argue for equality of conscience even when the conscience of individuals errs, but religion also ascribes all life to God. Human life is his. It is inviolable but not autonomous, at least not in its interactions with others—with family, neighbor, stranger. For religion, the human person, because it is dignified by God, is something to be built up. A society that exalts the individual or certain classes of individuals can actually threaten the dignity of its weaker members and the prosperity of society as a whole. Religion calls for the defense of all persons. It thus has a powerful contribution to make to human rights, challenging authoritarian states as well as societies that emphasize the rights of individuals over care for all.

To conclude, this book is by no means exhaustive when it comes to thinking about Christianity and Islam in tandem. The discussion is ongoing and can offer much fruit. The goal for this volume has been to illustrate one way of reflecting on religion, which, I hope many agree, is a stimulating path for both scholars and believers to take up—and perhaps even to do so together. Inquiry into religious pluralism is a great challenge to the prevailing notion of religion as identity marker. The possibility of common ground, however fragile, means that believers approach religion not simply as something their group does at certain times of the week but rather as a comprehensible phenomenon that can be explored and discussed in light of the wider human experience. Believers, then, are also rational in the way they comprehend and articulate beliefs. Therein lies the common ground whereby religion can be considered pluralistically.

Index